The Tarot Café

By
Sang-Sun Park
Jung-Su Kim
Volume 2

WITHDRAWN

HAMBURG // LONDON // LOS ANGELES // TOKYO

The Tarot Cafe Vol. 2
created by Sang-Sun Park
Written by Jung-Su Kim

Translation - Sukhee Ryu
English Adaptation - Kristin Bailey Murphy
Retouch and Lettering - Bench Comix
Production Artist - Gloria Wu
Cover Design - Matt Alford

Editor - Julie Taylor
Digital Imaging Manager - Chris Buford
Pre-Press Manager - Antonio DePietro
Production Managers - Jennifer Miller and Mutsumi Miyazaki
Art Director - Matt Alford
Managing Editor - Jill Freshney
VP of Production - Ron Klamert
Editor-in-Chief - Mike Kiley
President and C.O.O. - John Parker
Publisher and C.E.O. - Stuart Levy

A  Manga

TOKYOPOP Inc.
5900 Wilshire Blvd. Suite 2000
Los Angeles, CA 90036

E-mail: info@TOKYOPOP.com
Come visit us online at www.TOKYOPOP.com

ISBN: 1-59532-556-5

First TOKYOPOP printing: June 2005
10 9 8 7 6 5 4 3
Printed in the USA

Story so far...

Meet Pamela, a tarot card reader who helps supernatural beings living in the human world. She'll help any one whether they're a love-stricken cat, a vampire spending eternal life running from his one true love, an unattractive waitress looking for the man of her dreams, or even a magician who creates a humanoid doll to serve the woman he loves. Although she is good-natured, there is a deep dark secret that she must deal with before she can move on to the next life.

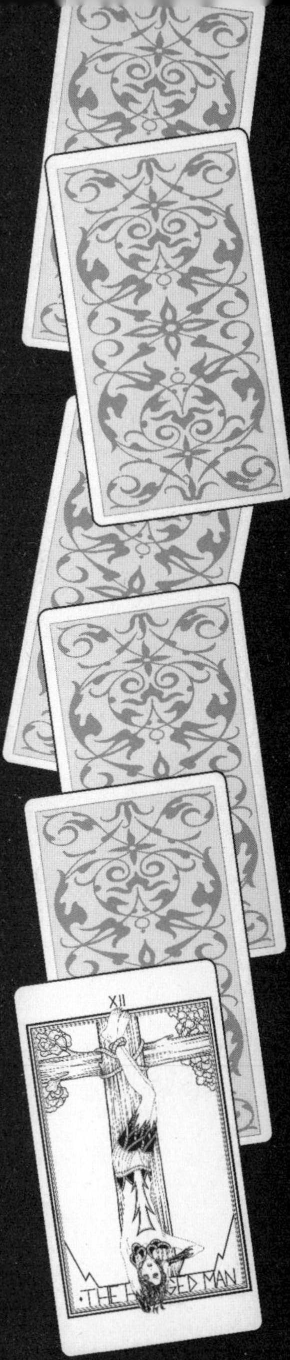
XII
THE

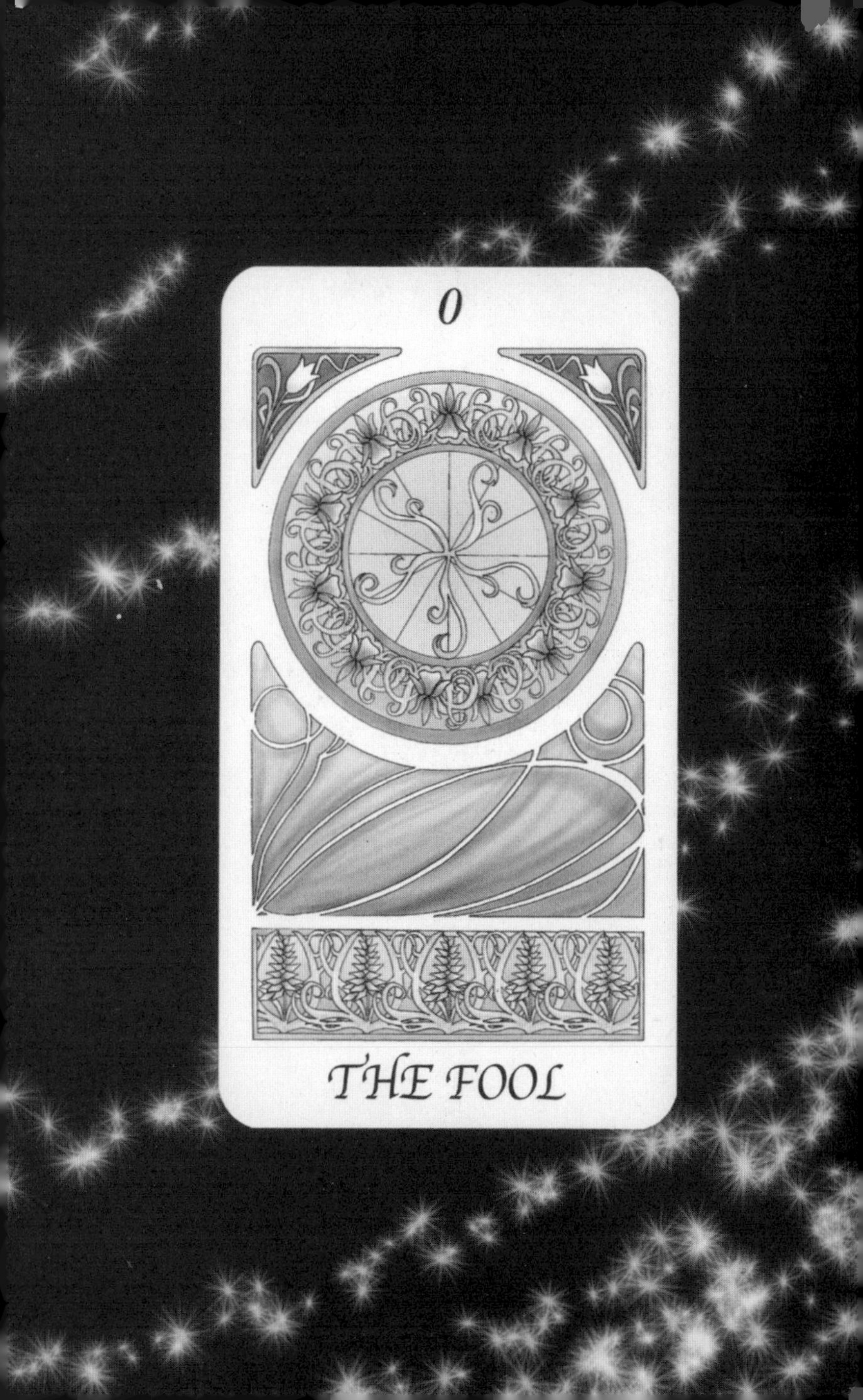
0
THE FOOL

Pamela

Table of Contents

Episode 5:
A Heartless Princess, an Alchemist
and a Jester (Part 2) -------------11

Episode 6:
The Werewolf Boy ----------------35

Episode 7:
The Witch Hunt -------------------107

JUSTICE
LA JUSTICE

VIII

DIE GERECHTIGKEIT
LA JUSTICIA

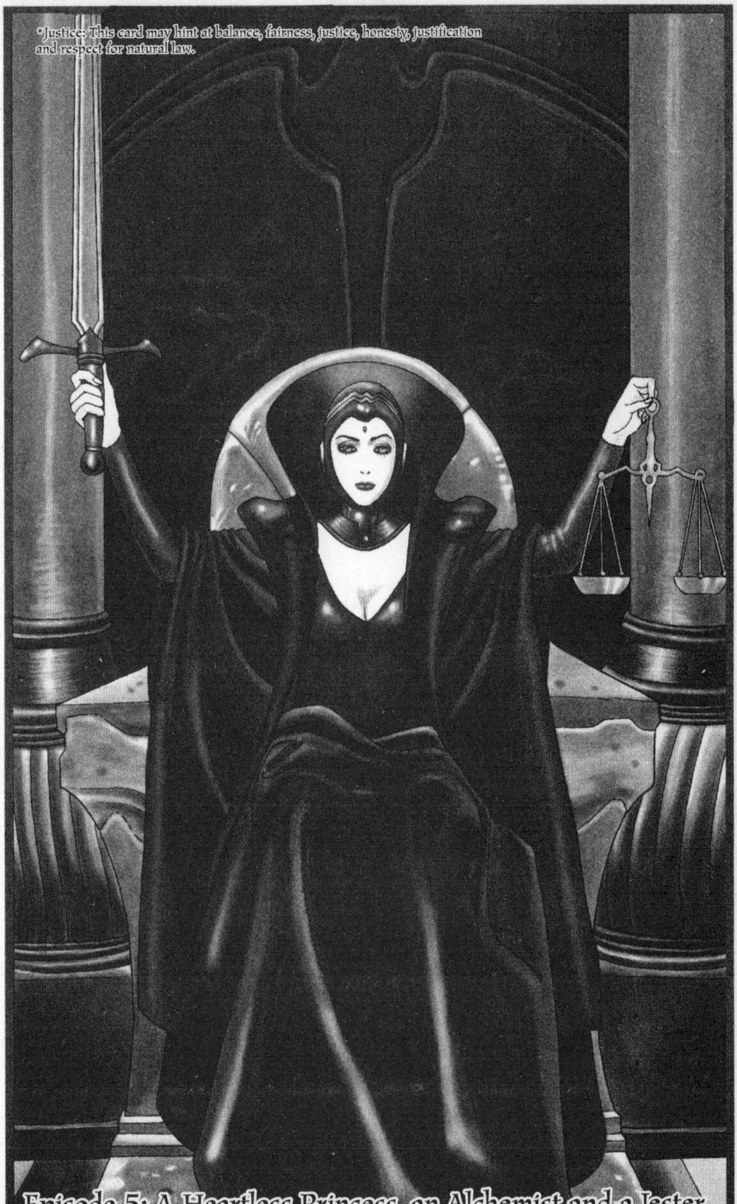
*Justice: This card may hint at balance, fairness, justice, honesty, justification and respect for natural law.

Episode 5: A Heartless Princess, an Alchemist and a Jester (Part 2)

LA GIUSTIZIA

ILLUSTRATION FROM SECRET TAROT

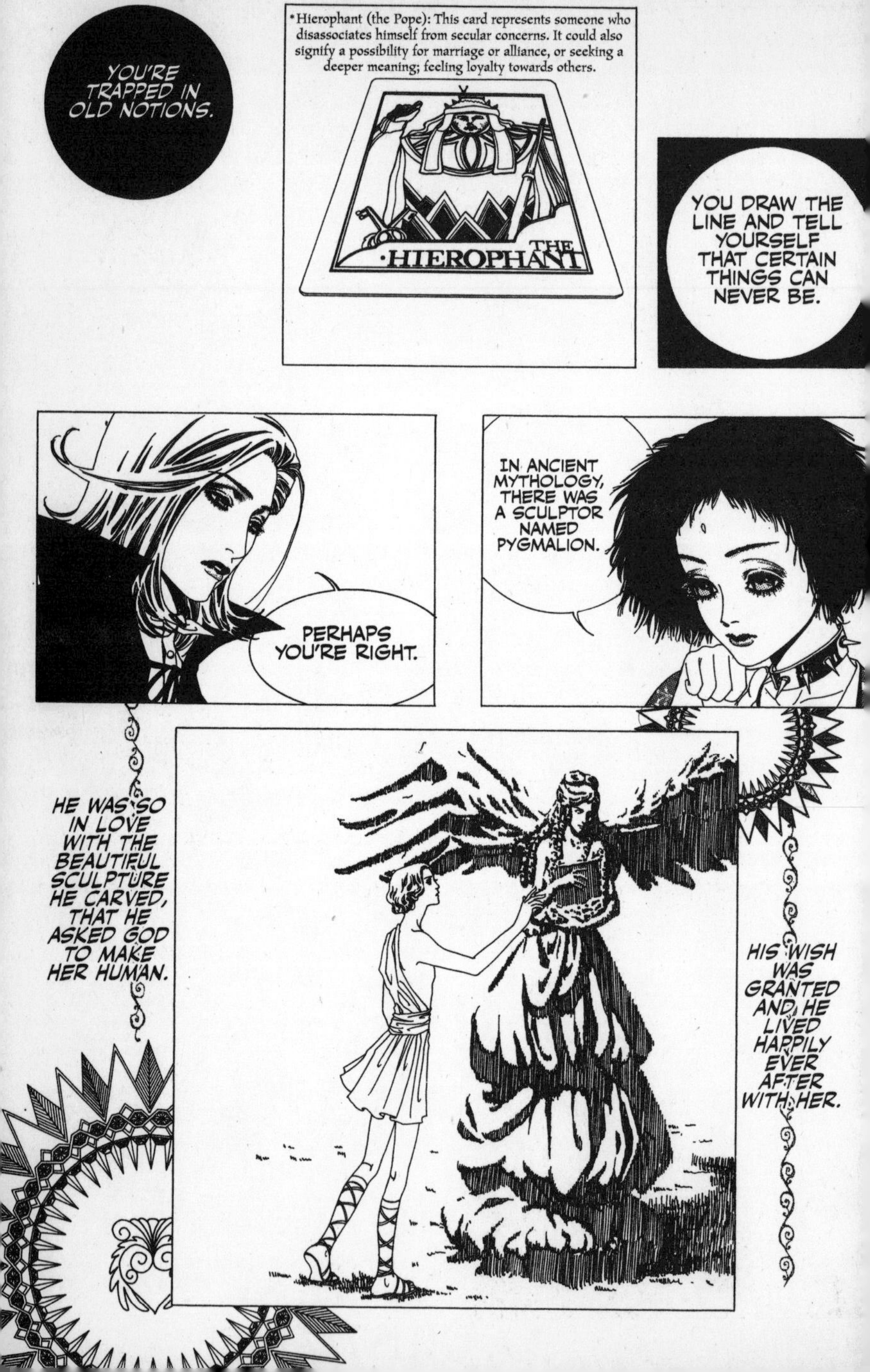
YOU'RE TRAPPED IN OLD NOTIONS.
*Hierophant (the Pope): This card represents someone who disassociates himself from secular concerns. It could also signify a possibility for marriage or alliance, or seeking a deeper meaning; feeling loyalty towards others.
THE HIEROPHANT
YOU DRAW THE LINE AND TELL YOURSELF THAT CERTAIN THINGS CAN NEVER BE.
PERHAPS YOU'RE RIGHT.
IN ANCIENT MYTHOLOGY, THERE WAS A SCULPTOR NAMED PYGMALION.
HE WAS SO IN LOVE WITH THE BEAUTIFUL SCULPTURE HE CARVED, THAT HE ASKED GOD TO MAKE HER HUMAN.
HIS WISH WAS GRANTED AND HE LIVED HAPPILY EVER AFTER WITH HER.

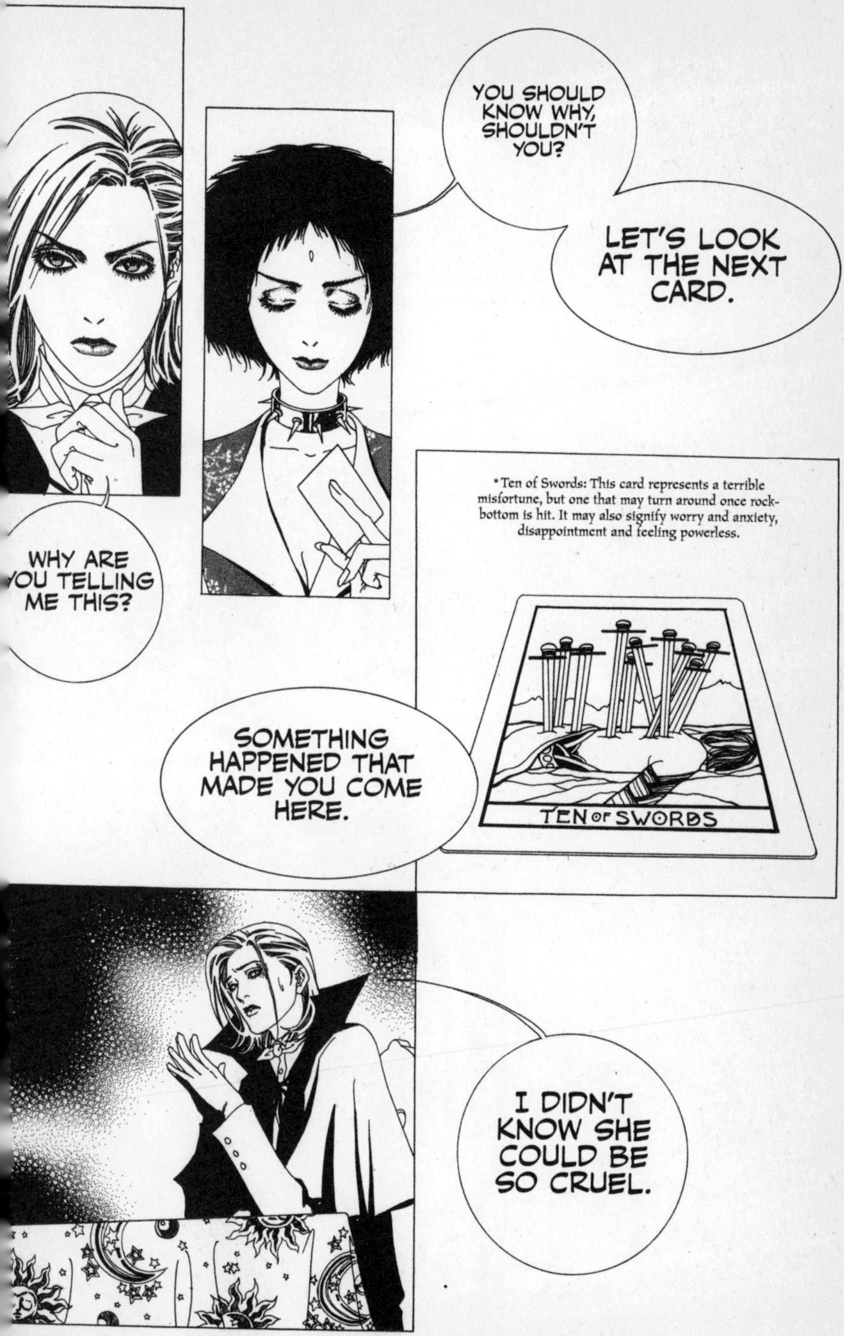
WHY ARE YOU TELLING ME THIS?
YOU SHOULD KNOW WHY, SHOULDN'T YOU?
LET'S LOOK AT THE NEXT CARD.
SOMETHING HAPPENED THAT MADE YOU COME HERE.
*Ten of Swords: This card represents a terrible misfortune, but one that may turn around once rock-bottom is hit. It may also signify worry and anxiety, disappointment and feeling powerless.
TEN OF SWORDS
I DIDN'T KNOW SHE COULD BE SO CRUEL.

PRINCESS, LOOK HERE!

THIS IS BORING, JUST AS I EXPECTED.

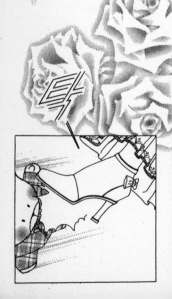

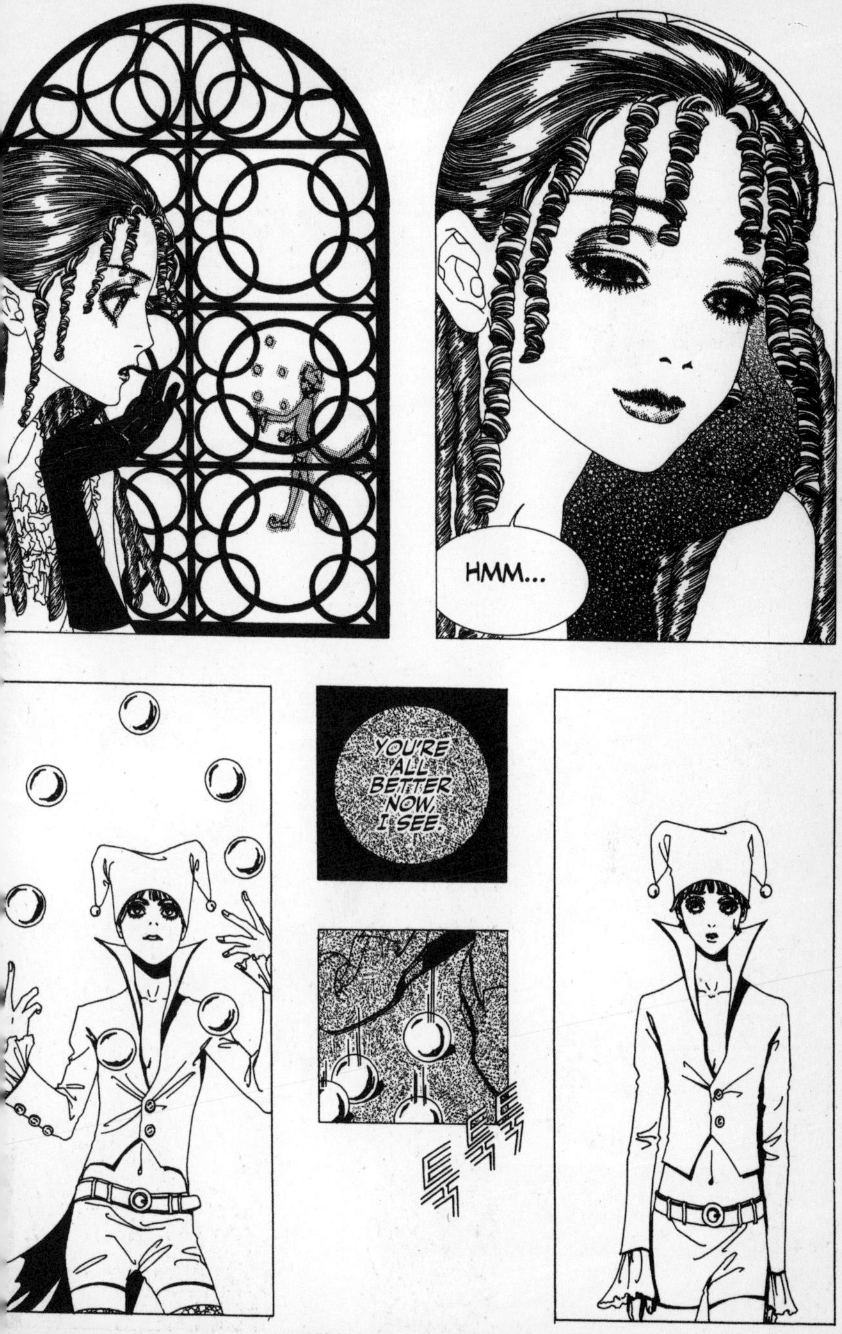
HMM...
YOU'RE ALL BETTER NOW, I SEE.

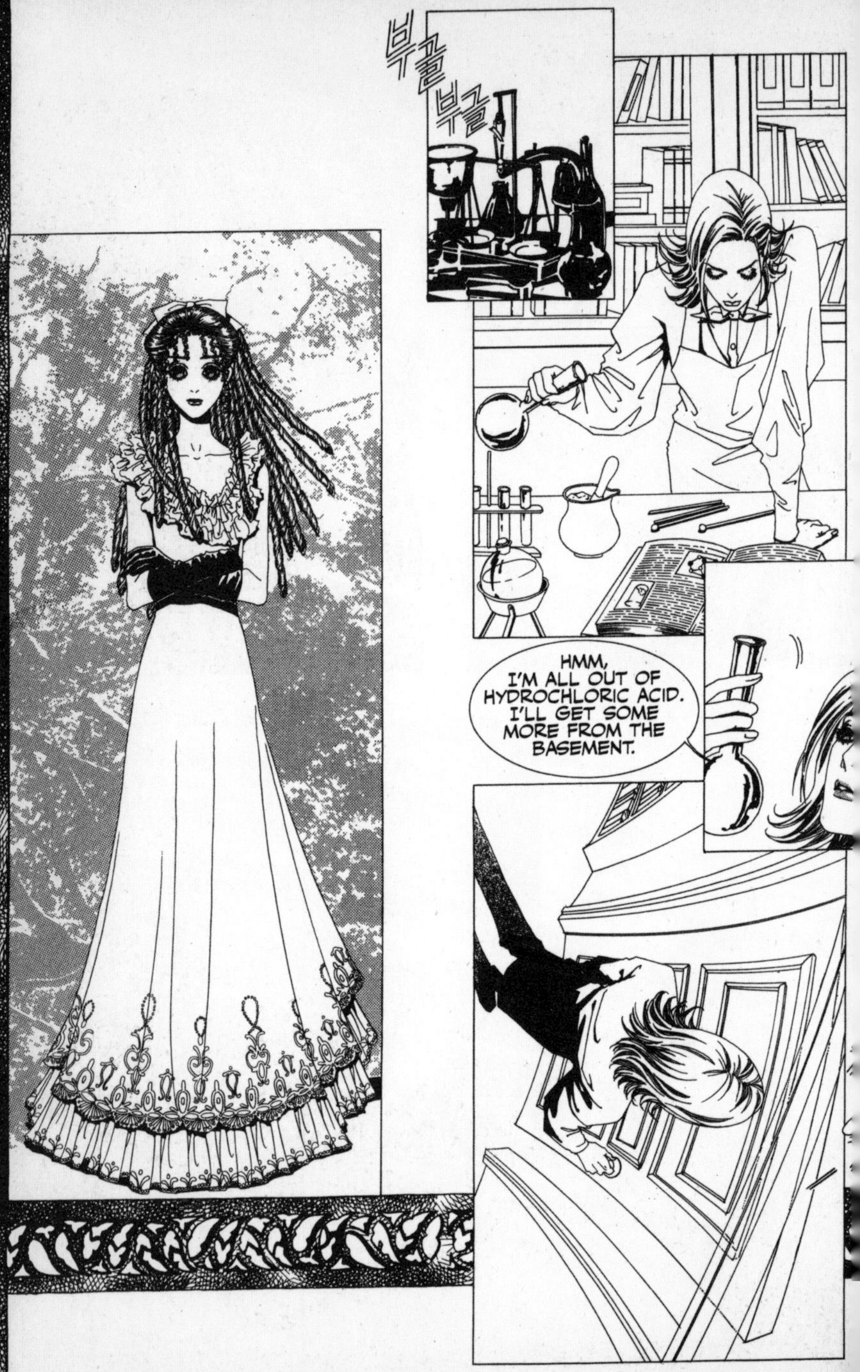
부글부글
HMM, I'M ALL OUT OF HYDROCHLORIC ACID. I'LL GET SOME MORE FROM THE BASEMENT.

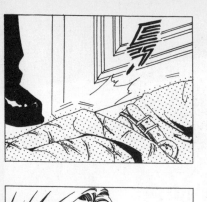

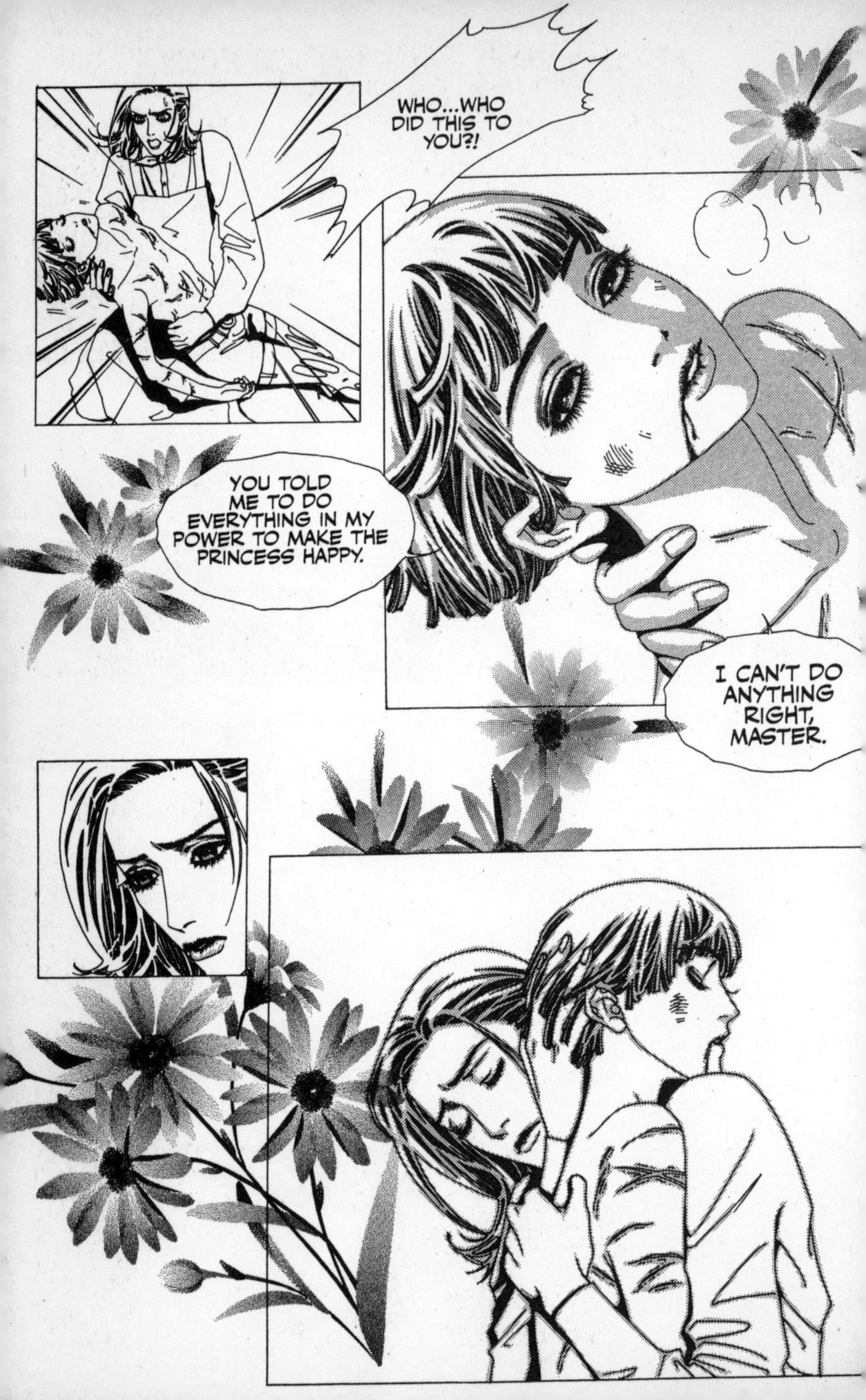
WHO...WHO DID THIS TO YOU?!
YOU TOLD ME TO DO EVERYTHING IN MY POWER TO MAKE THE PRINCESS HAPPY.
I CAN'T DO ANYTHING RIGHT, MASTER.

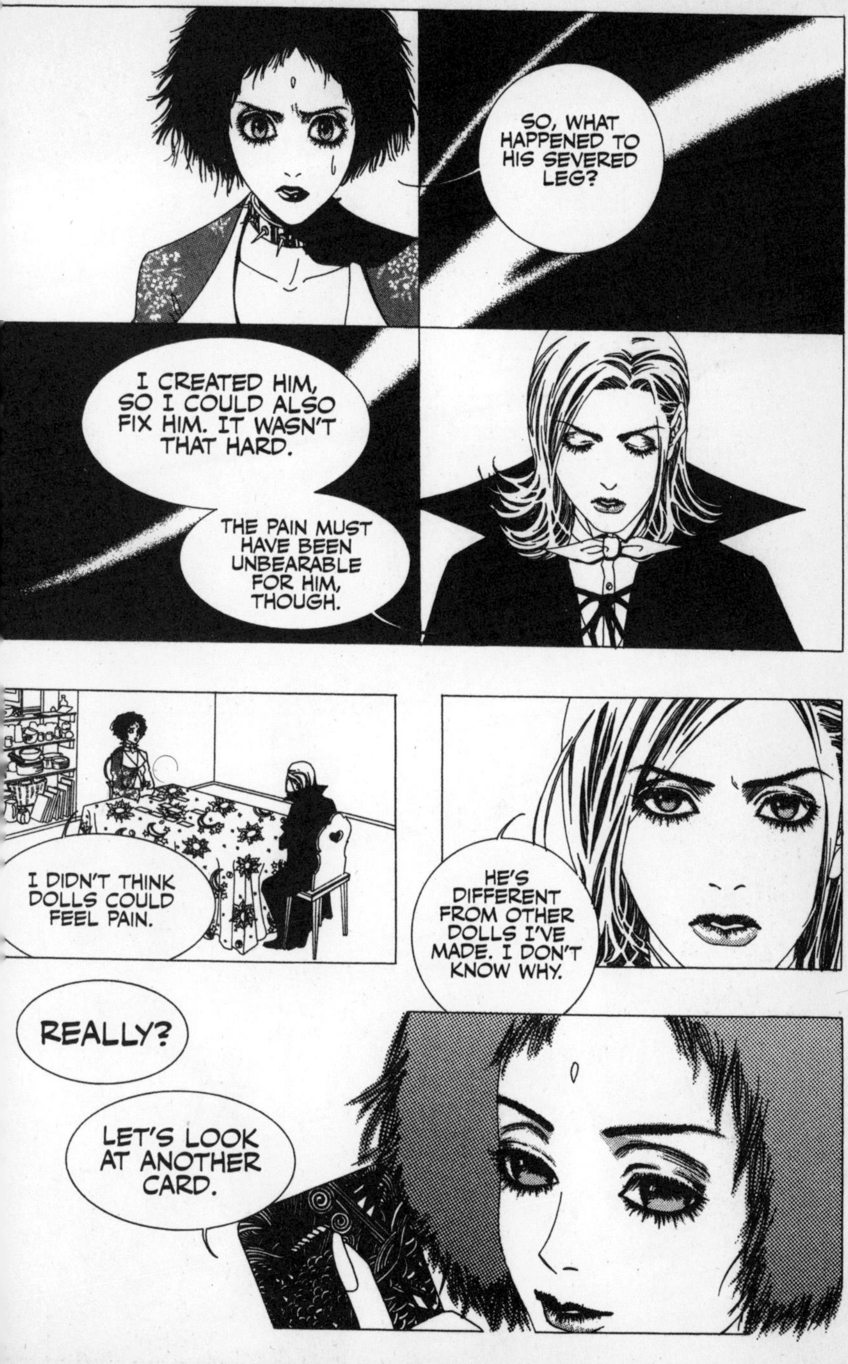
SO, WHAT HAPPENED TO HIS SEVERED LEG?
I CREATED HIM, SO I COULD ALSO FIX HIM. IT WASN'T THAT HARD.
THE PAIN MUST HAVE BEEN UNBEARABLE FOR HIM, THOUGH.
I DIDN'T THINK DOLLS COULD FEEL PAIN.
HE'S DIFFERENT FROM OTHER DOLLS I'VE MADE. I DON'T KNOW WHY.
REALLY?
LET'S LOOK AT ANOTHER CARD.

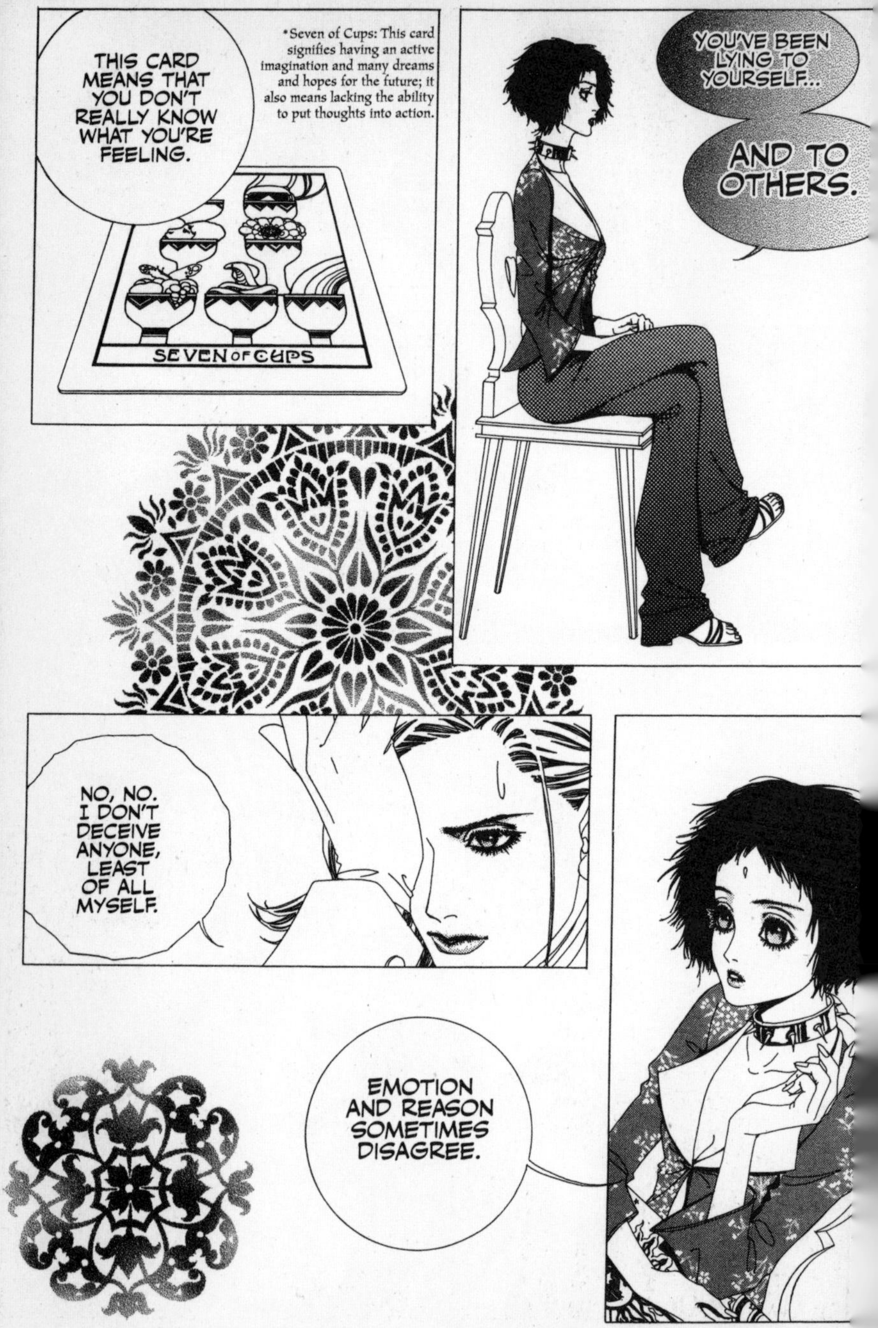
THIS CARD MEANS THAT YOU DON'T REALLY KNOW WHAT YOU'RE FEELING.
*Seven of Cups: This card signifies having an active imagination and many dreams and hopes for the future; it also means lacking the ability to put thoughts into action.
SEVEN OF CUPS
YOU'VE BEEN LYING TO YOURSELF...
AND TO OTHERS.
NO, NO. I DON'T DECEIVE ANYONE, LEAST OF ALL MYSELF.
EMOTION AND REASON SOMETIMES DISAGREE.

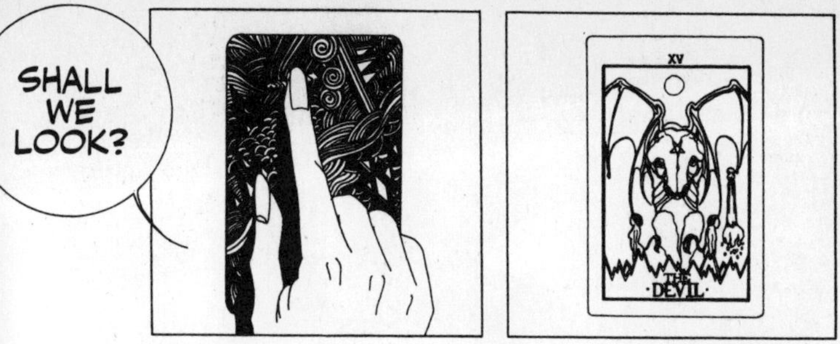
SHALL WE LOOK?
XV
THE DEVIL

*The Devil: The card hints at a lack of humanity. It may also signify a focus on material gain to the detriment of others, or being tied down against your will; enslaved.

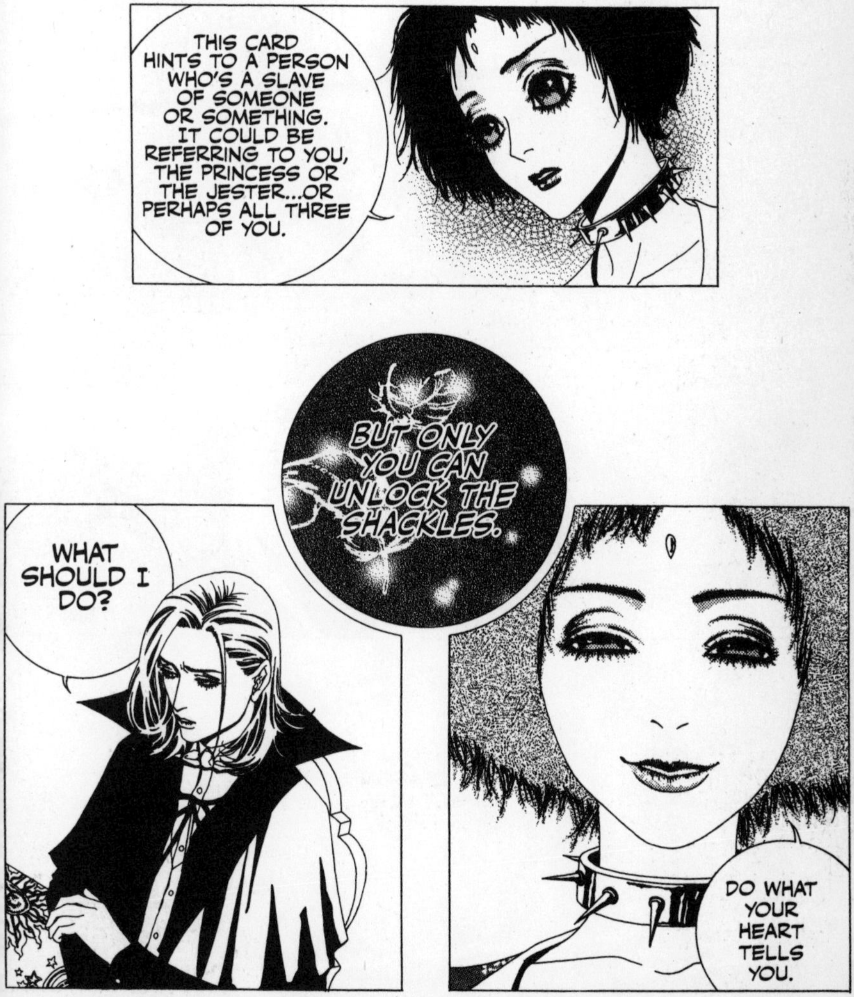
THIS CARD HINTS TO A PERSON WHO'S A SLAVE OF SOMEONE OR SOMETHING. IT COULD BE REFERRING TO YOU, THE PRINCESS OR THE JESTER...OR PERHAPS ALL THREE OF YOU.
BUT ONLY YOU CAN UNLOCK THE SHACKLES.
WHAT SHOULD I DO?
DO WHAT YOUR HEART TELLS YOU.

I THINK I KNOW WHAT YOU MEAN.

THANK YOU FOR YOUR ADVICE.

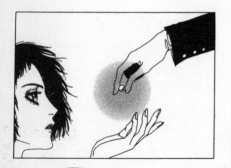

MAY I ASK YOU ONE MORE THING?

THIS BEAD IS FROM BERIAL'S NECKLACE.

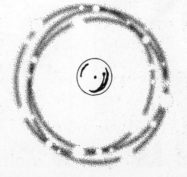

WHY DO YOU HAVE THIS BEAD?

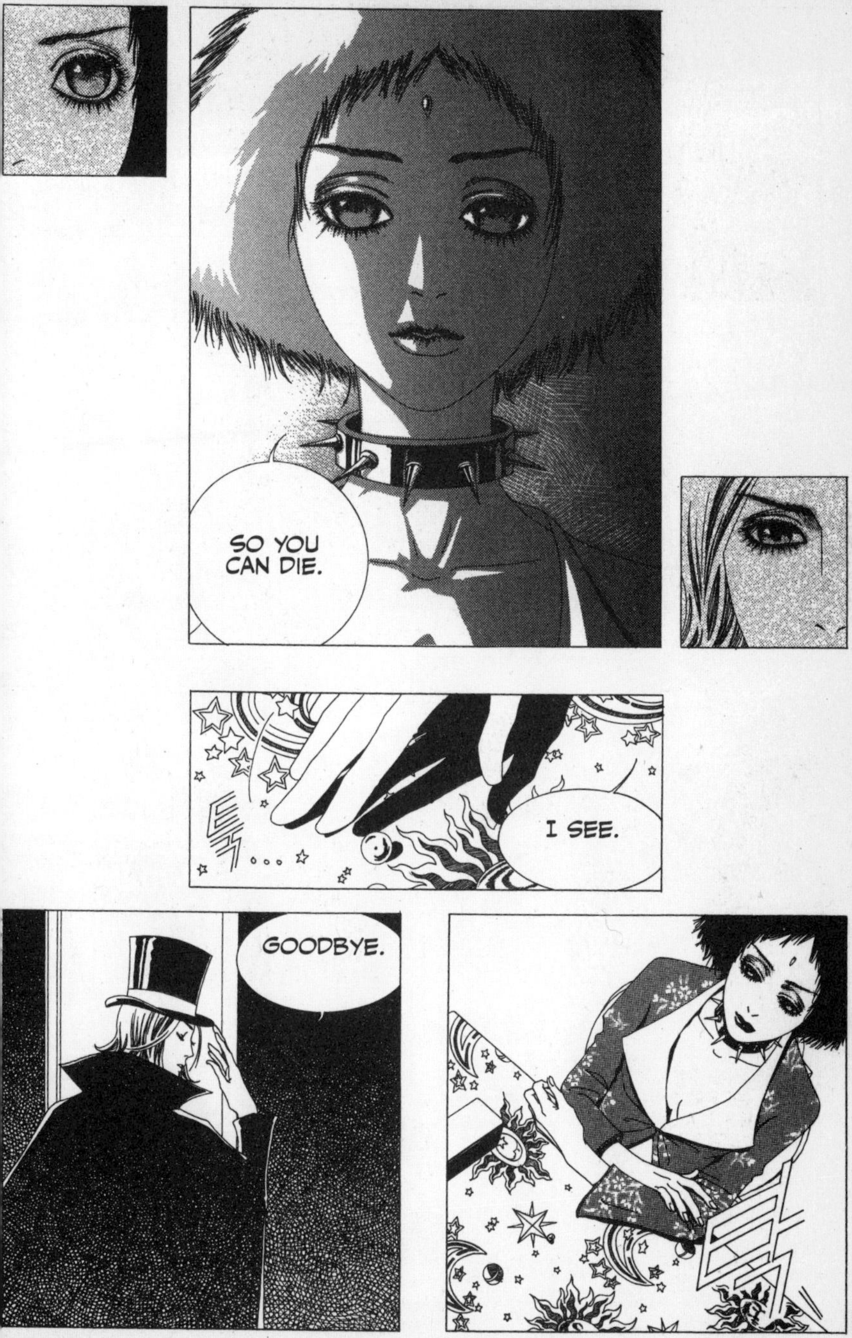
SO YOU CAN DIE.
I SEE.
GOODBYE.

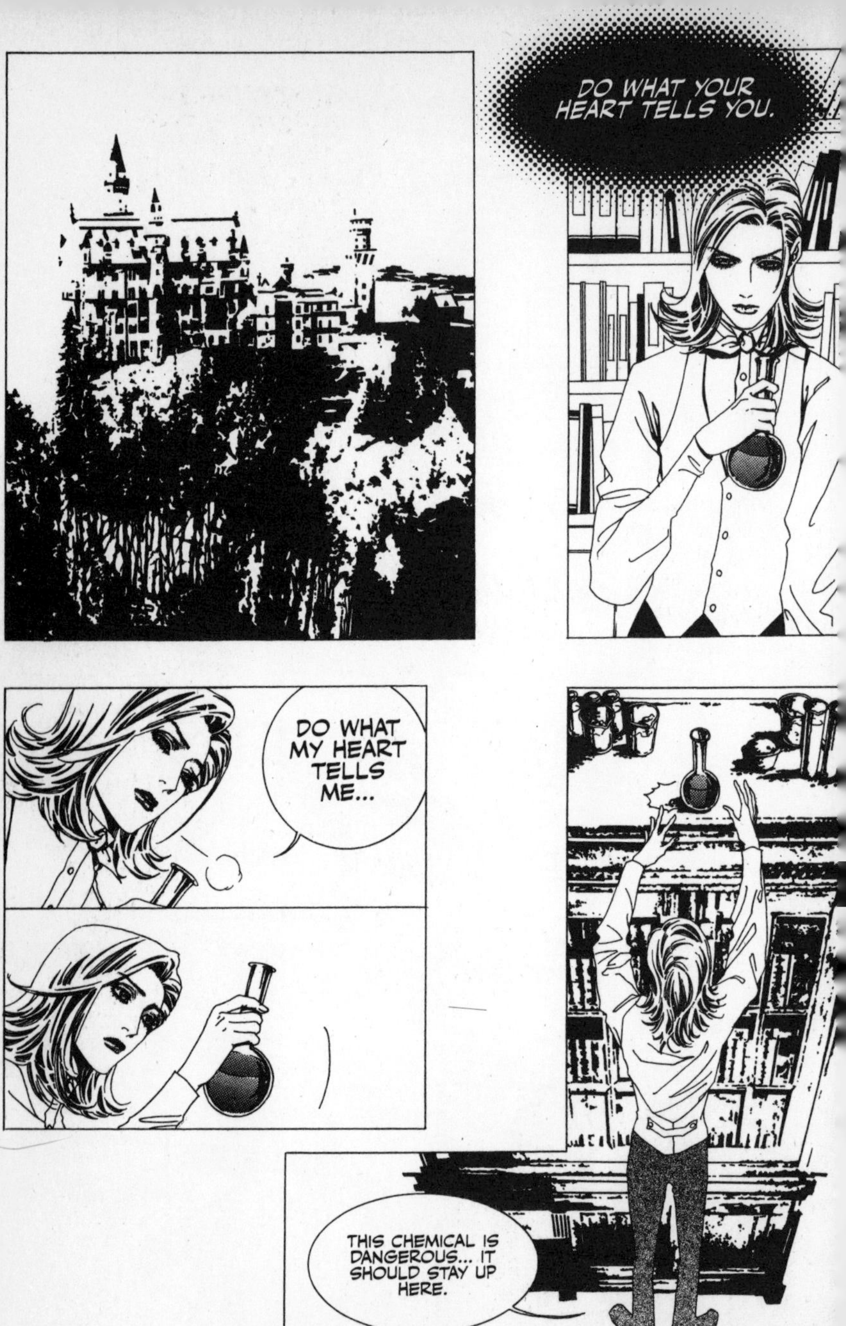
DO WHAT YOUR HEART TELLS YOU.
DO WHAT MY HEART TELLS ME...
THIS CHEMICAL IS DANGEROUS... IT SHOULD STAY UP HERE.

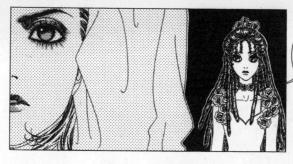

WHERE IS THE JESTER?

GWYNETH...

WE WERE IN THE MIDDLE OF A VERY INTERESTING GAME. BUT I GUESS HE WASN'T ENJOYING HIMSELF SO MUCH!

MASTER! HERE ARE THE FLOWERS YOU ASKED FOR.

WELL, LOOK AT THAT! YOUR LEG IS ALL FIXED NOW!

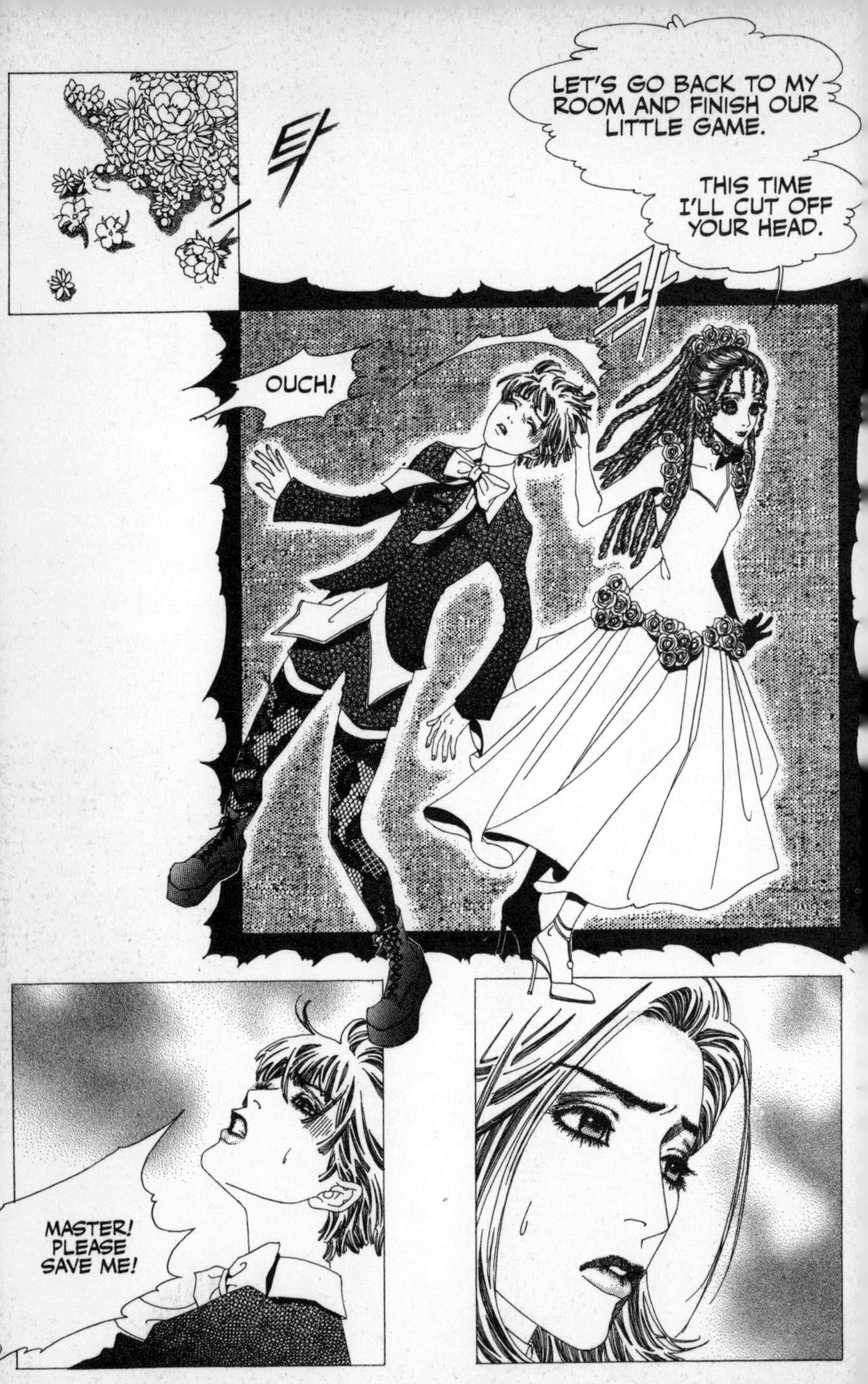

탁
LET'S GO BACK TO MY ROOM AND FINISH OUR LITTLE GAME.
THIS TIME I'LL CUT OFF YOUR HEAD.
콱
OUCH!
MASTER! PLEASE SAVE ME!

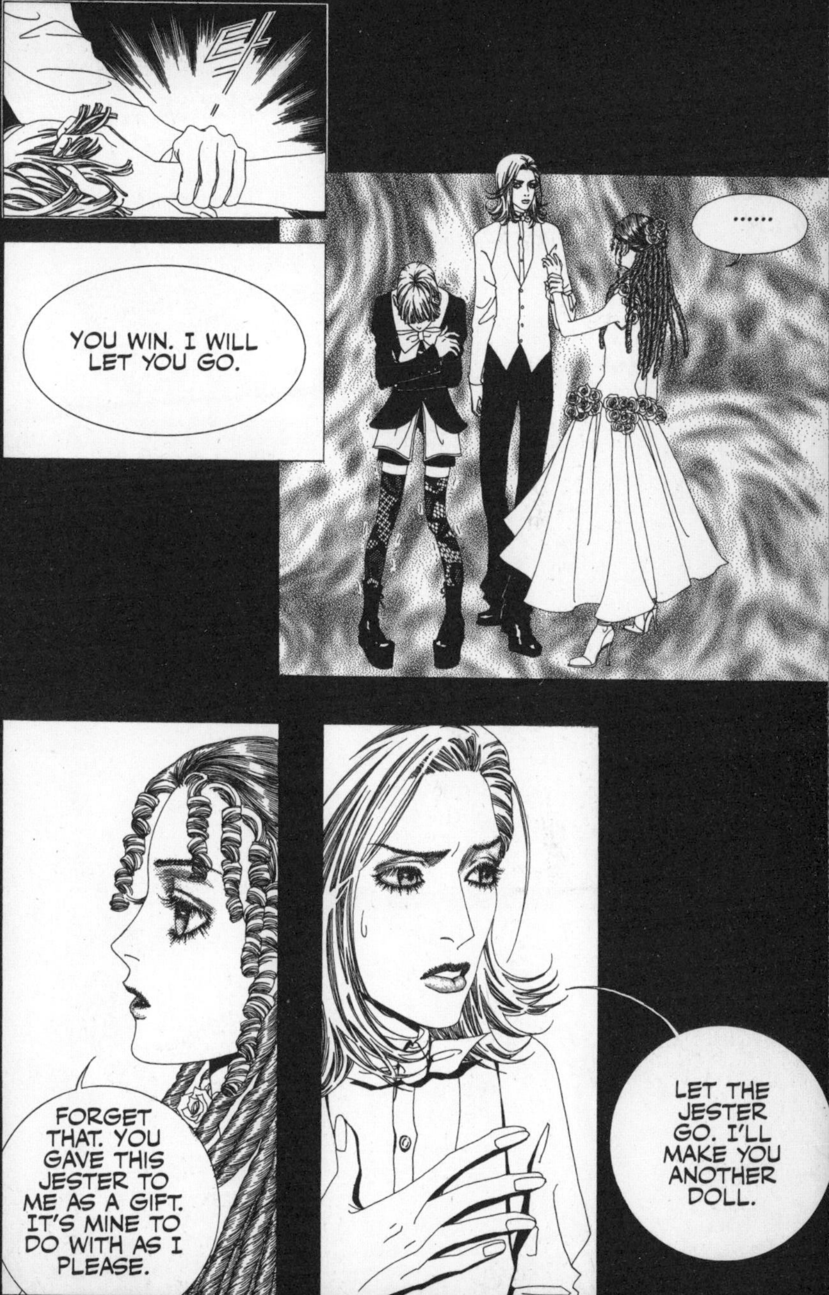
YOU WIN. I WILL LET YOU GO.
......
FORGET THAT. YOU GAVE THIS JESTER TO ME AS A GIFT. IT'S MINE TO DO WITH AS I PLEASE.
LET THE JESTER GO. I'LL MAKE YOU ANOTHER DOLL.

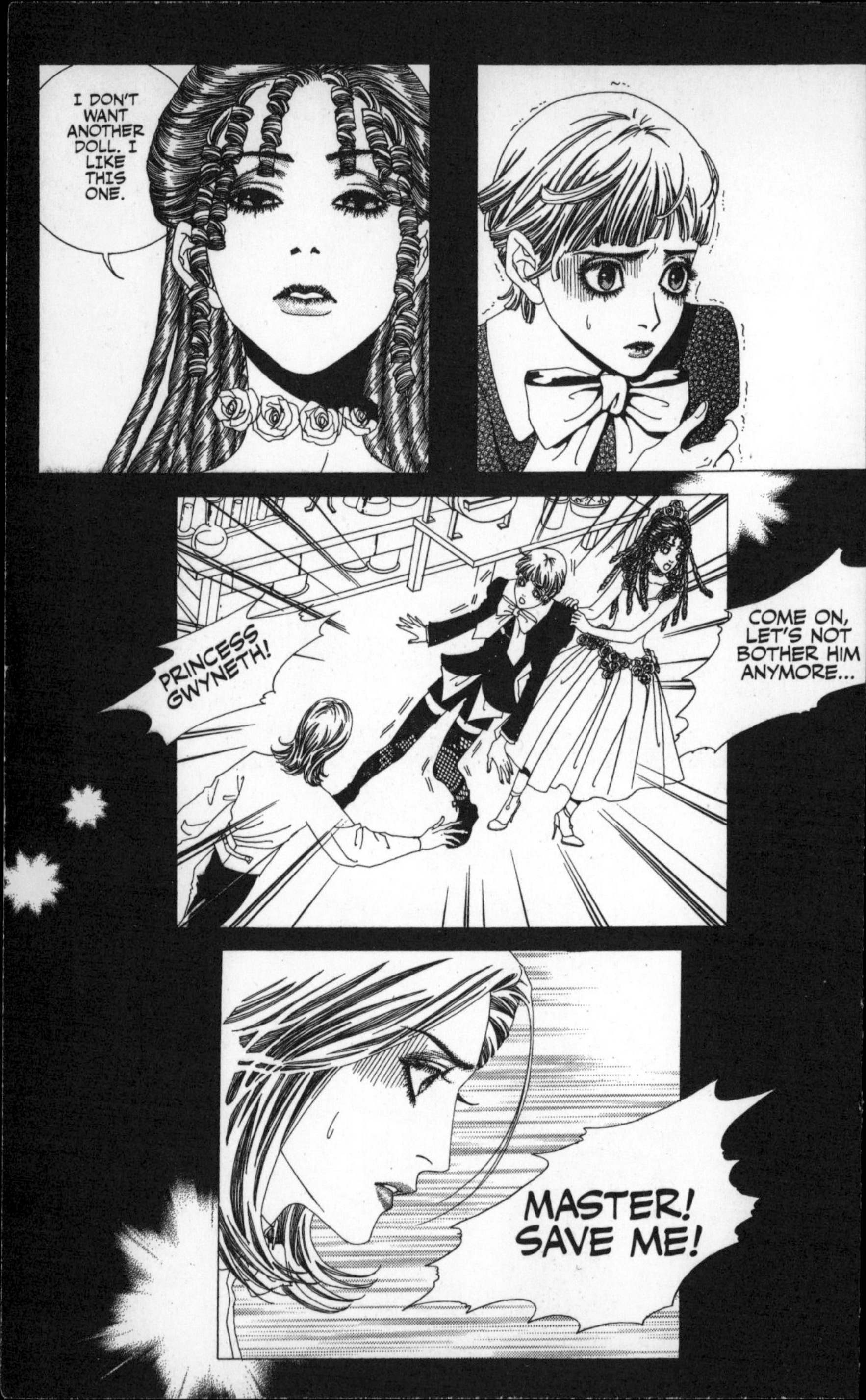
I DON'T WANT ANOTHER DOLL. I LIKE THIS ONE.
PRINCESS GWYNETH!
COME ON, LET'S NOT BOTHER HIM ANYMORE...
MASTER! SAVE ME!

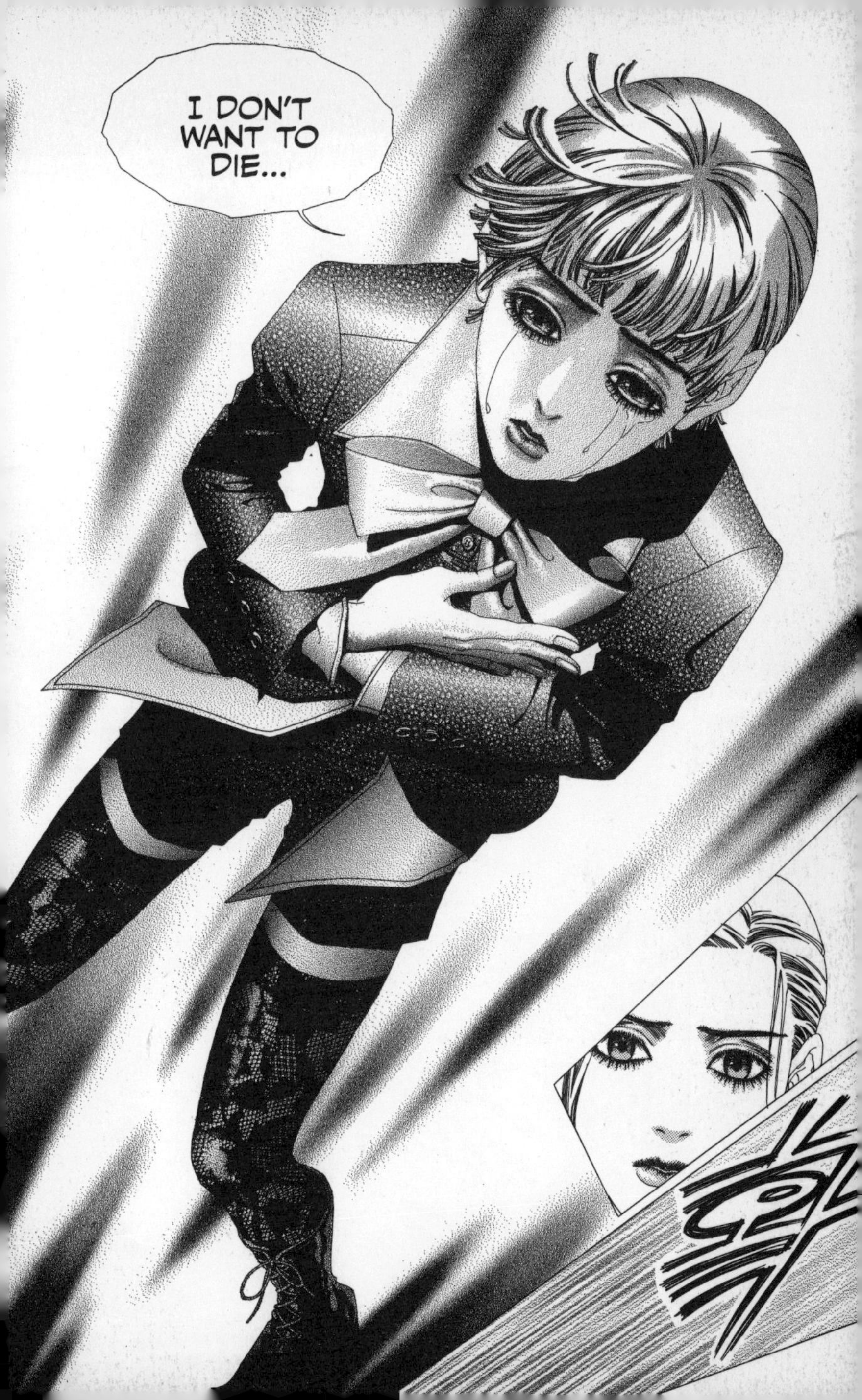
I DON'T WANT TO DIE...

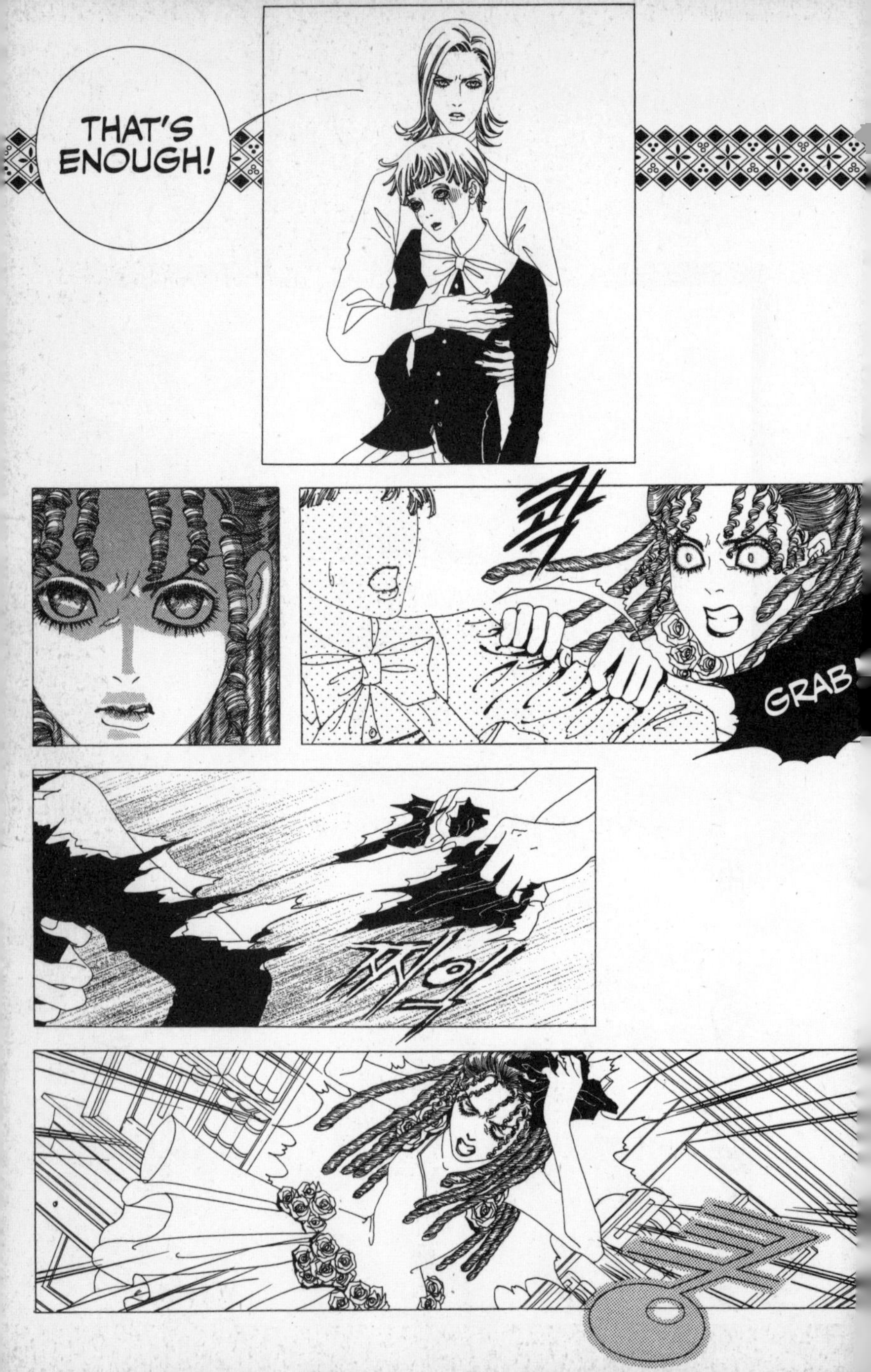
THAT'S ENOUGH!
콱
GRAB

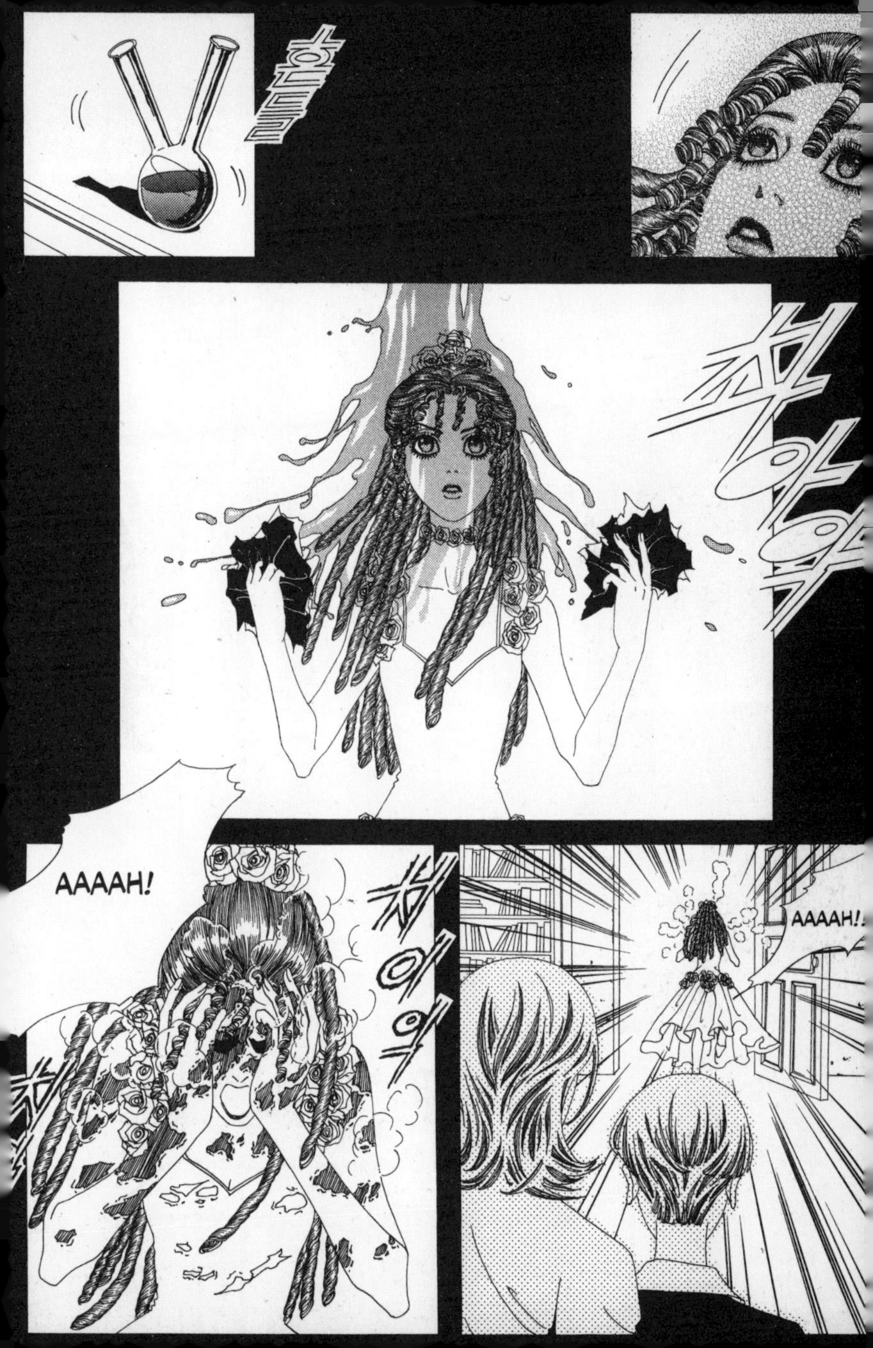
흔들
촤아악
AAAAH!
치이익
AAAAH!!

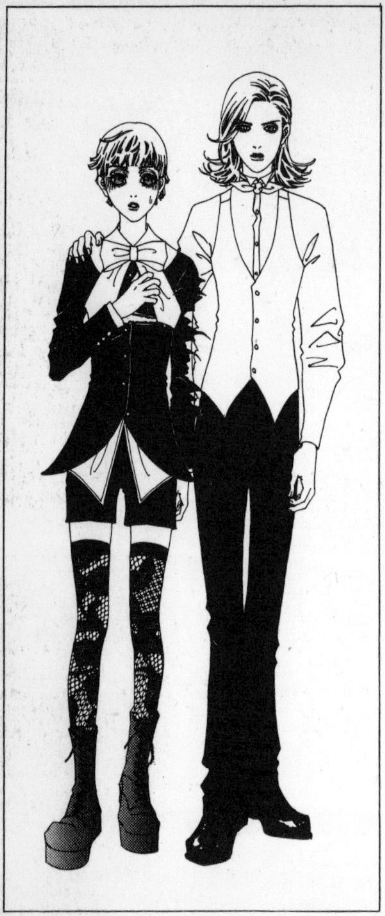

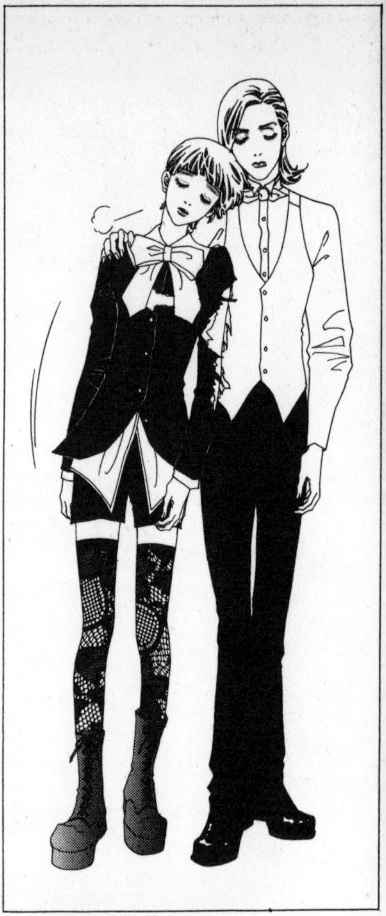

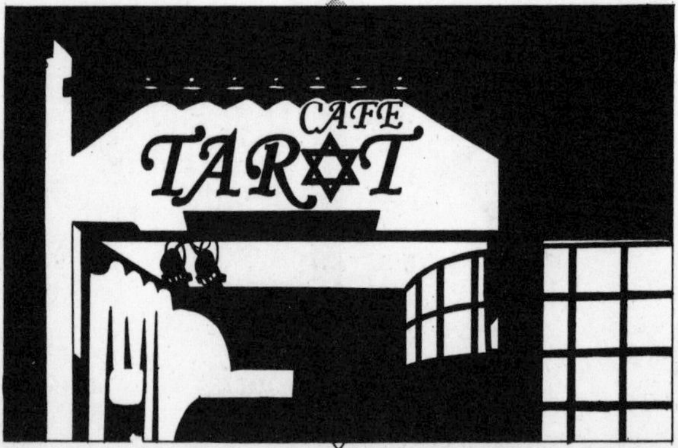
CAFE
TAROT

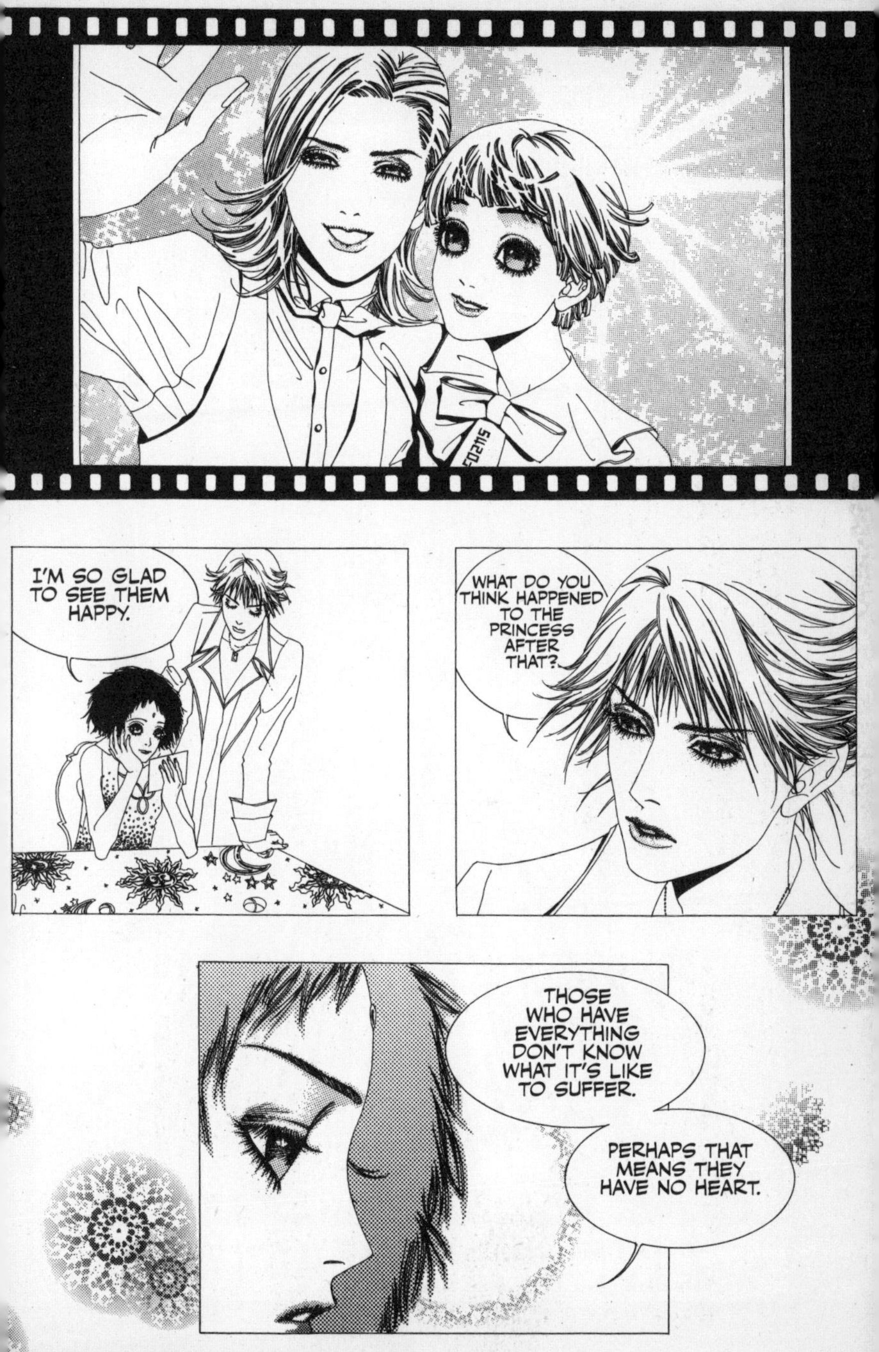
I'M SO GLAD TO SEE THEM HAPPY.
WHAT DO YOU THINK HAPPENED TO THE PRINCESS AFTER THAT?
THOSE WHO HAVE EVERYTHING DON'T KNOW WHAT IT'S LIKE TO SUFFER.
PERHAPS THAT MEANS THEY HAVE NO HEART.

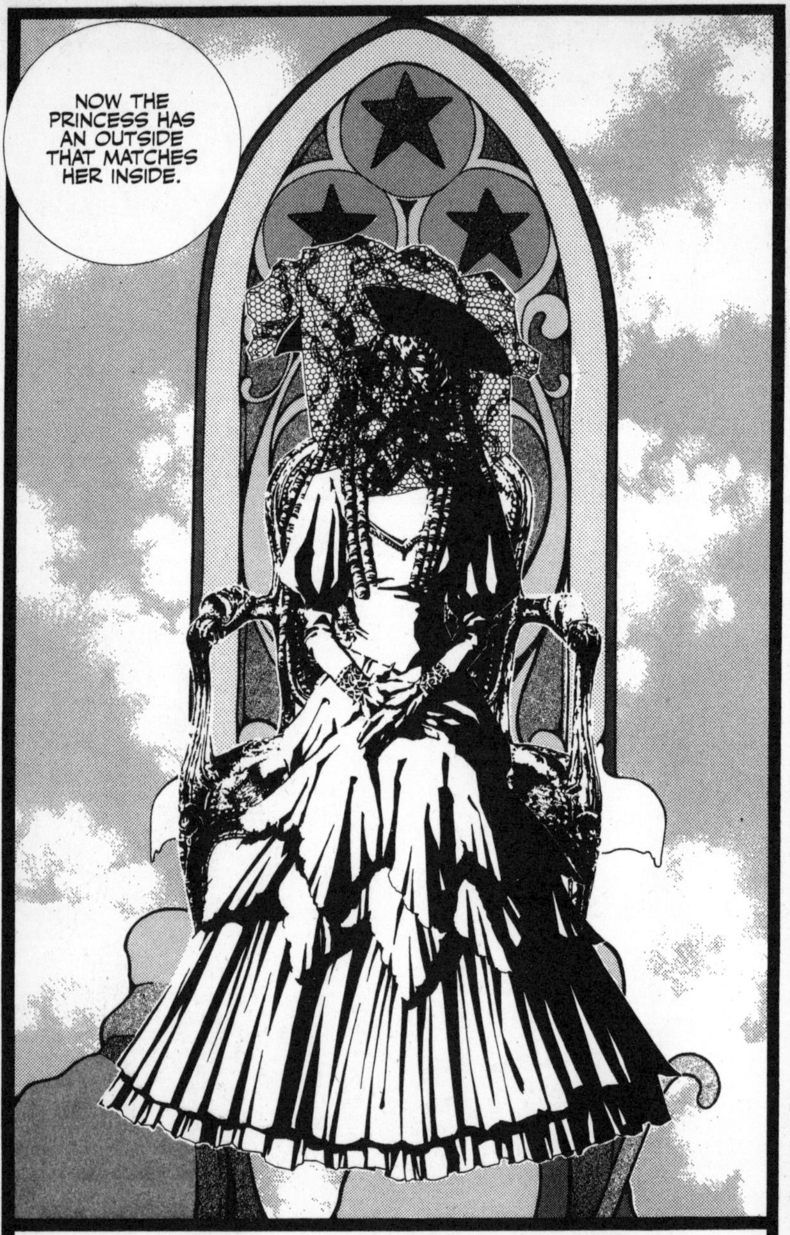
NOW THE PRINCESS HAS AN OUTSIDE THAT MATCHES HER INSIDE.
FIVE OF PENTACLES

*Five of Pentacles: This card represents lacking what one needs. It may also hint at ill health, poverty and rejection.

ILLUSTRATION FROM TAROT OF THE WOLVES

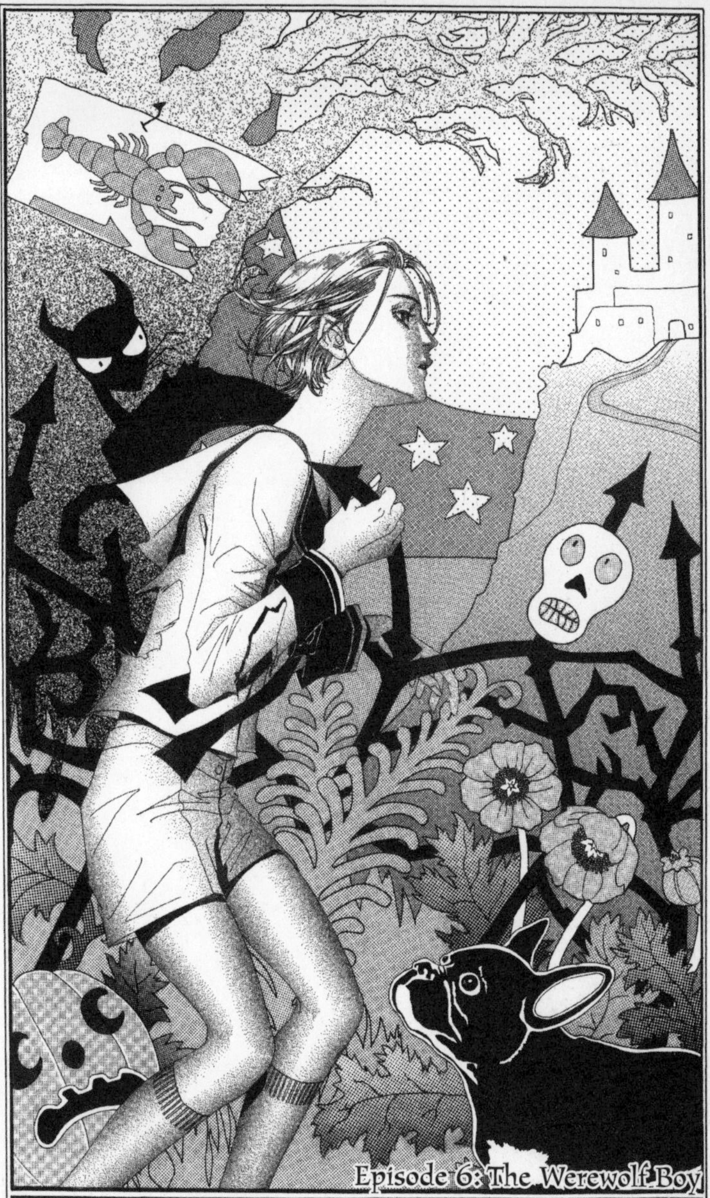
Episode 6: The Werewolf Boy

XVIII The Moon

*The Moon (Werewolf): This card represents fear of hidden danger. It may also hint at being deceived by yourself or others, misinterpreting the truth, wildness, savagery or aimless wandering.

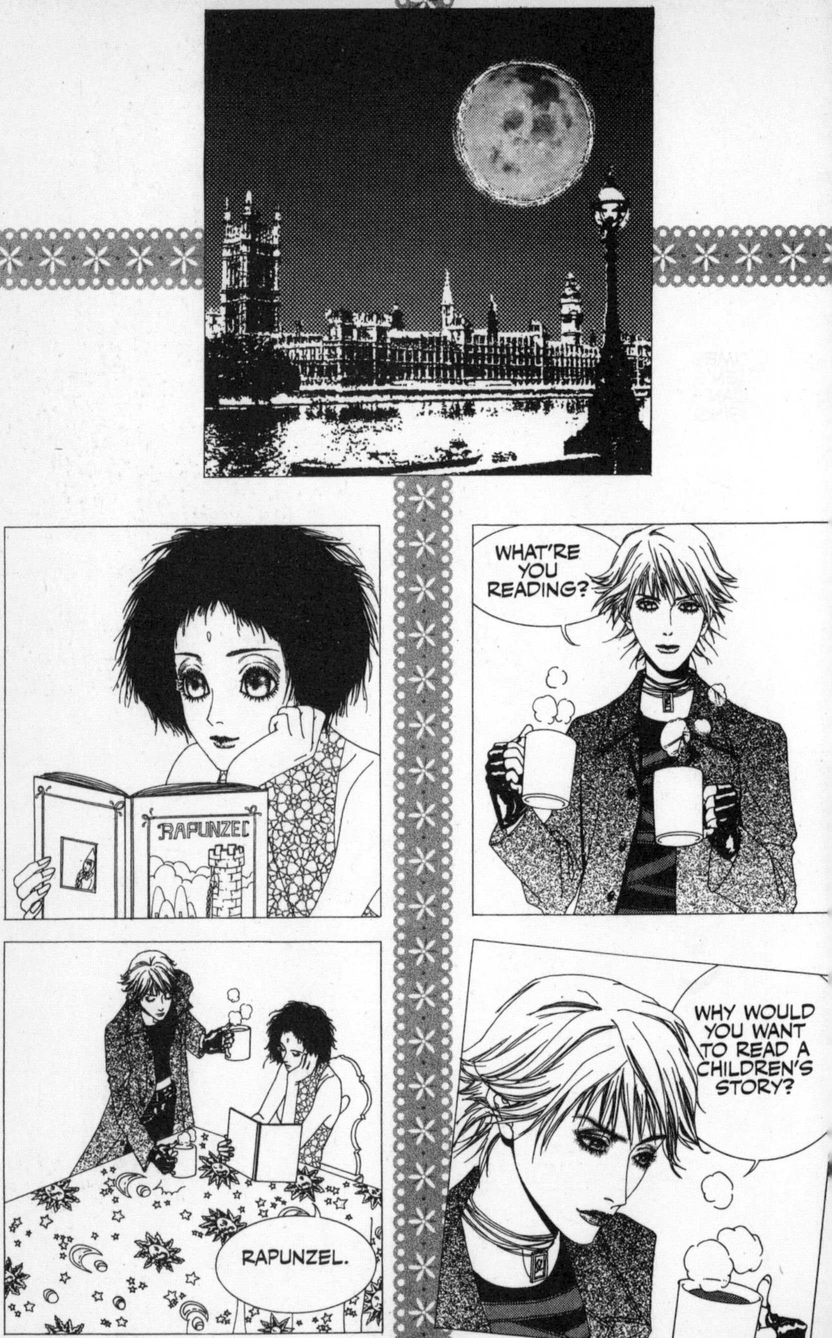
RAPUNZEL
WHAT'RE YOU READING?
RAPUNZEL.
WHY WOULD YOU WANT TO READ A CHILDREN'S STORY?

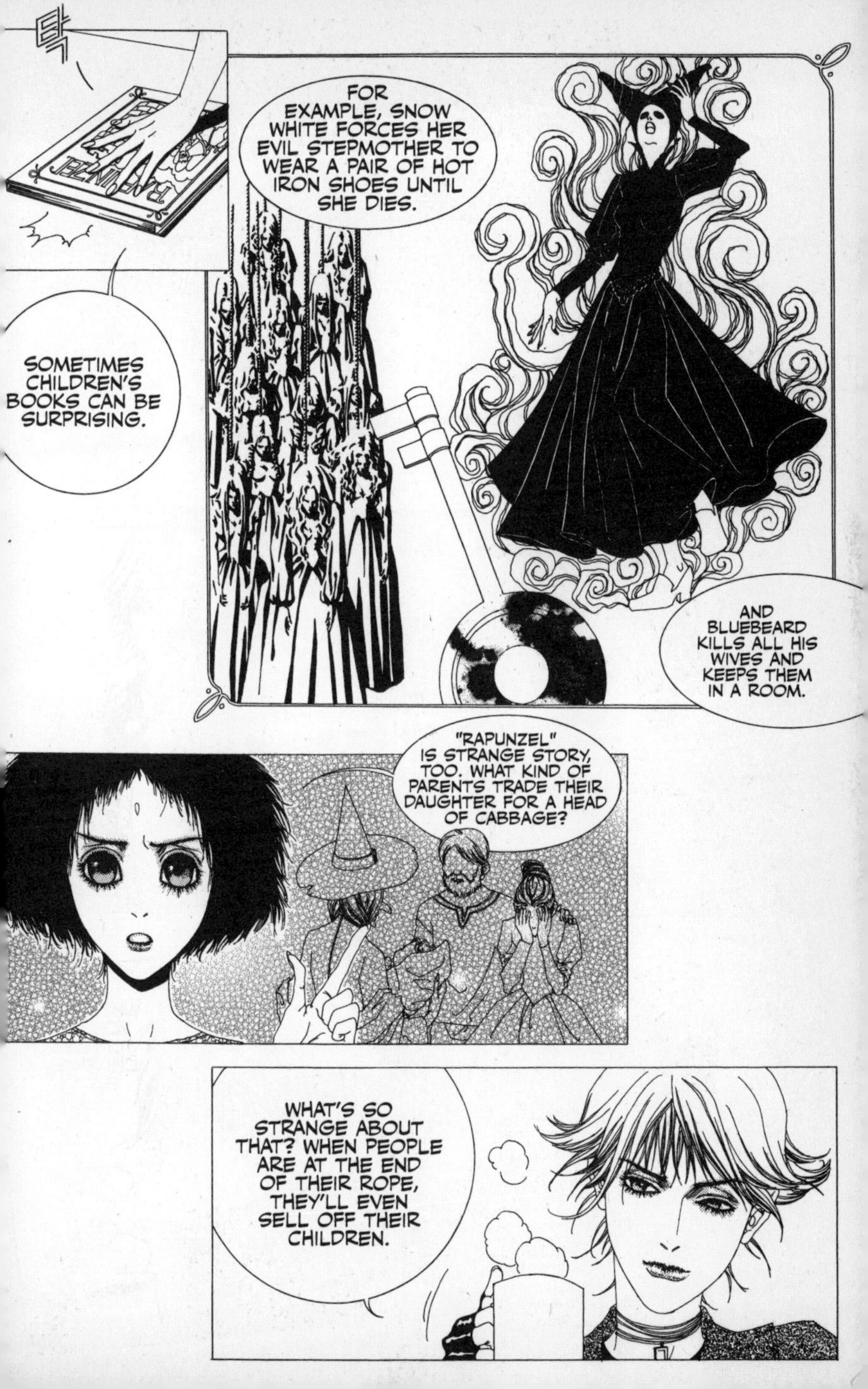
RAPUNZEL
FOR EXAMPLE, SNOW WHITE FORCES HER EVIL STEPMOTHER TO WEAR A PAIR OF HOT IRON SHOES UNTIL SHE DIES.
SOMETIMES CHILDREN'S BOOKS CAN BE SURPRISING.
AND BLUEBEARD KILLS ALL HIS WIVES AND KEEPS THEM IN A ROOM.
"RAPUNZEL" IS STRANGE STORY, TOO. WHAT KIND OF PARENTS TRADE THEIR DAUGHTER FOR A HEAD OF CABBAGE?
WHAT'S SO STRANGE ABOUT THAT? WHEN PEOPLE ARE AT THE END OF THEIR ROPE, THEY'LL EVEN SELL OFF THEIR CHILDREN.

......

I DON'T LIKE TALKING ABOUT THIS STUFF.

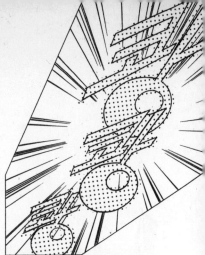

?

?

I'M SORRY, BUT WE'RE CLOSED.

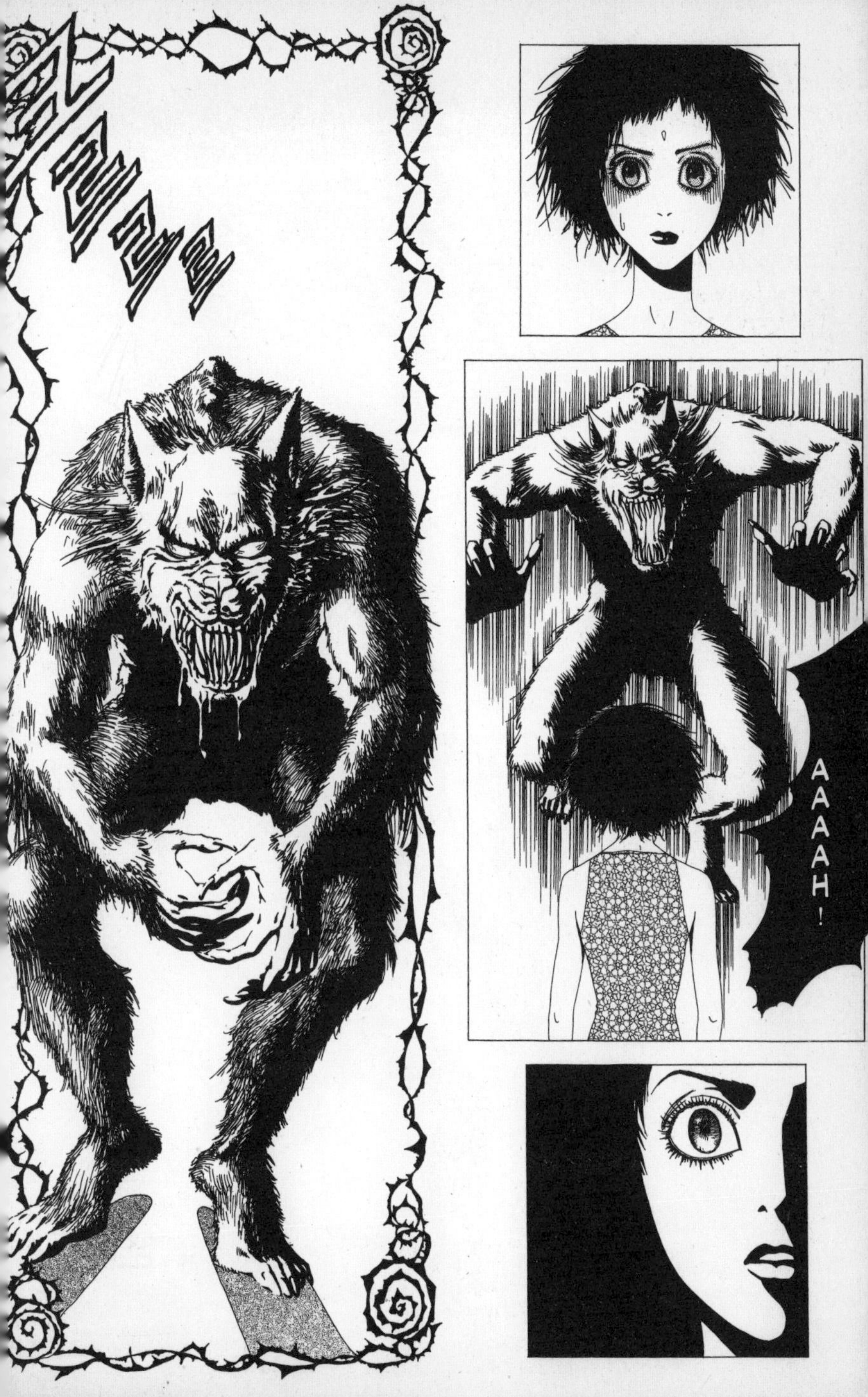
AAAAAH!

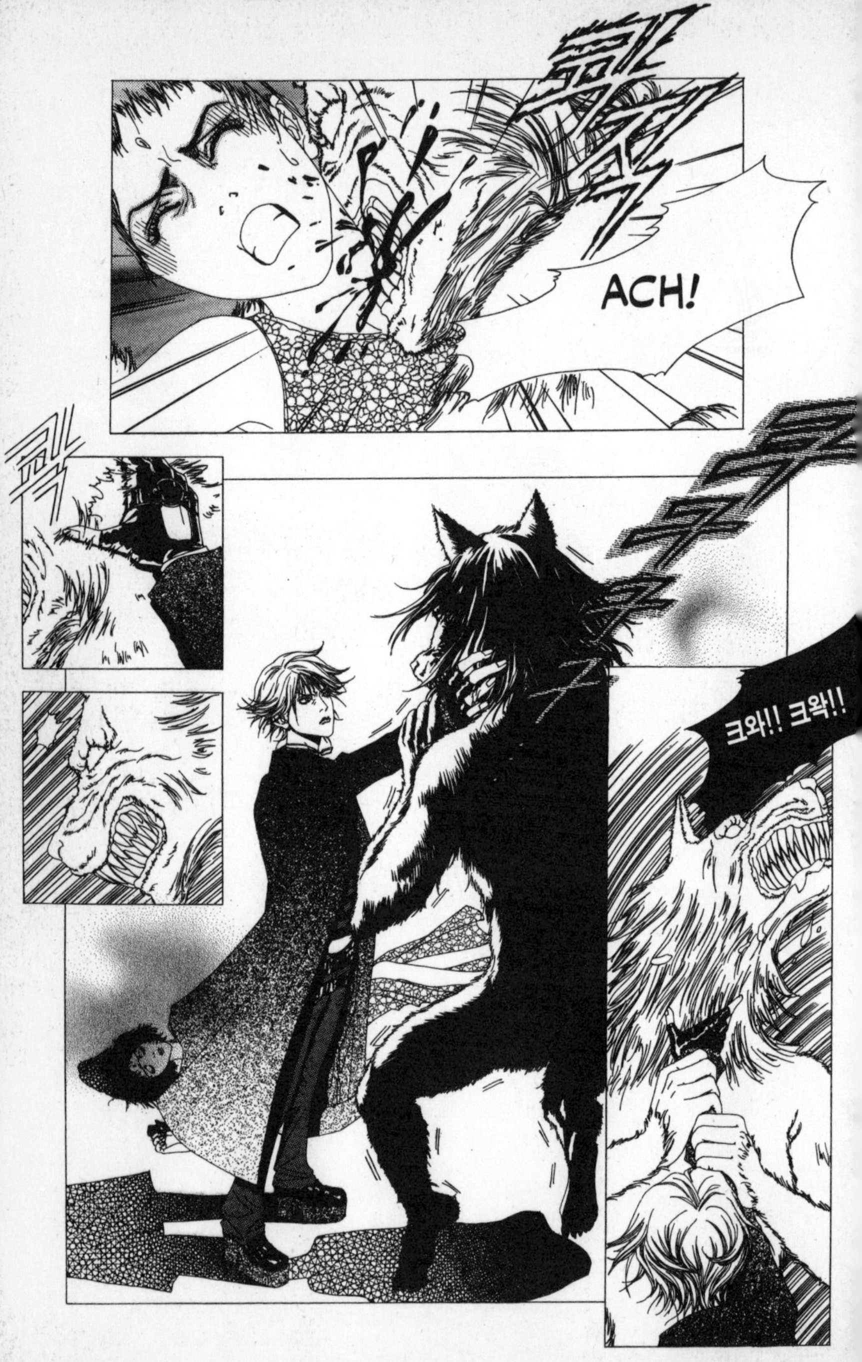
ACH!
크와!! 크왁!!

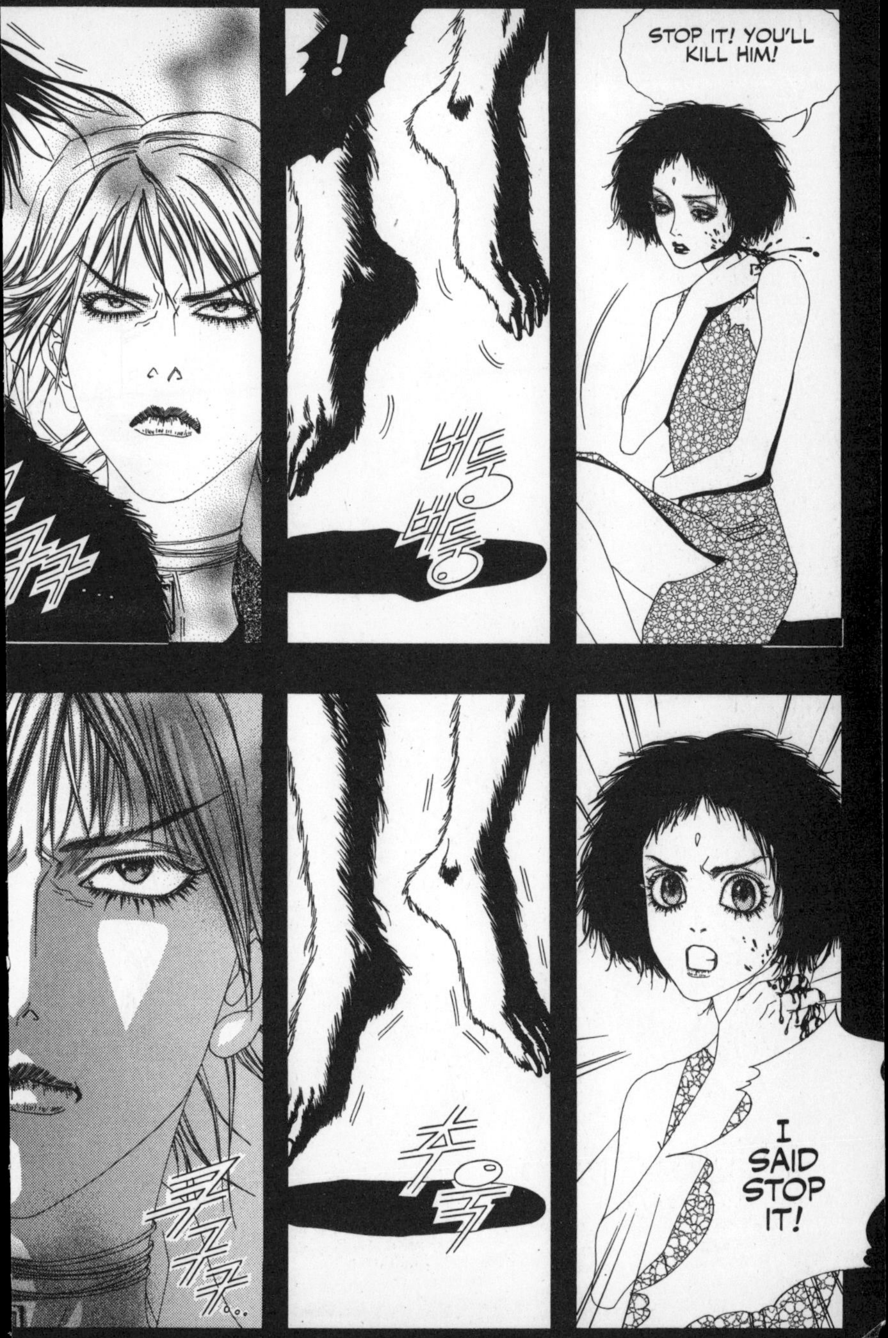
!
STOP IT! YOU'LL KILL HIM!
I SAID STOP IT!

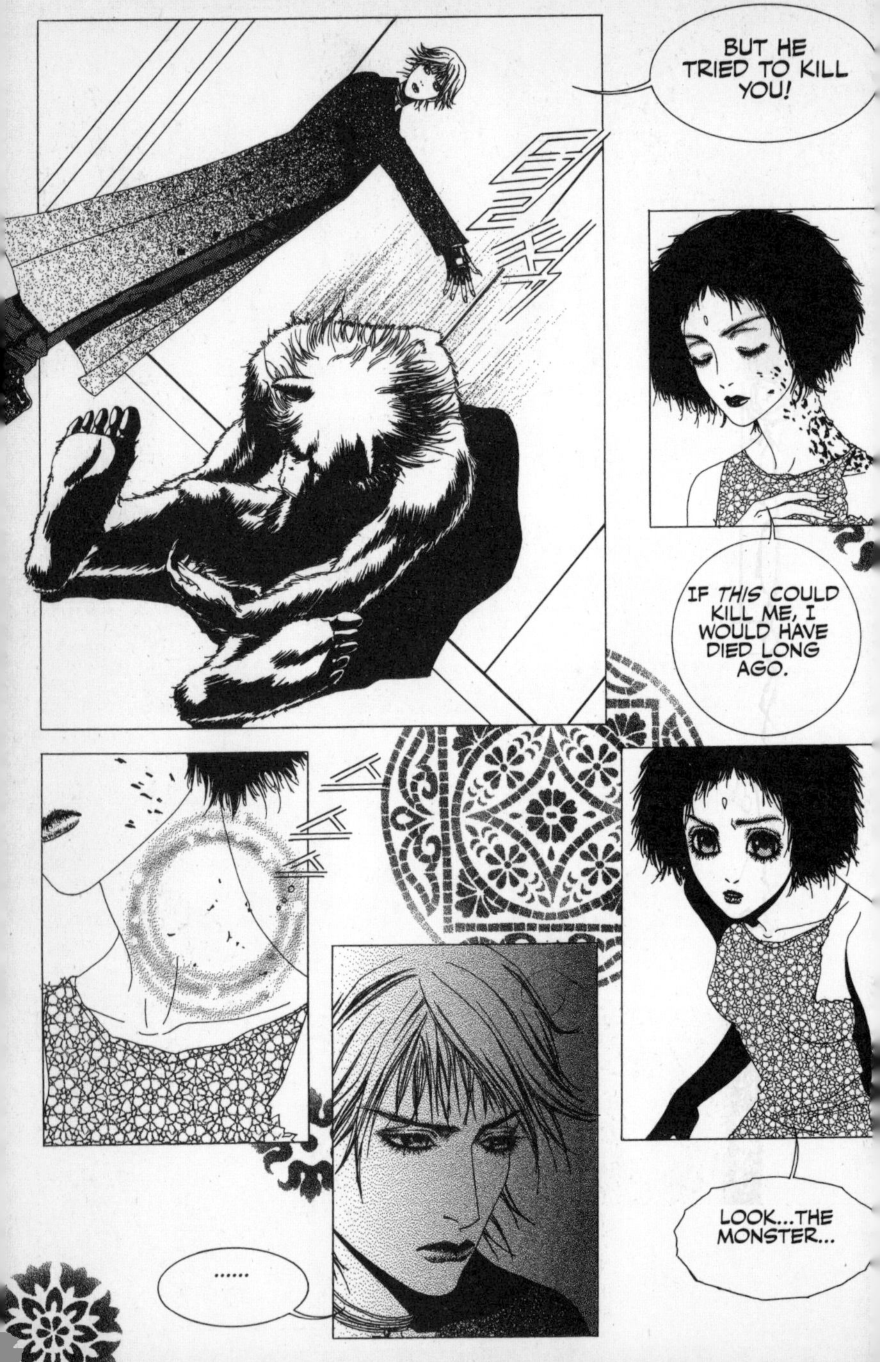
BUT HE TRIED TO KILL YOU!
IF *THIS* COULD KILL ME, I WOULD HAVE DIED LONG AGO.
LOOK...THE MONSTER...
......

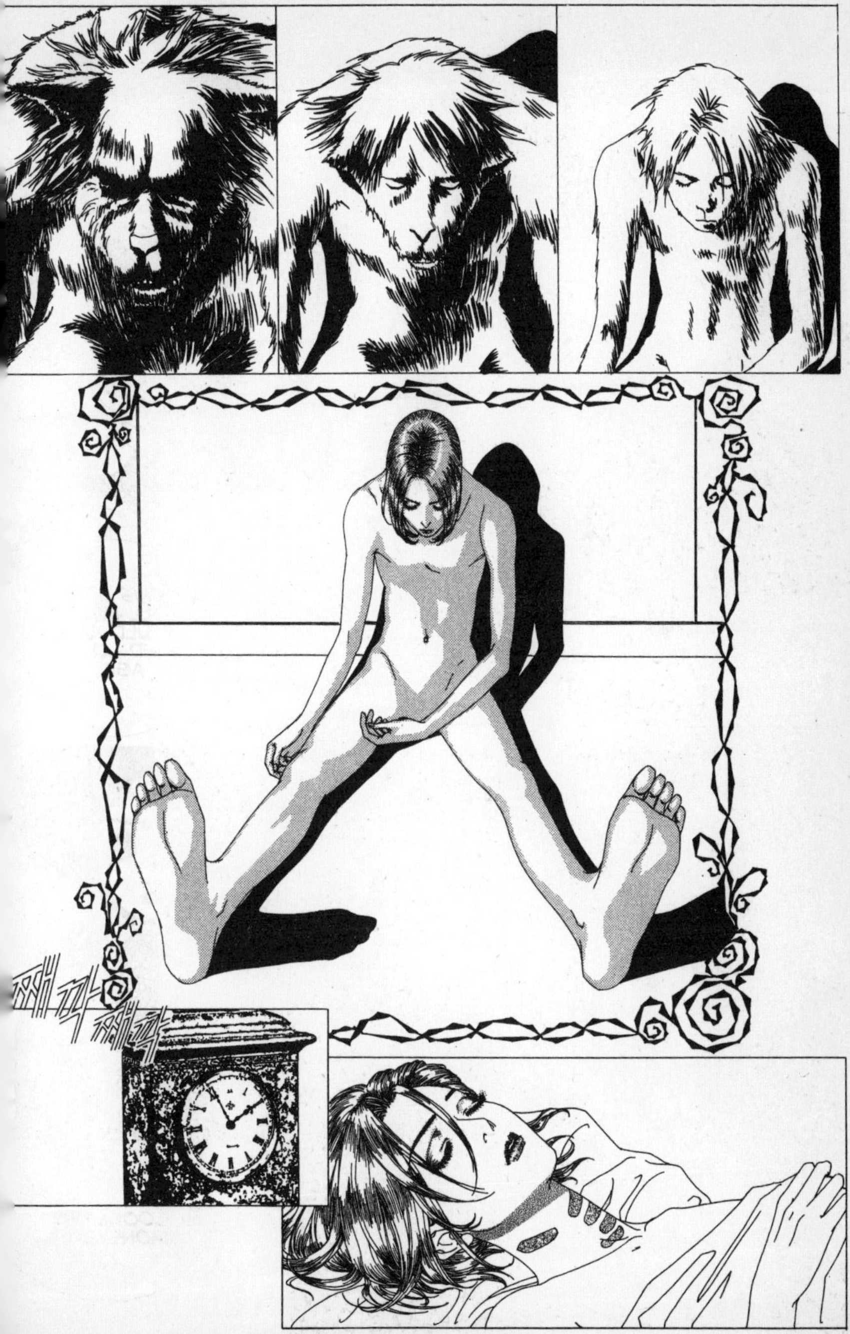

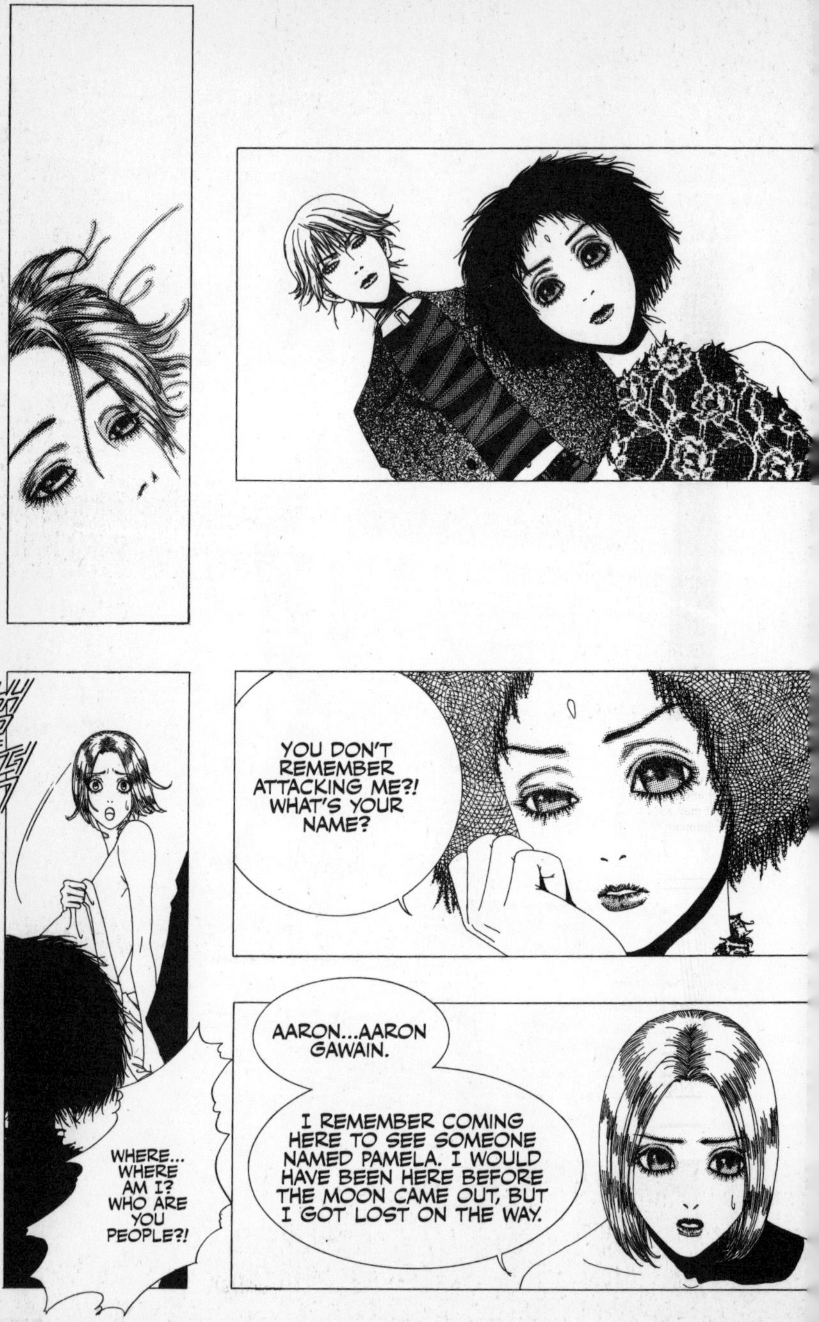
WHERE... WHERE AM I? WHO ARE YOU PEOPLE?!
YOU DON'T REMEMBER ATTACKING ME?! WHAT'S YOUR NAME?
AARON...AARON GAWAIN.
I REMEMBER COMING HERE TO SEE SOMEONE NAMED PAMELA. I WOULD HAVE BEEN HERE BEFORE THE MOON CAME OUT, BUT I GOT LOST ON THE WAY.

SO YOU CAME TO THE RIGHT PLACE AFTER ALL.

YOU WERE ABANDONED BY SOMEONE VERY CLOSE TO YOU.

LIKE ONE OF YOUR PARENTS. IT MUST HAVE HURT YOU DEEPLY.

* Ten of Swords: This card represents a terrible misfortune, but one that may turn around once rock-bottom is hit. It may also signify worry and anxiety, disappointment, and feeling powerless.

TEN OF SWORDS

MY MOTHER DIED WHEN I WAS A CHILD, SO I LIVED ALONE WITH MY FATHER. HE WAS AN ALCOHOLIC.

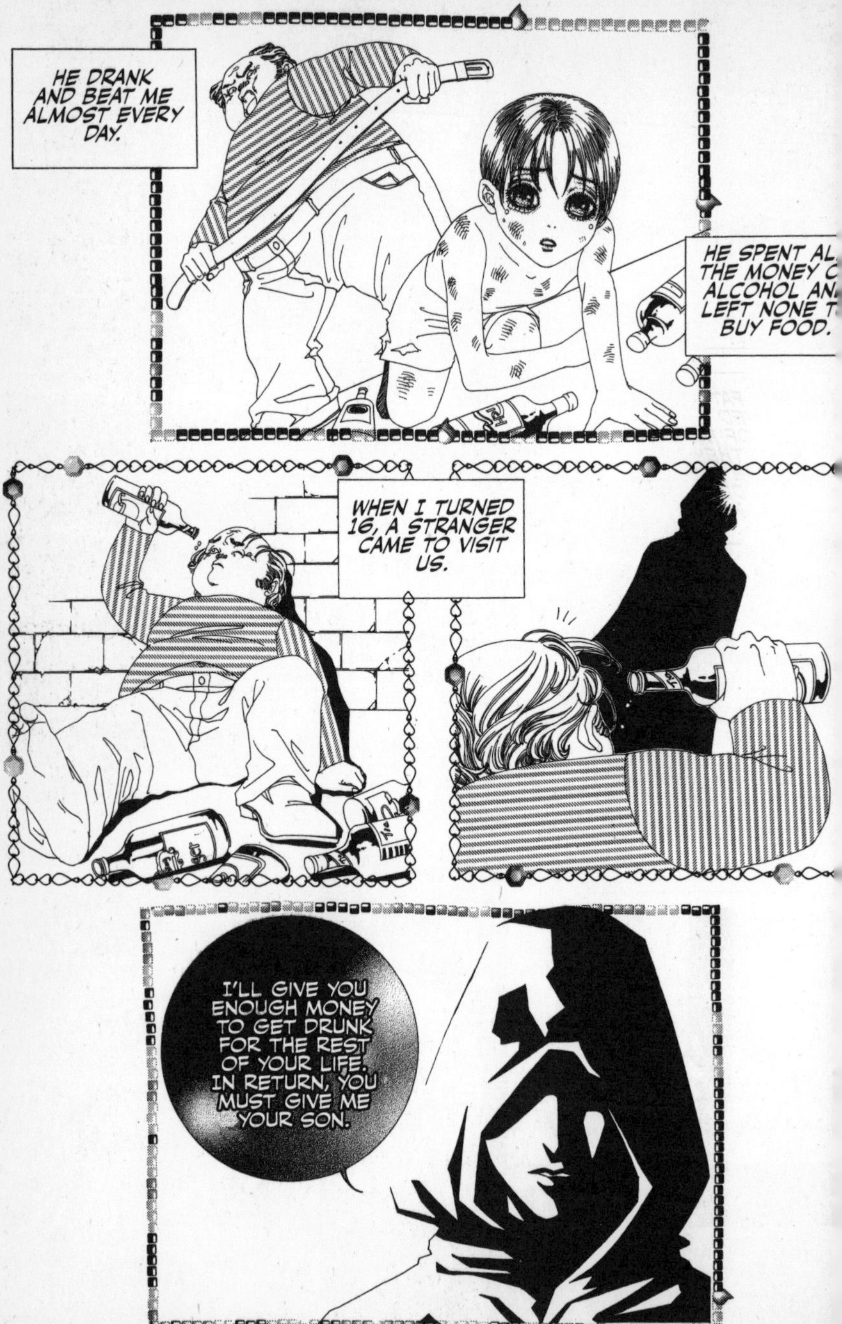
HE DRANK AND BEAT ME ALMOST EVERY DAY.
HE SPENT AL THE MONEY C ALCOHOL AN LEFT NONE T BUY FOOD.
WHEN I TURNED 16, A STRANGER CAME TO VISIT US.
I'LL GIVE YOU ENOUGH MONEY TO GET DRUNK FOR THE REST OF YOUR LIFE. IN RETURN, YOU MUST GIVE ME YOUR SON.

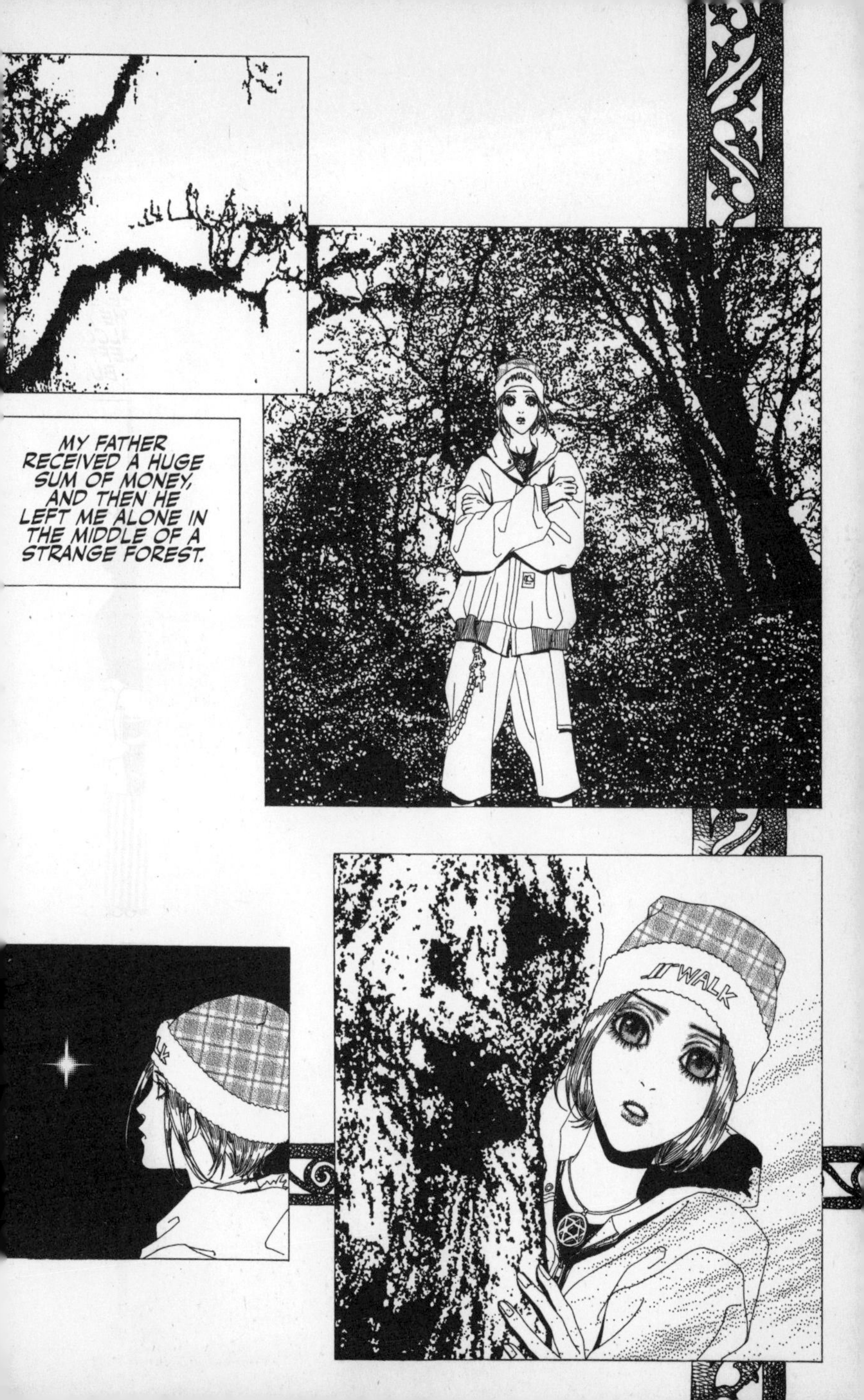
MY FATHER RECEIVED A HUGE SUM OF MONEY, AND THEN HE LEFT ME ALONE IN THE MIDDLE OF A STRANGE FOREST.

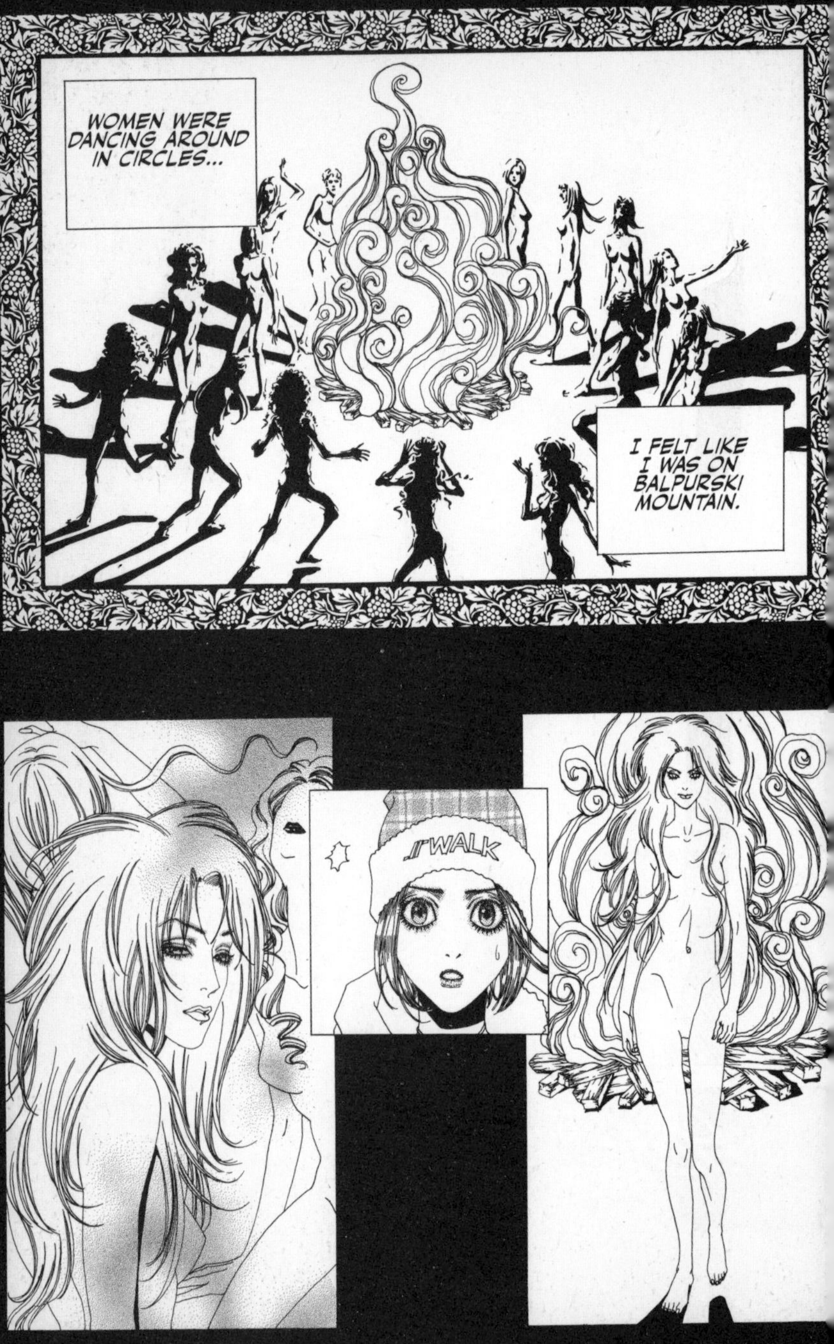
WOMEN WERE DANCING AROUND IN CIRCLES...
I FELT LIKE I WAS ON BALPURSKI MOUNTAIN.
J'WALK
!

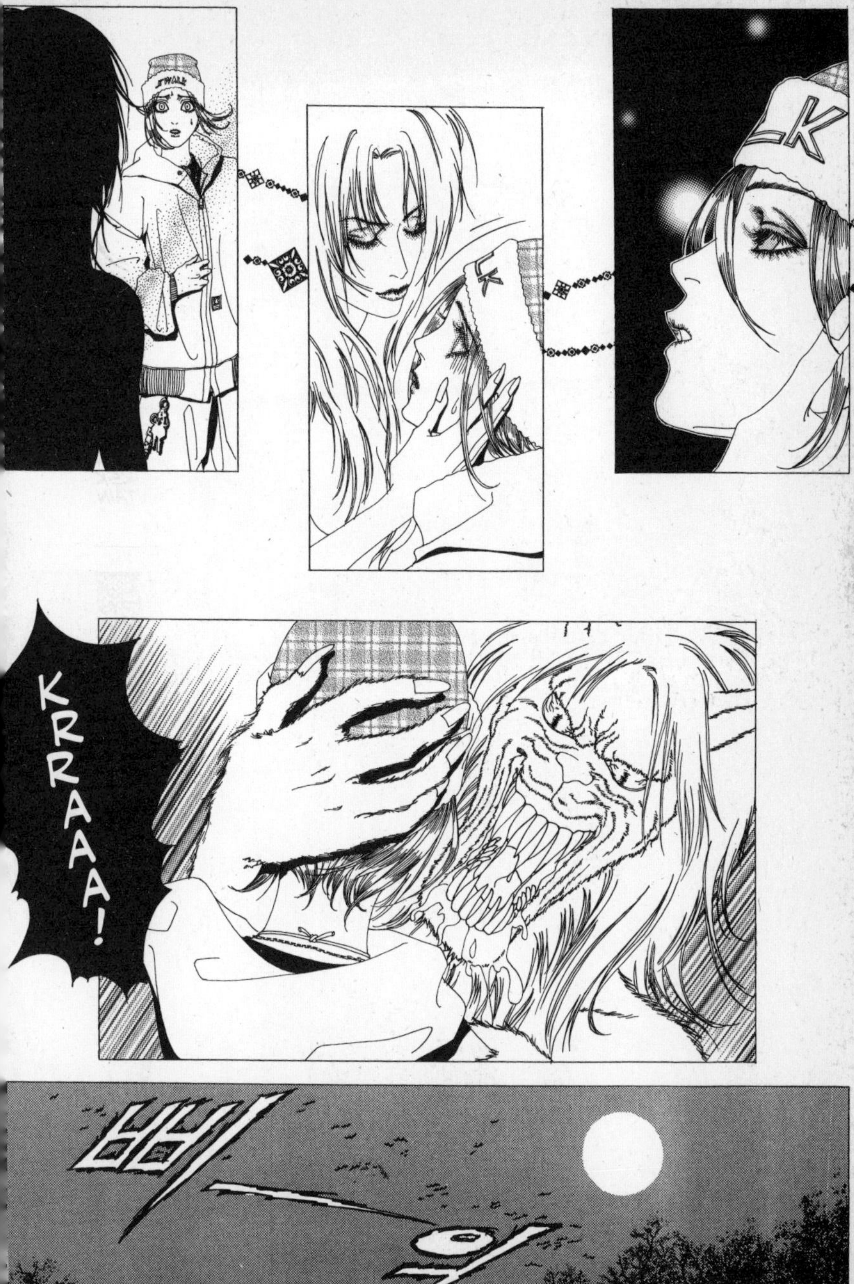
KRRAAA!
빠-악

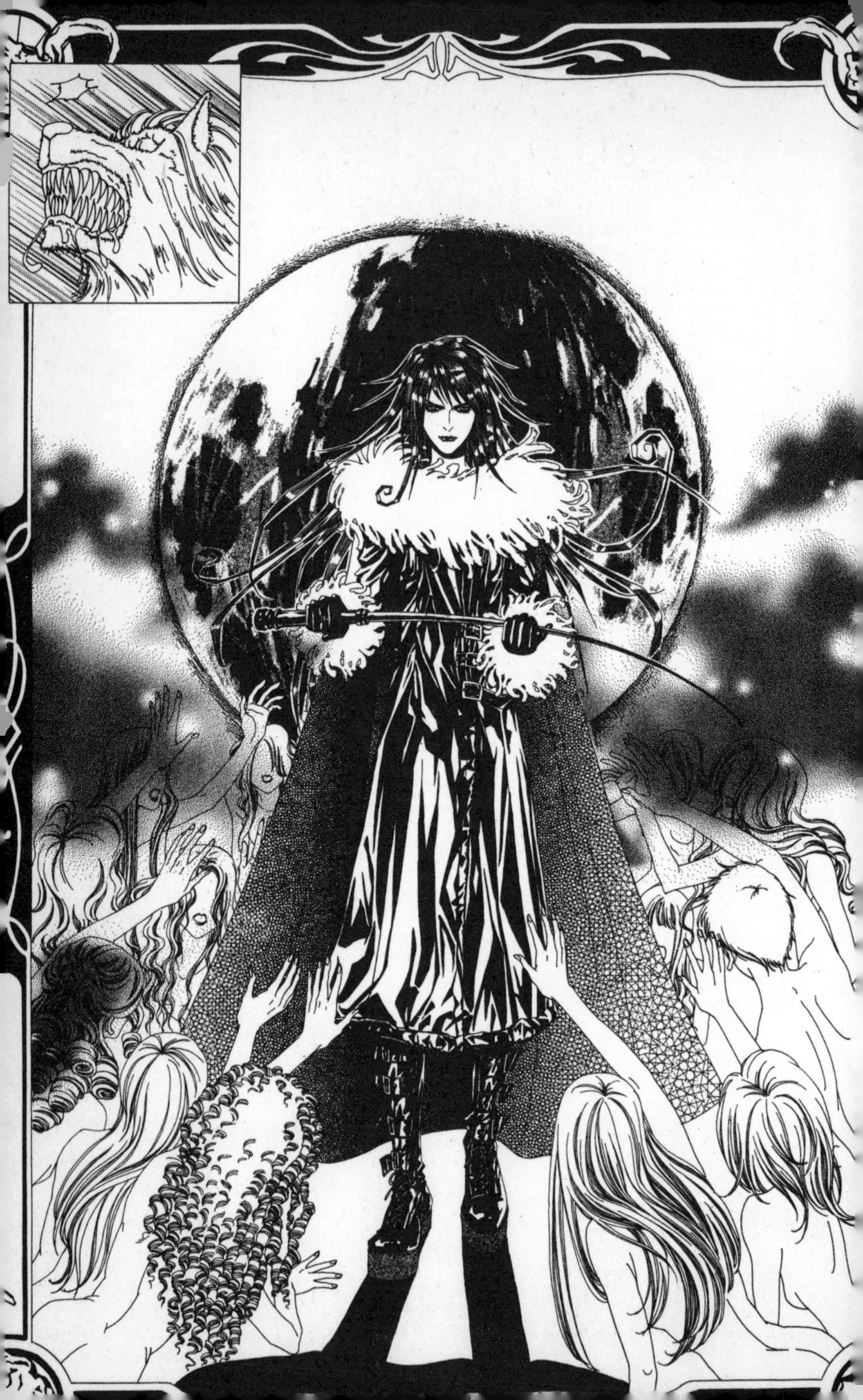

MASTER, PLEASE...I-I JUST...

AAAAH!

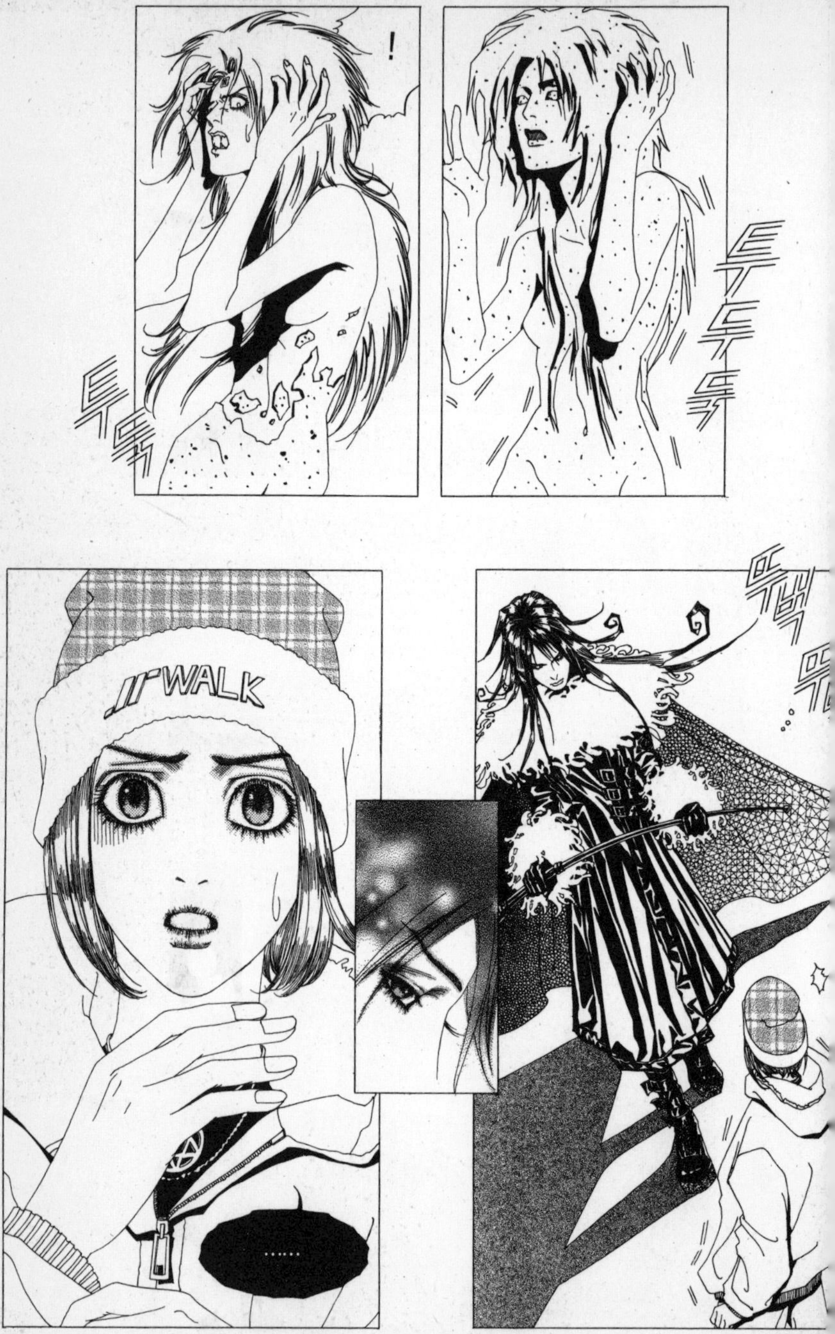
!
투둑
투두둑
WALK
......
뚜벅
!

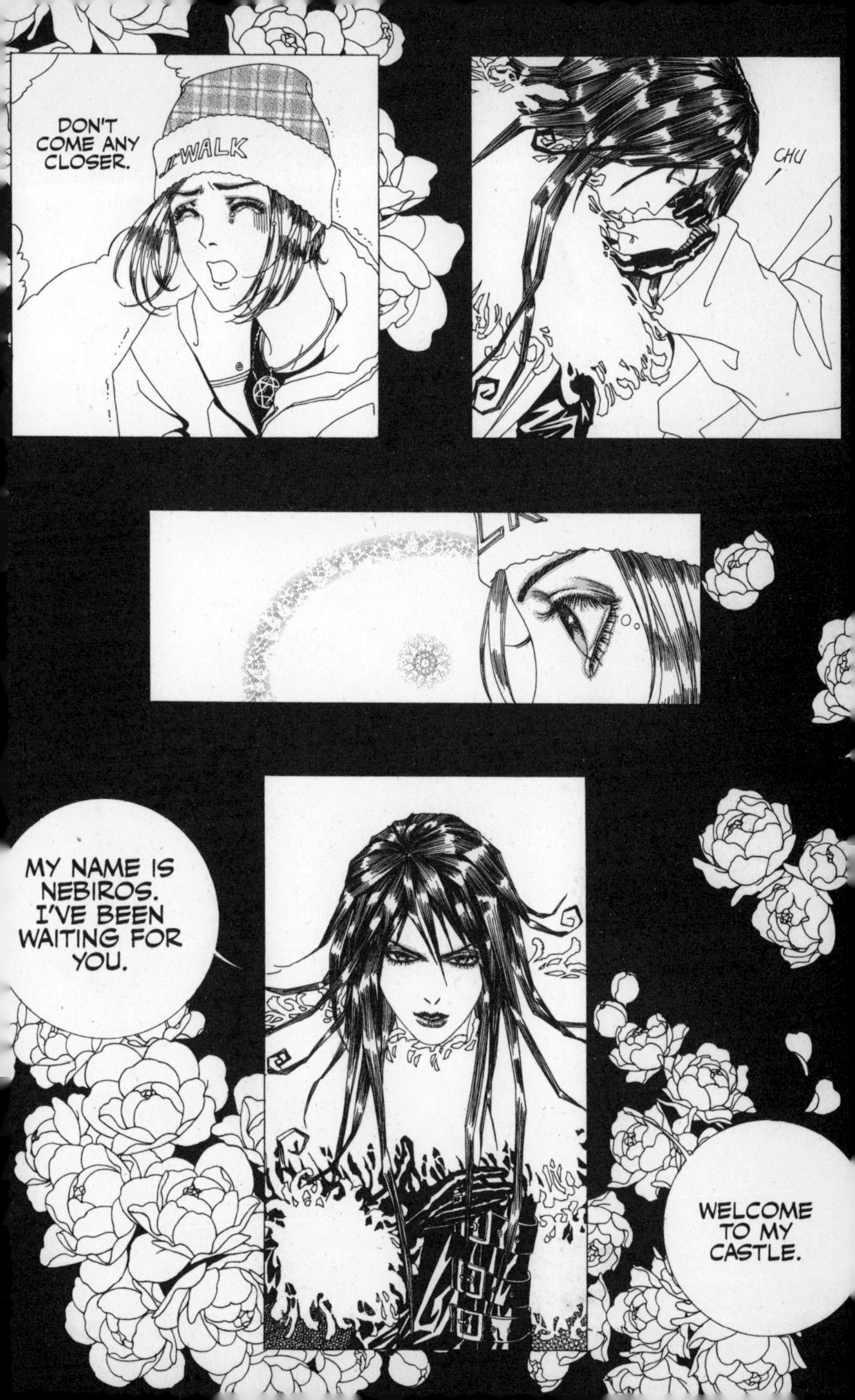
DON'T COME ANY CLOSER.
CHU
MY NAME IS NEBIROS. I'VE BEEN WAITING FOR YOU.
WELCOME TO MY CASTLE.

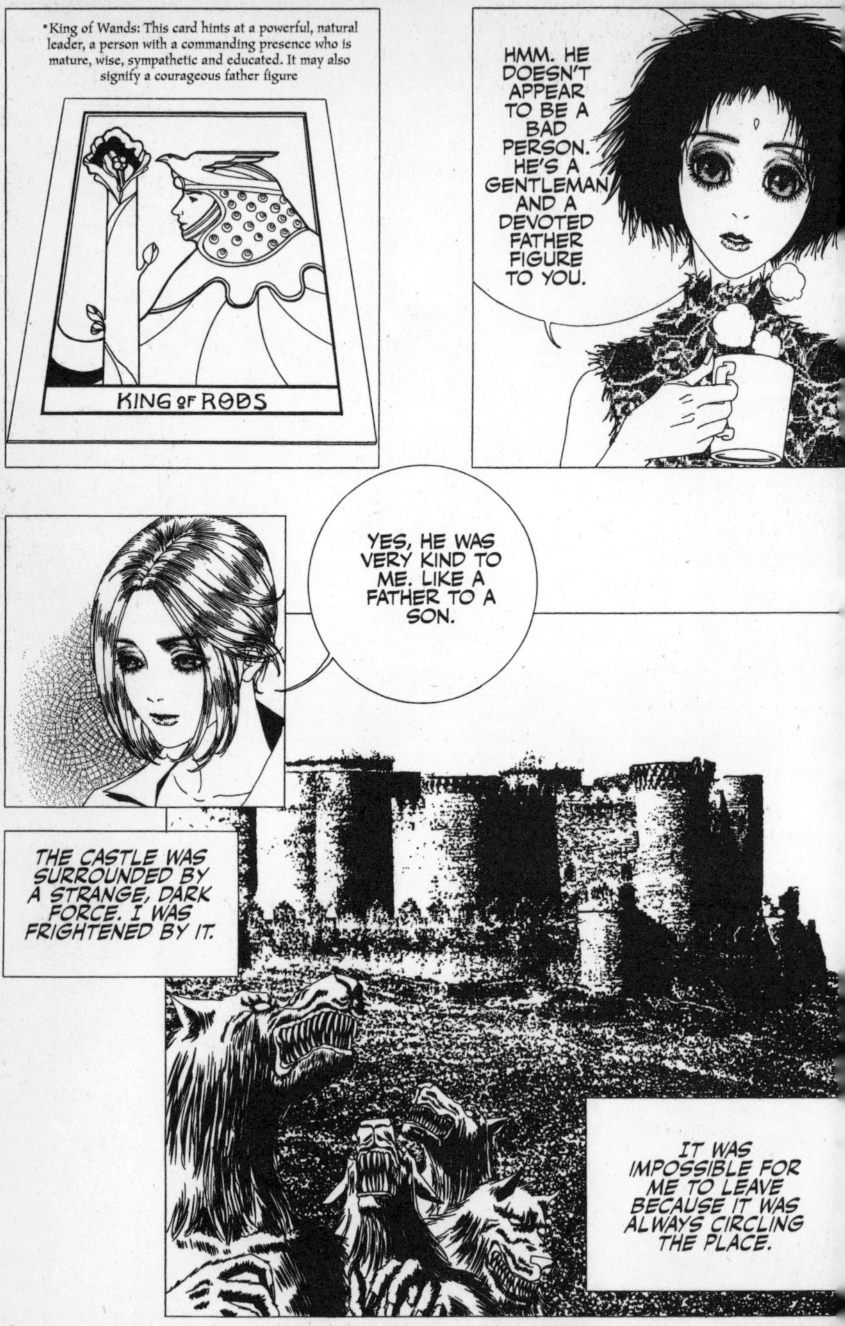
*King of Wands: This card hints at a powerful, natural leader, a person with a commanding presence who is mature, wise, sympathetic and educated. It may also signify a courageous father figure
KING OF RODS
HMM. HE DOESN'T APPEAR TO BE A BAD PERSON. HE'S A GENTLEMAN AND A DEVOTED FATHER FIGURE TO YOU.
YES, HE WAS VERY KIND TO ME. LIKE A FATHER TO A SON.
THE CASTLE WAS SURROUNDED BY A STRANGE, DARK FORCE. I WAS FRIGHTENED BY IT.
IT WAS IMPOSSIBLE FOR ME TO LEAVE BECAUSE IT WAS ALWAYS CIRCLING THE PLACE.

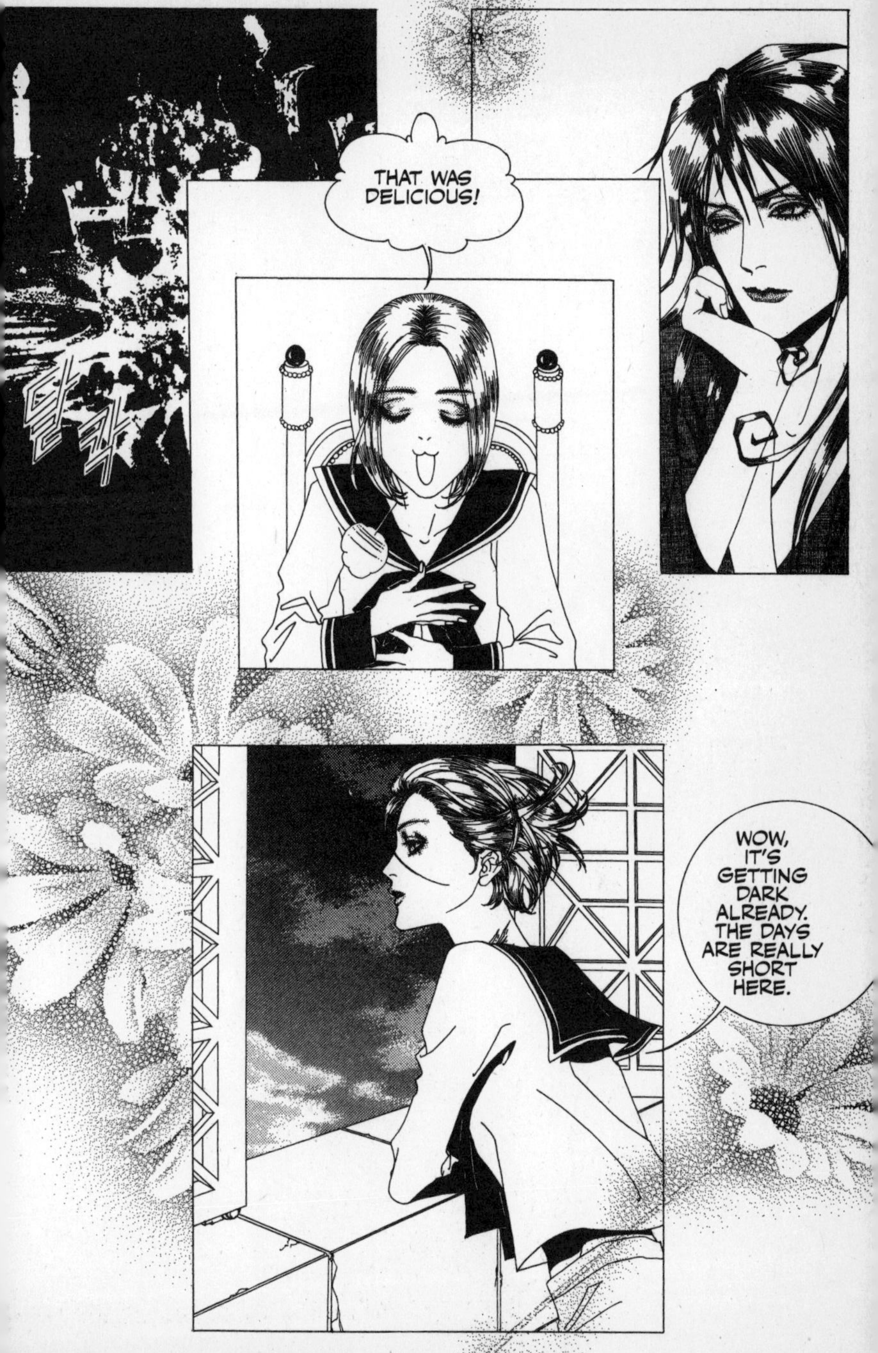
달칵
THAT WAS DELICIOUS!
WOW, IT'S GETTING DARK ALREADY. THE DAYS ARE REALLY SHORT HERE.

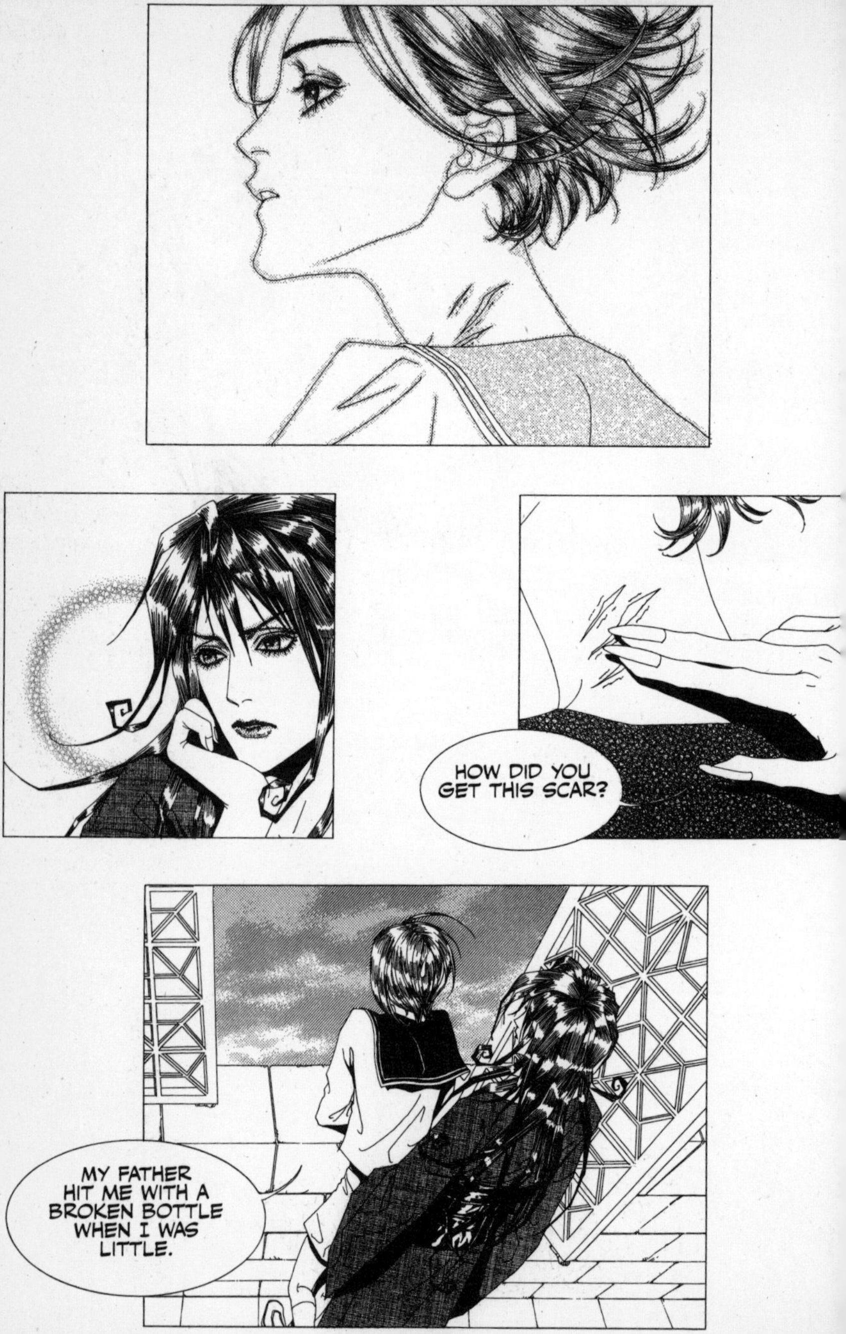
HOW DID YOU GET THIS SCAR?
MY FATHER HIT ME WITH A BROKEN BOTTLE WHEN I WAS LITTLE.

THOSE WOLVES... THEY SEEM TO ALWAYS BE GUARDING THIS PLACE.

ARE THEY TRYING TO KEEP ME FROM RUNNING AWAY?

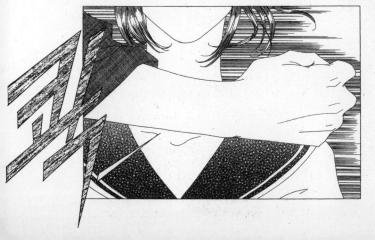

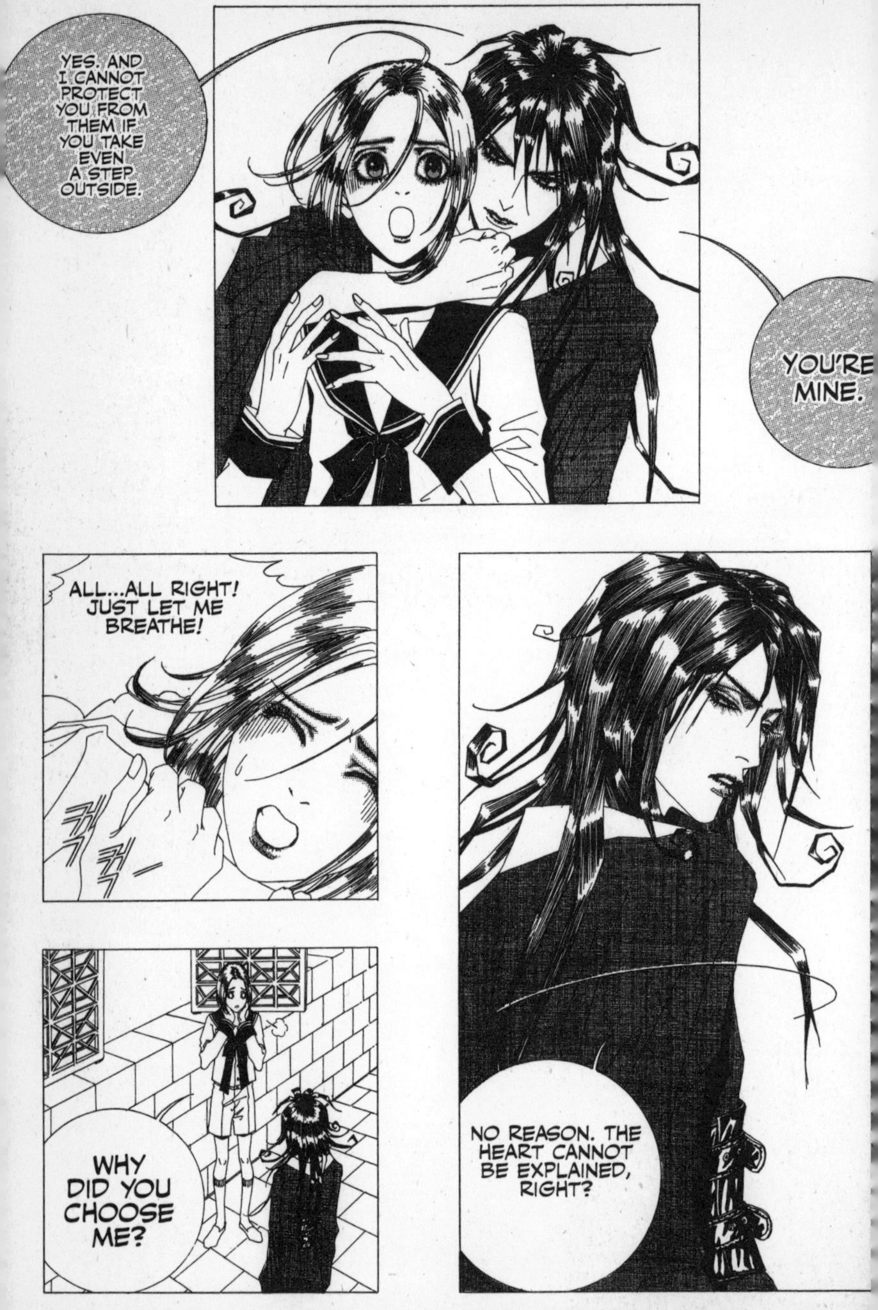
YES. AND I CANNOT PROTECT YOU FROM THEM IF YOU TAKE EVEN A STEP OUTSIDE.
YOU'RE MINE.
ALL...ALL RIGHT! JUST LET ME BREATHE!
WHY DID YOU CHOOSE ME?
NO REASON. THE HEART CANNOT BE EXPLAINED, RIGHT?

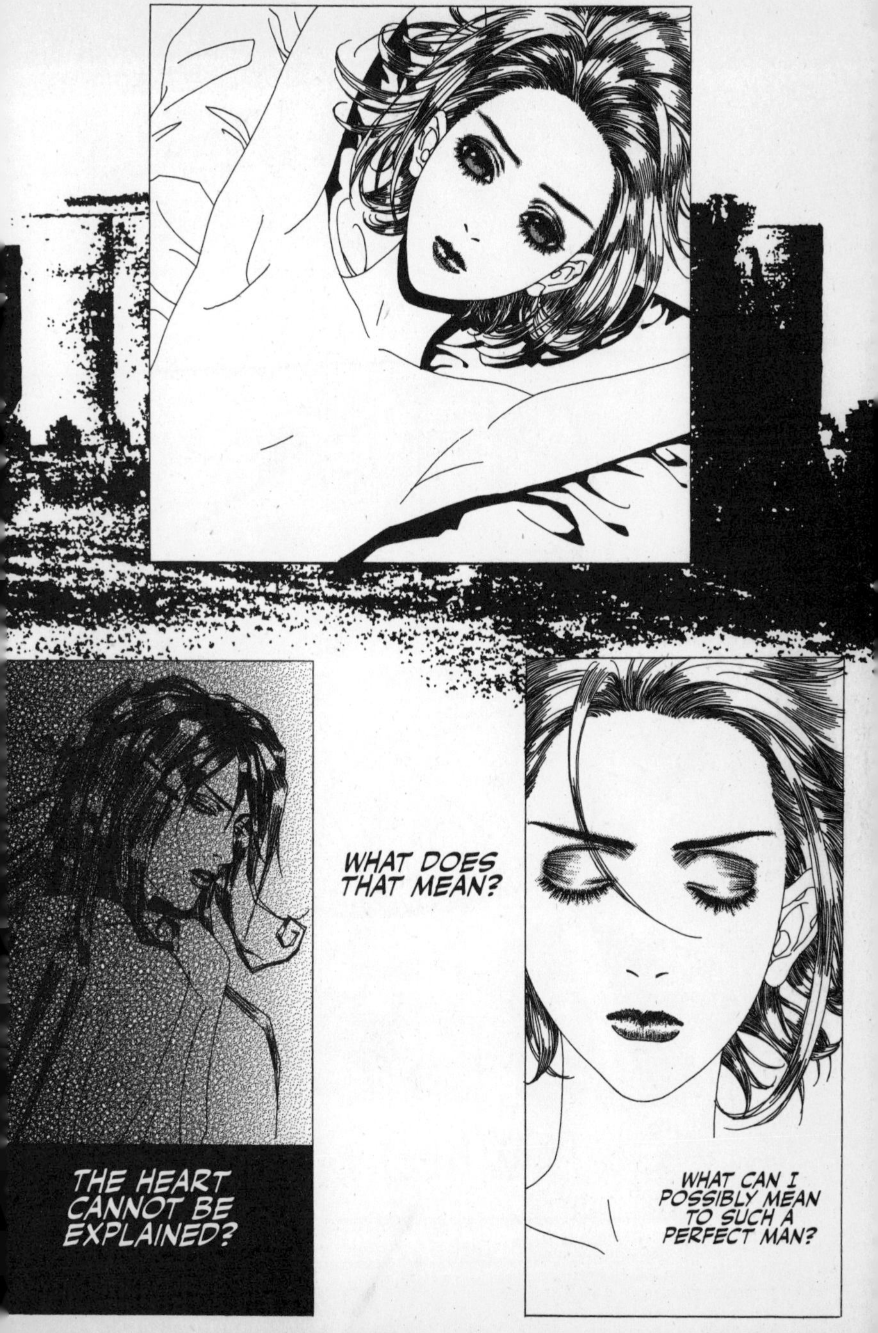
THE HEART CANNOT BE EXPLAINED?
WHAT DOES THAT MEAN?
WHAT CAN I POSSIBLY MEAN TO SUCH A PERFECT MAN?

ILLUSTRATION FROM HALLOWEEN TAROT.

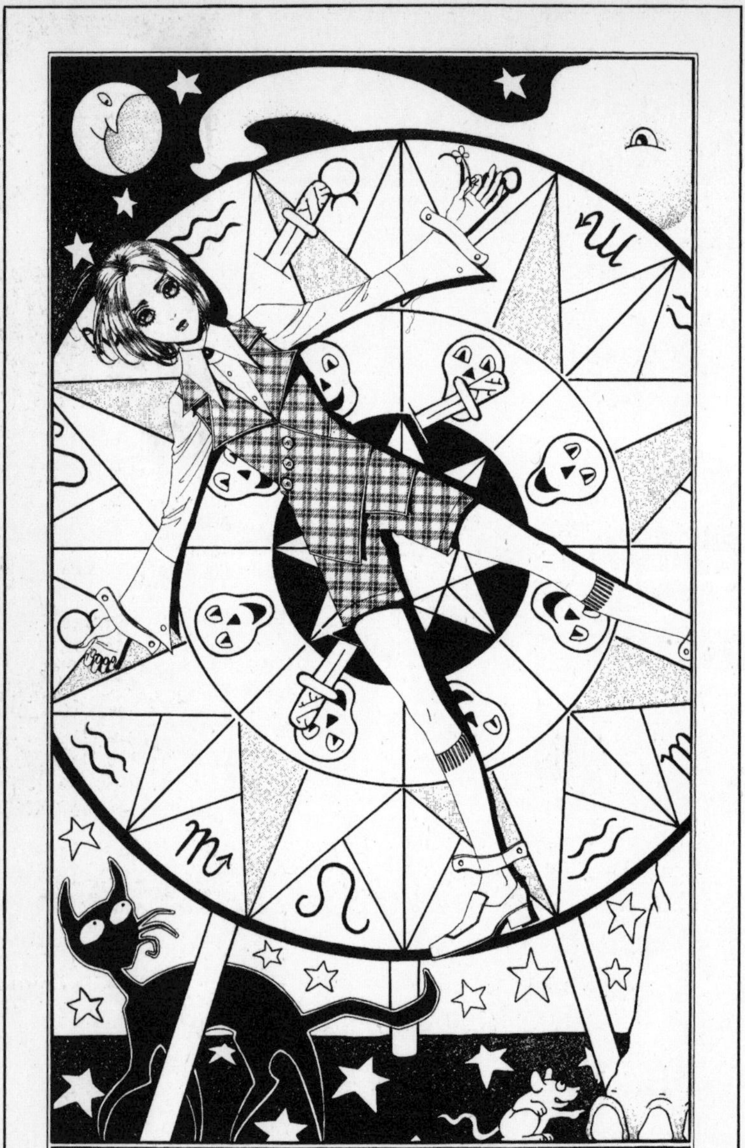
X
The Wheel of Fortune

*The Wheel of Fortune: This card represents the unpredictable turn of life events; destiny. It signifies unexpected change, new choices, and a new environment. It may also hint at motivation and energy.

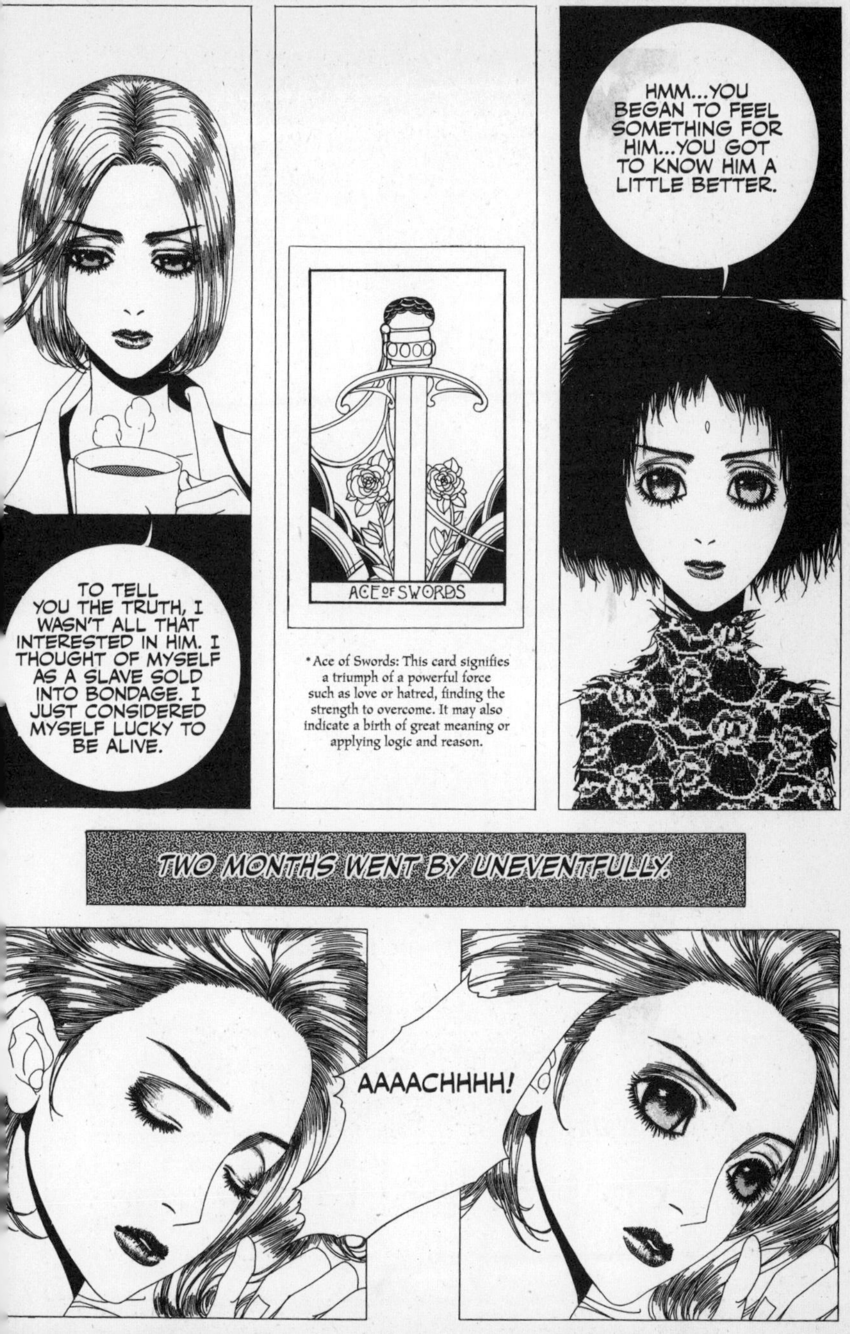
TO TELL YOU THE TRUTH, I WASN'T ALL THAT INTERESTED IN HIM. I THOUGHT OF MYSELF AS A SLAVE SOLD INTO BONDAGE. I JUST CONSIDERED MYSELF LUCKY TO BE ALIVE.
ACE OF SWORDS
*Ace of Swords: This card signifies a triumph of a powerful force such as love or hatred, finding the strength to overcome. It may also indicate a birth of great meaning or applying logic and reason.
HMM...YOU BEGAN TO FEEL SOMETHING FOR HIM...YOU GOT TO KNOW HIM A LITTLE BETTER.
TWO MONTHS WENT BY UNEVENTFULLY.
AAAACHHHH!

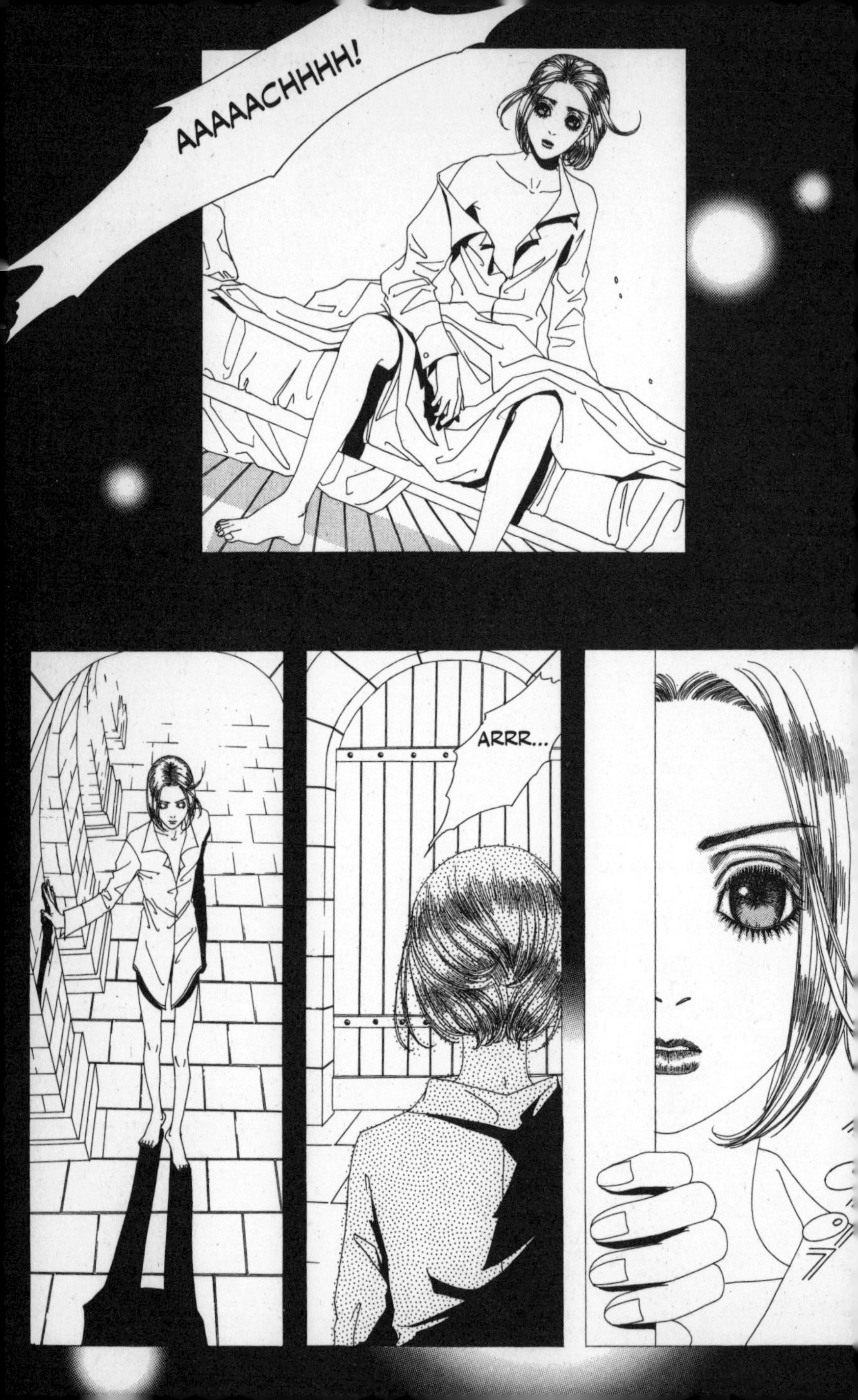
AAAAACHHHH!
ARRR...

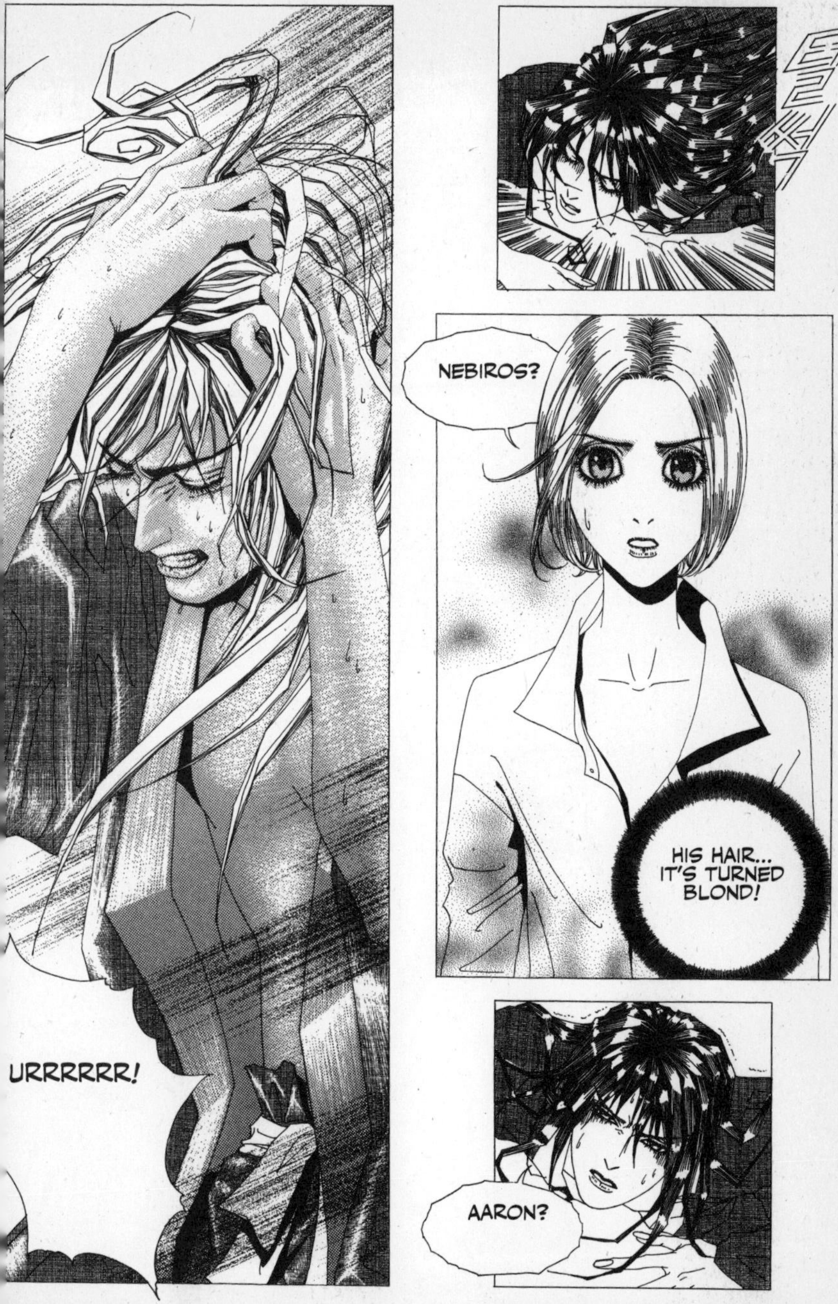
URRRRRR!
NEBIROS?
HIS HAIR... IT'S TURNED BLOND!
AARON?

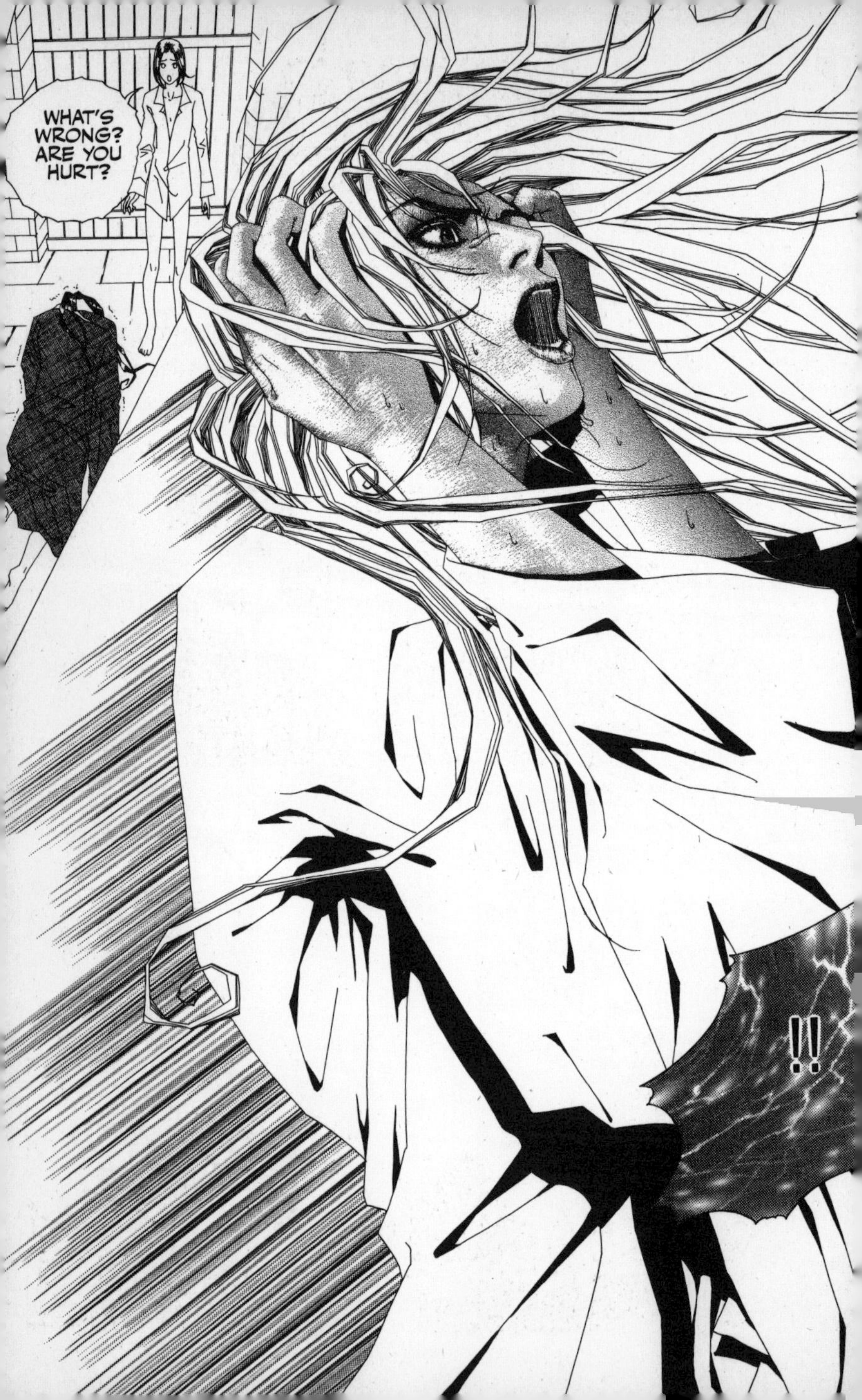
WHAT'S WRONG? ARE YOU HURT?
!!

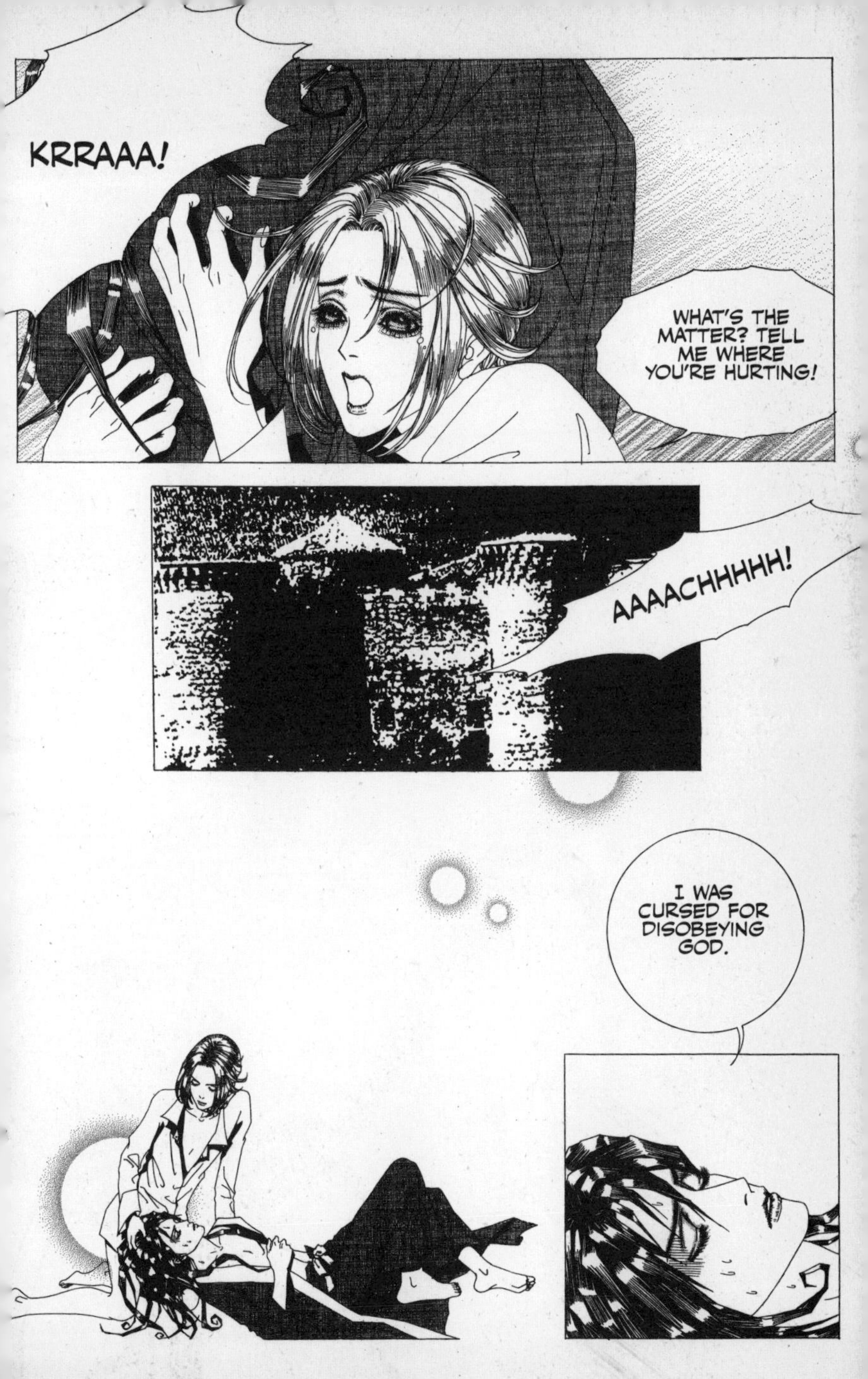
KRRAAA!
WHAT'S THE MATTER? TELL ME WHERE YOU'RE HURTING!
AAAACHHHHH!
I WAS CURSED FOR DISOBEYING GOD.

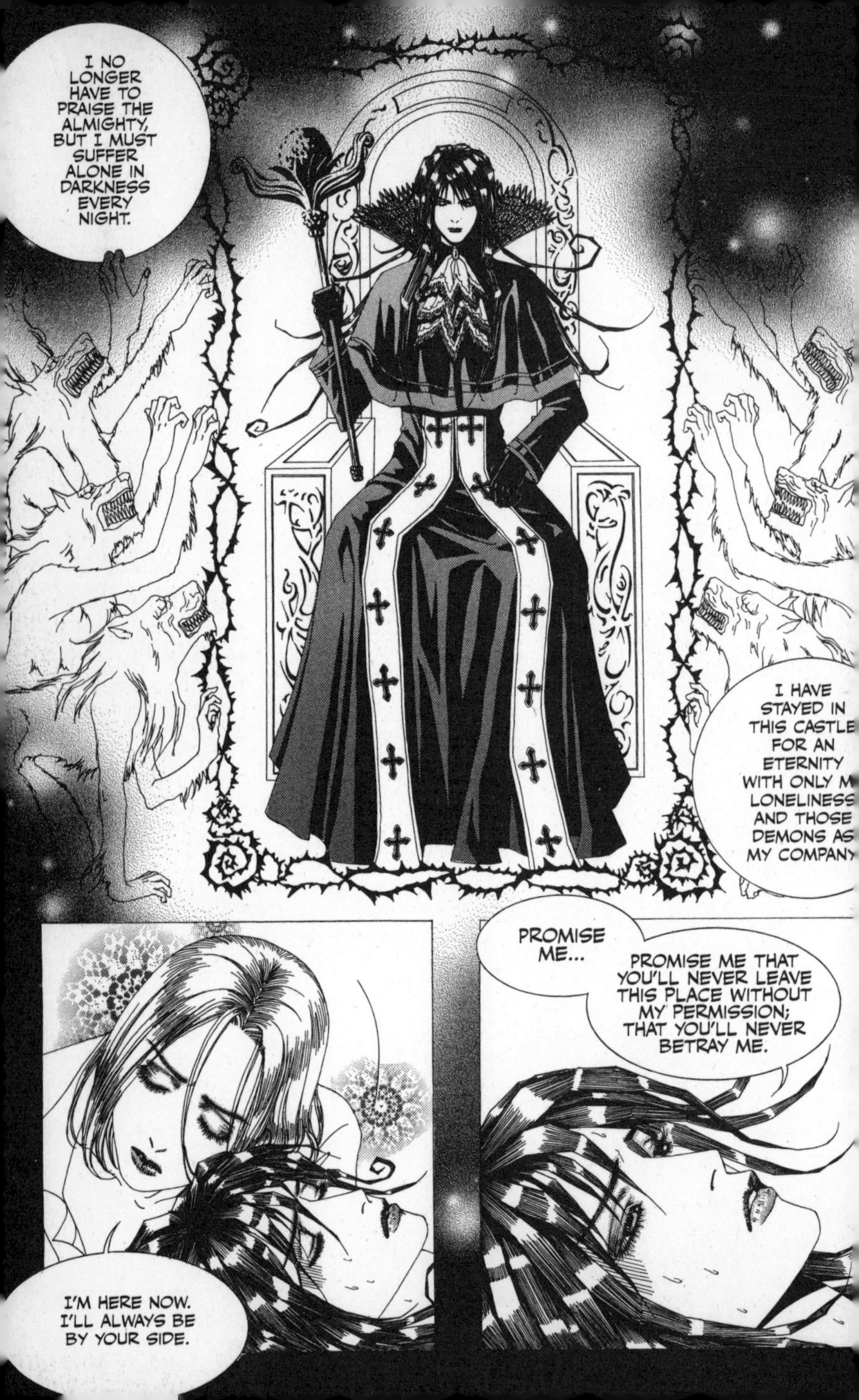
I NO LONGER HAVE TO PRAISE THE ALMIGHTY, BUT I MUST SUFFER ALONE IN DARKNESS EVERY NIGHT.
I HAVE STAYED IN THIS CASTLE FOR AN ETERNITY WITH ONLY M LONELINESS AND THOSE DEMONS AS MY COMPANY
I'M HERE NOW. I'LL ALWAYS BE BY YOUR SIDE.
PROMISE ME...
PROMISE ME THAT YOU'LL NEVER LEAVE THIS PLACE WITHOUT MY PERMISSION; THAT YOU'LL NEVER BETRAY ME.

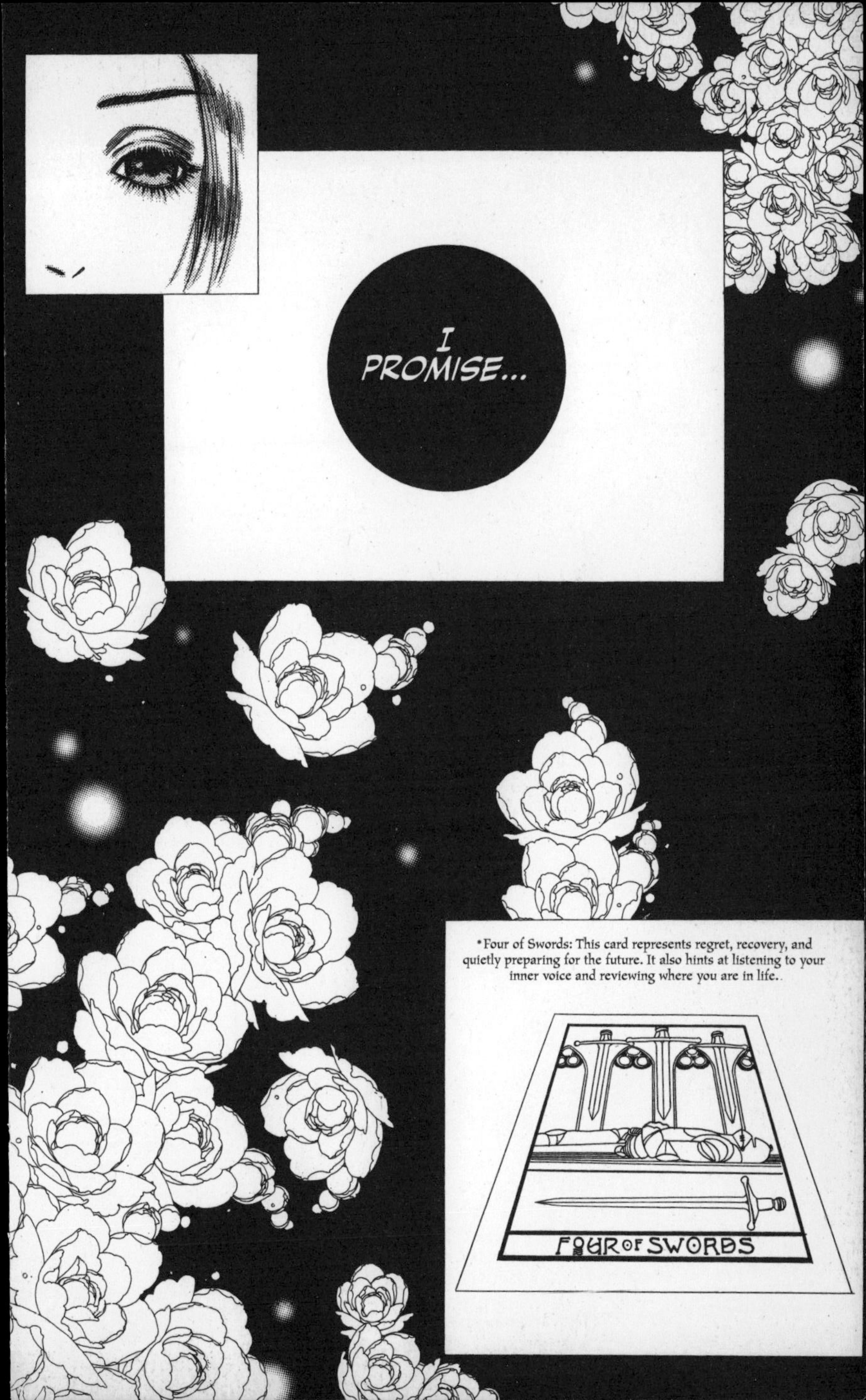
I PROMISE...

*Four of Swords: This card represents regret, recovery, and quietly preparing for the future. It also hints at listening to your inner voice and reviewing where you are in life..

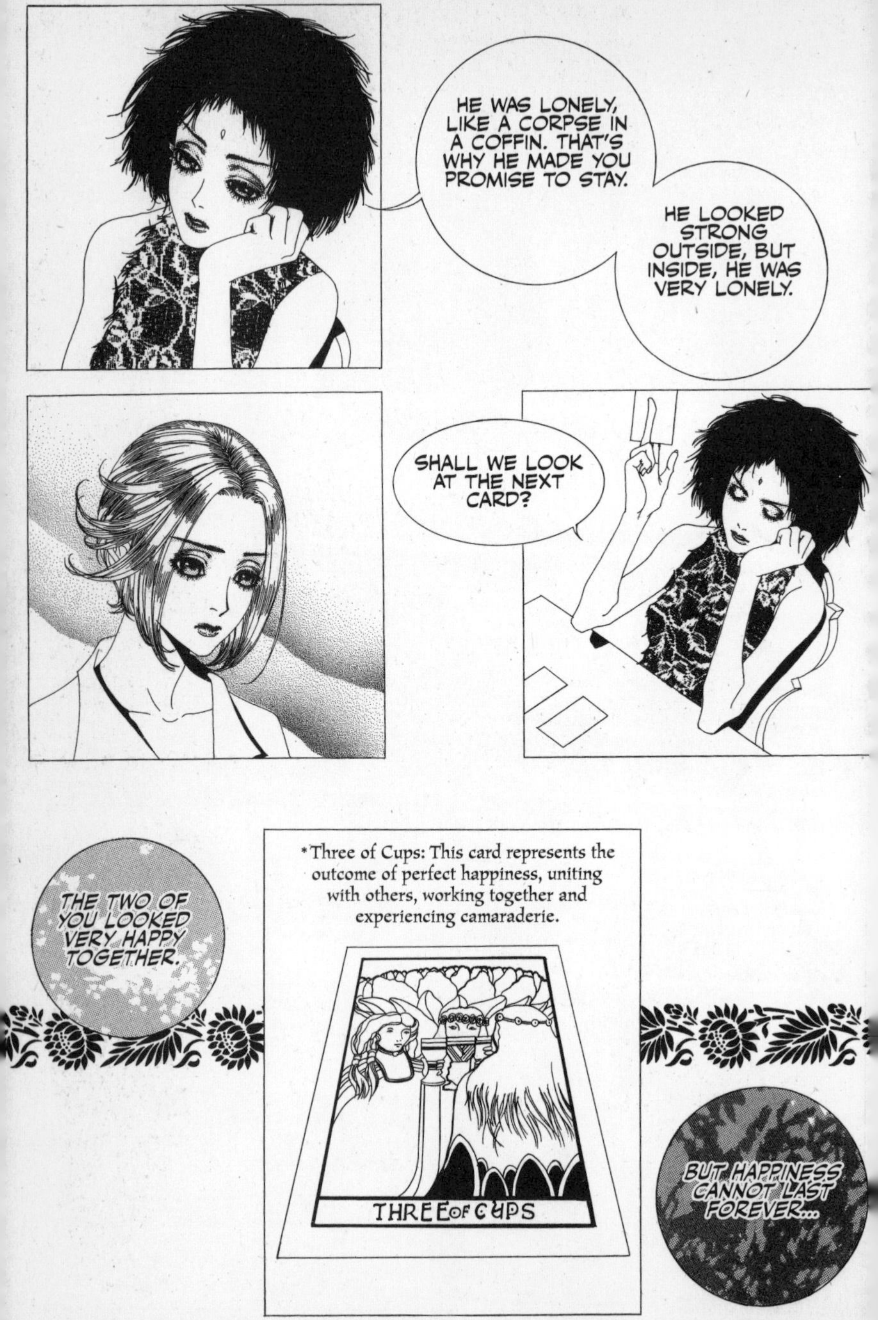
HE WAS LONELY, LIKE A CORPSE IN A COFFIN. THAT'S WHY HE MADE YOU PROMISE TO STAY.
HE LOOKED STRONG OUTSIDE, BUT INSIDE, HE WAS VERY LONELY.
SHALL WE LOOK AT THE NEXT CARD?
THE TWO OF YOU LOOKED VERY HAPPY TOGETHER.
*Three of Cups: This card represents the outcome of perfect happiness, uniting with others, working together and experiencing camaraderie.
THREE OF CUPS
BUT HAPPINESS CANNOT LAST FOREVER...

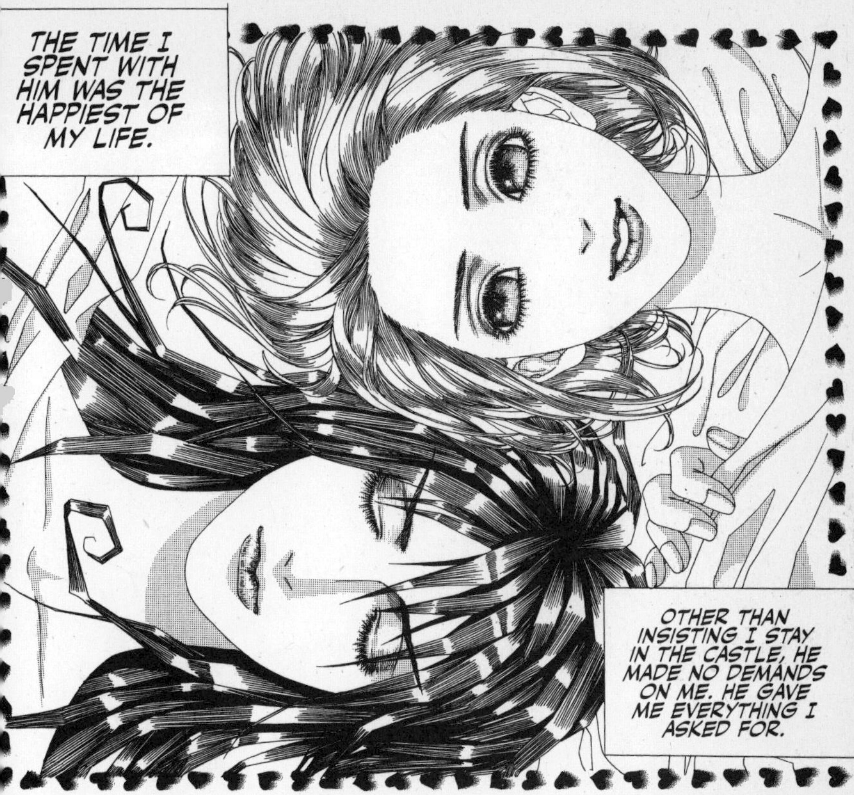
THE TIME I SPENT WITH HIM WAS THE HAPPIEST OF MY LIFE.
OTHER THAN INSISTING I STAY IN THE CASTLE, HE MADE NO DEMANDS ON ME. HE GAVE ME EVERYTHING I ASKED FOR.
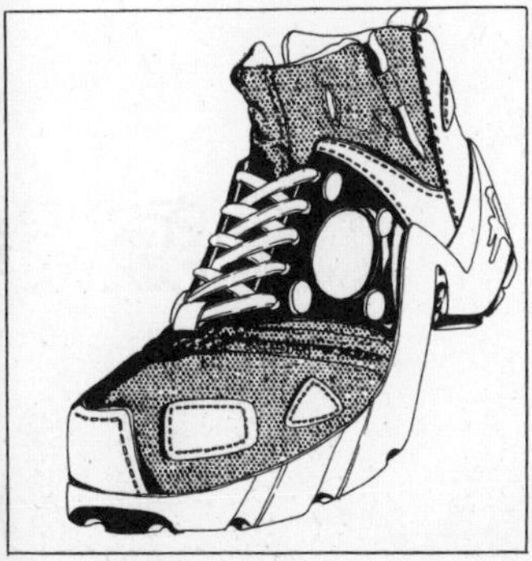
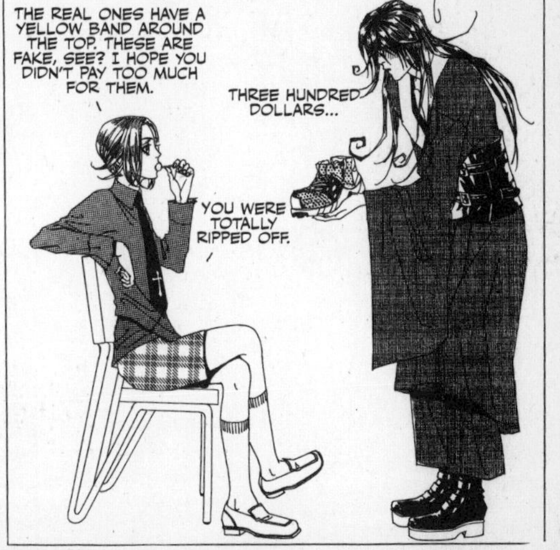
THE REAL ONES HAVE A YELLOW BAND AROUND THE TOP. THESE ARE FAKE, SEE? I HOPE YOU DIDN'T PAY TOO MUCH FOR THEM.
THREE HUNDRED DOLLARS...
YOU WERE TOTALLY RIPPED OFF.

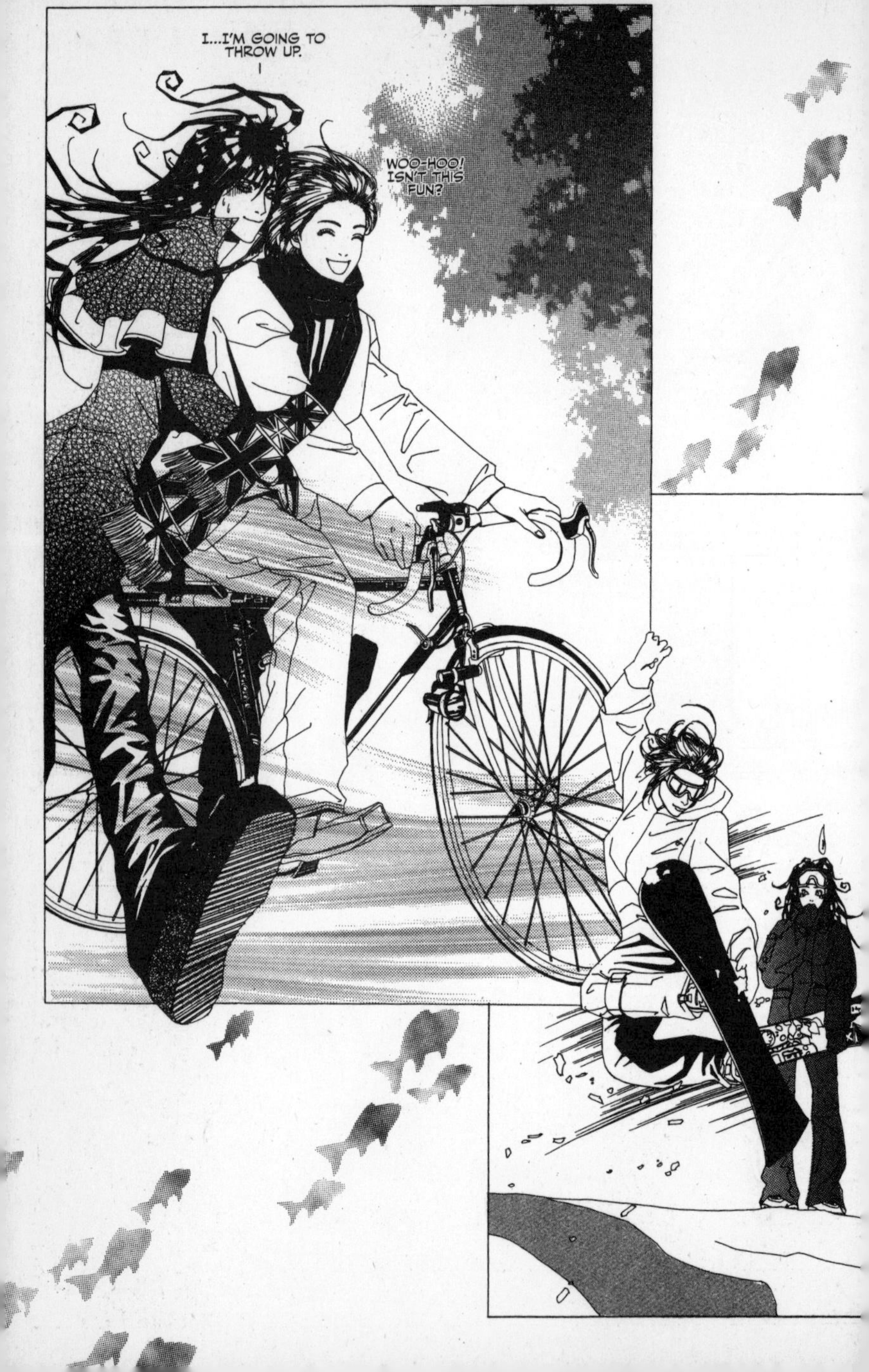
I...I'M GOING TO THROW UP.
WOO-HOO! ISN'T THIS FUN?

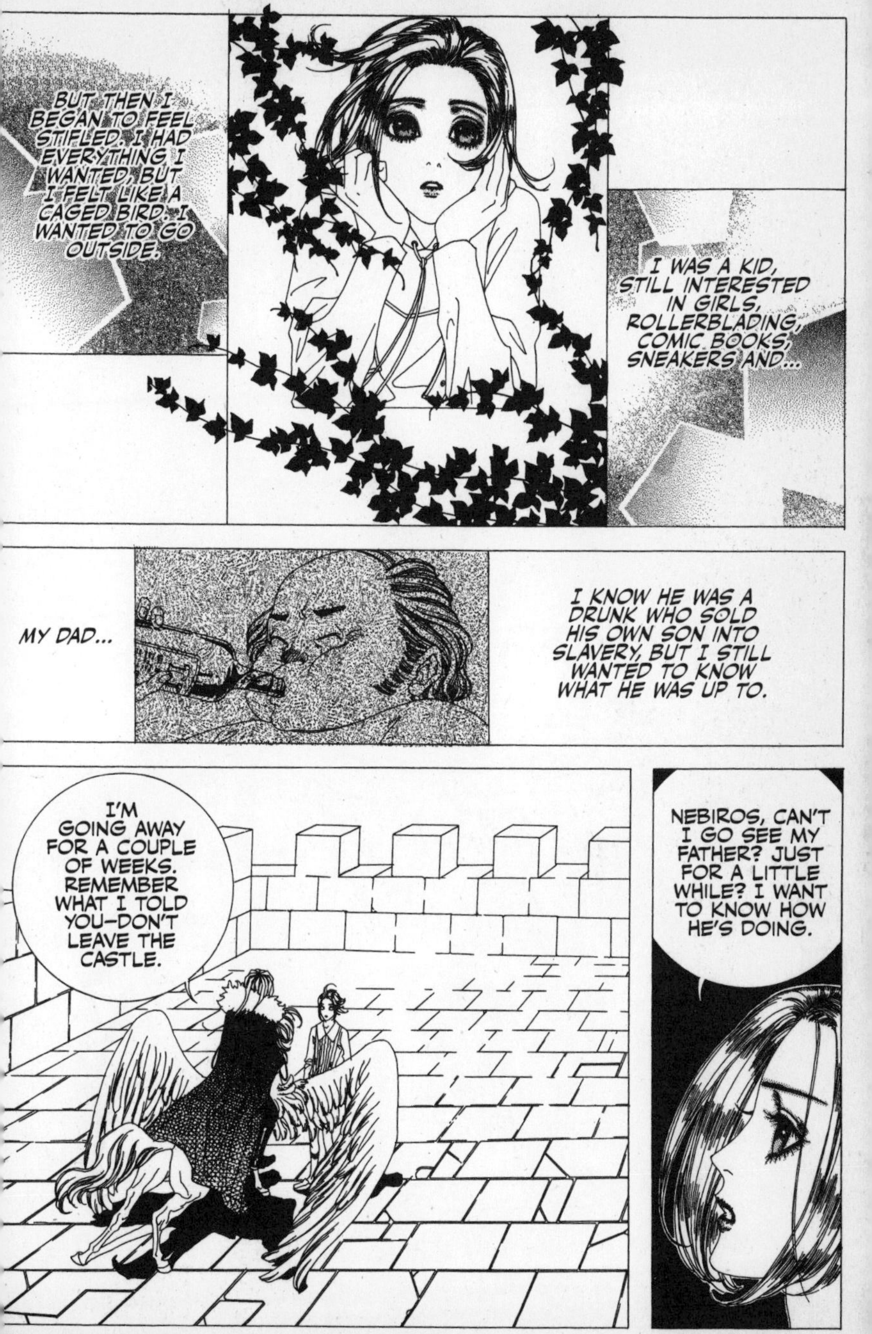
BUT THEN I BEGAN TO FEEL STIFLED. I HAD EVERYTHING I WANTED, BUT I FELT LIKE A CAGED BIRD. I WANTED TO GO OUTSIDE.
I WAS A KID, STILL INTERESTED IN GIRLS, ROLLERBLADING, COMIC BOOKS, SNEAKERS AND...
MY DAD...
I KNOW HE WAS A DRUNK WHO SOLD HIS OWN SON INTO SLAVERY, BUT I STILL WANTED TO KNOW WHAT HE WAS UP TO.
I'M GOING AWAY FOR A COUPLE OF WEEKS. REMEMBER WHAT I TOLD YOU–DON'T LEAVE THE CASTLE.
NEBIROS, CAN'T I GO SEE MY FATHER? JUST FOR A LITTLE WHILE? I WANT TO KNOW HOW HE'S DOING.

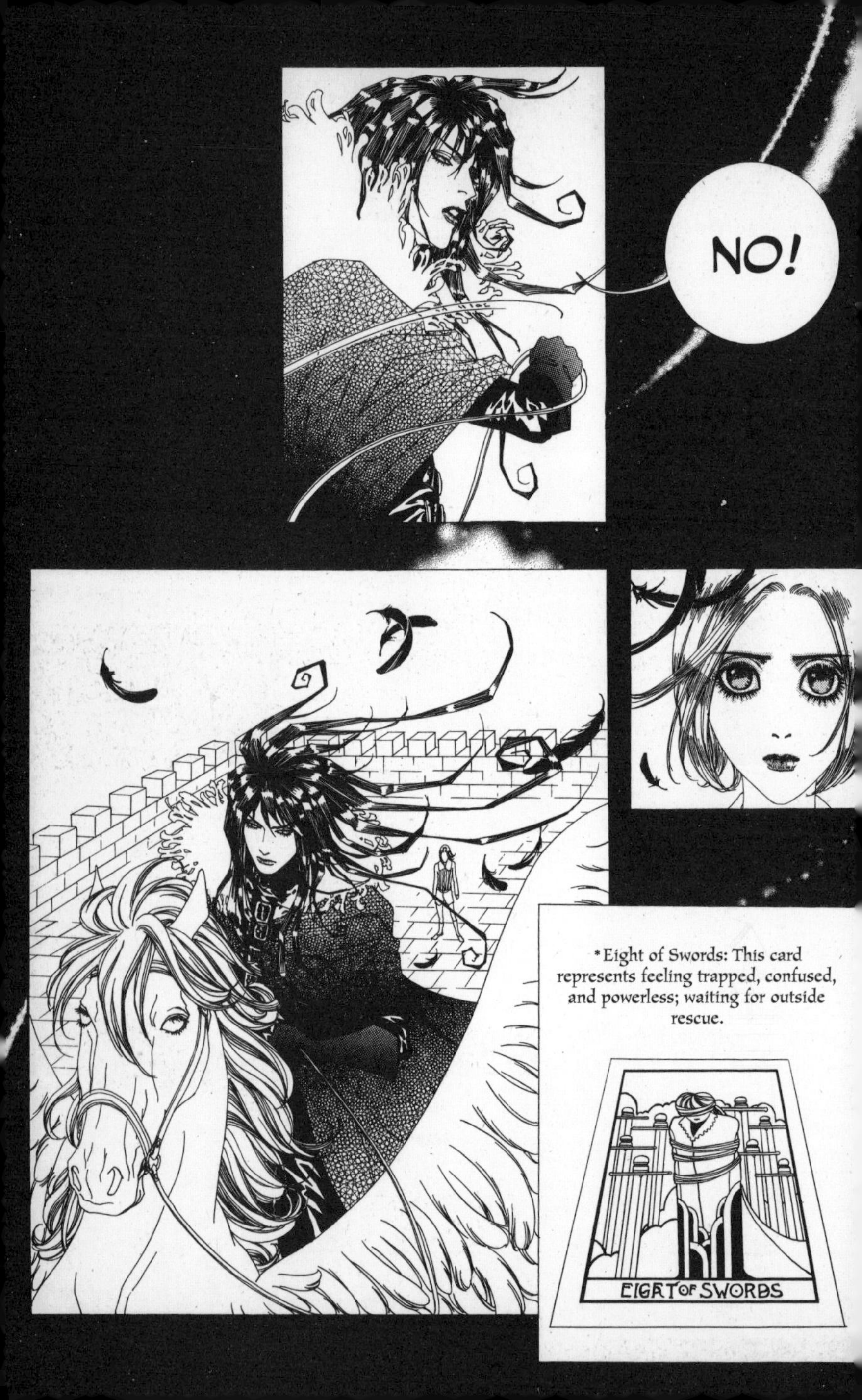
NO!
*Eight of Swords: This card represents feeling trapped, confused, and powerless; waiting for outside rescue.
EIGHT OF SWORDS

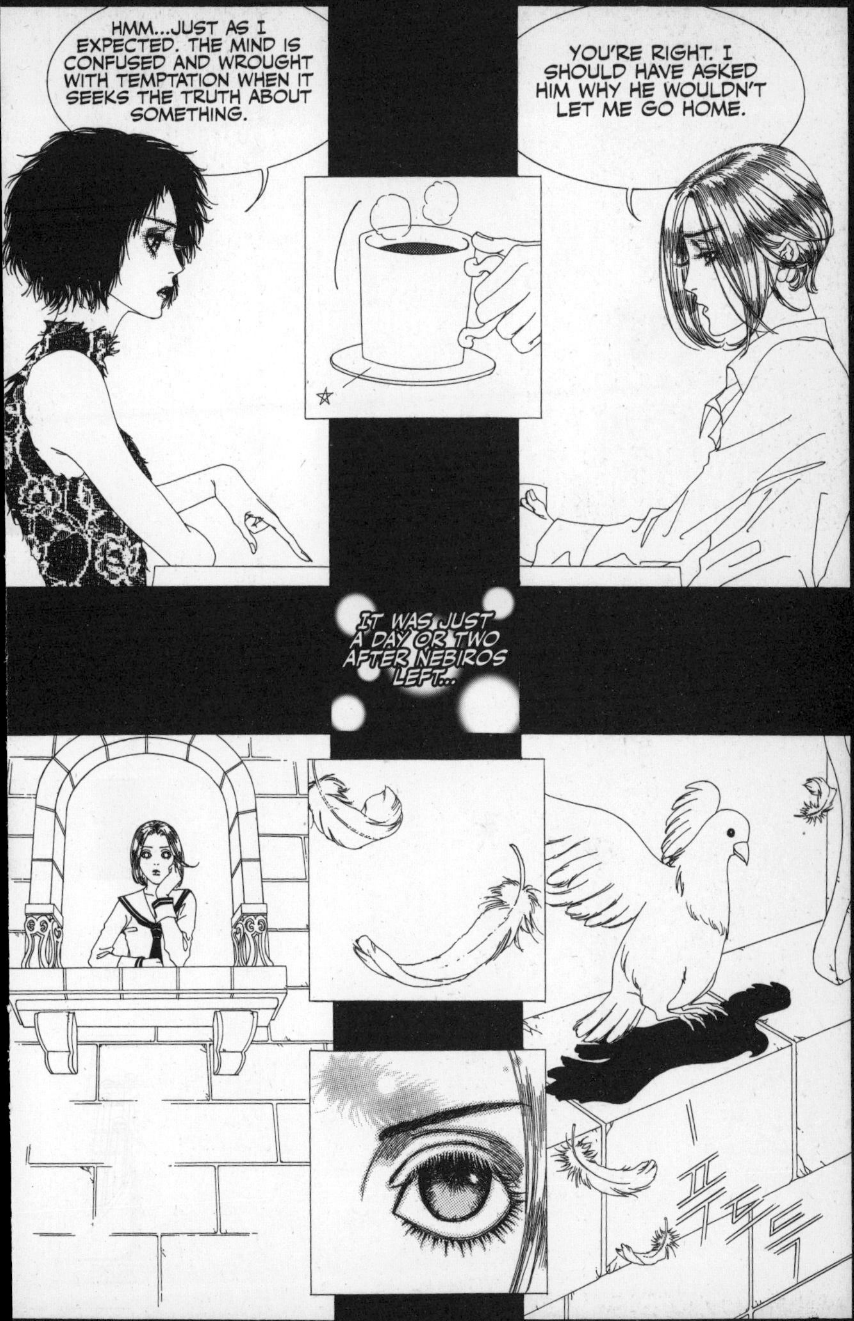
HMM...JUST AS I EXPECTED. THE MIND IS CONFUSED AND WROUGHT WITH TEMPTATION WHEN IT SEEKS THE TRUTH ABOUT SOMETHING.
YOU'RE RIGHT. I SHOULD HAVE ASKED HIM WHY HE WOULDN'T LET ME GO HOME.
IT WAS JUST A DAY OR TWO AFTER NEBIROS LEFT...

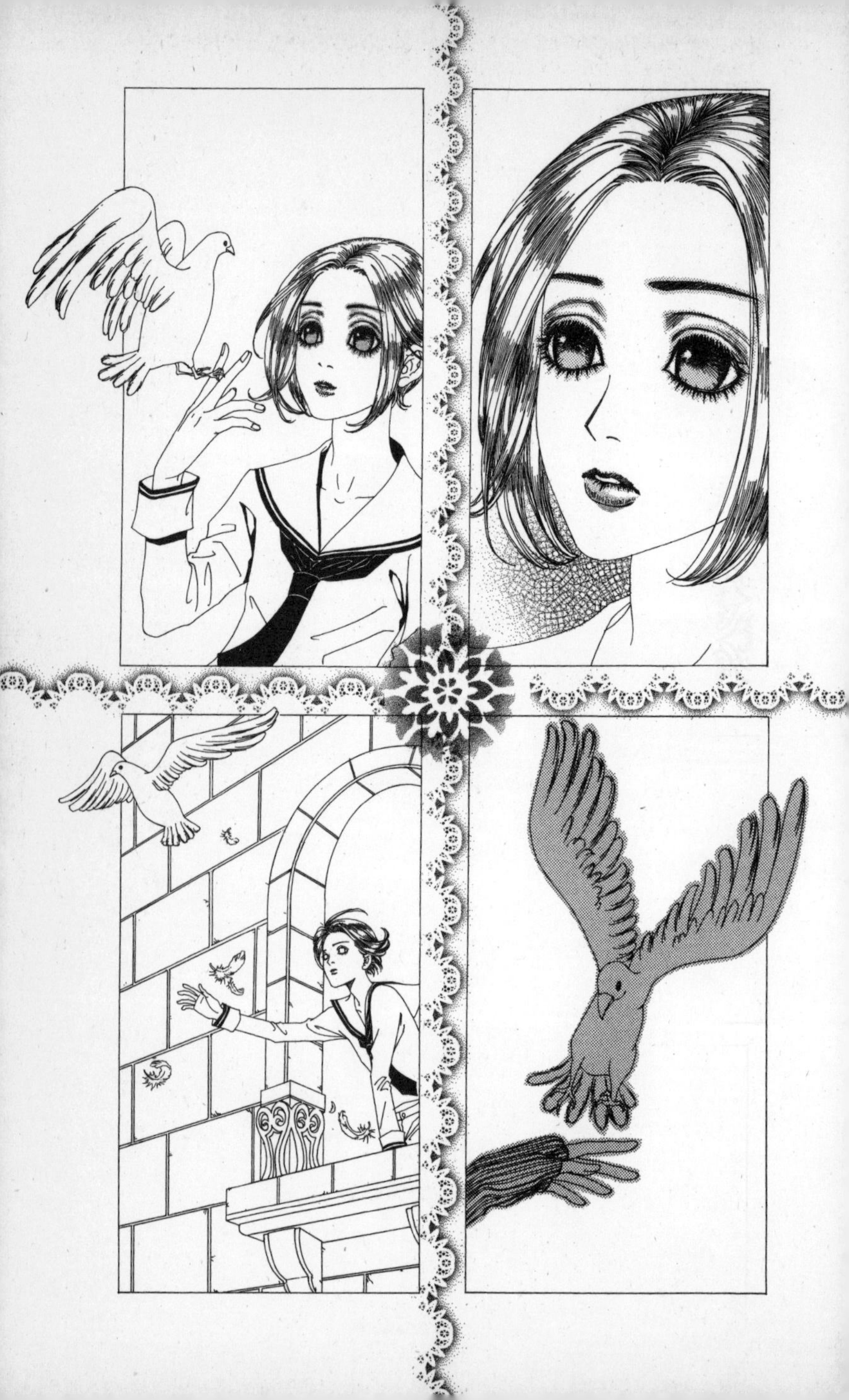

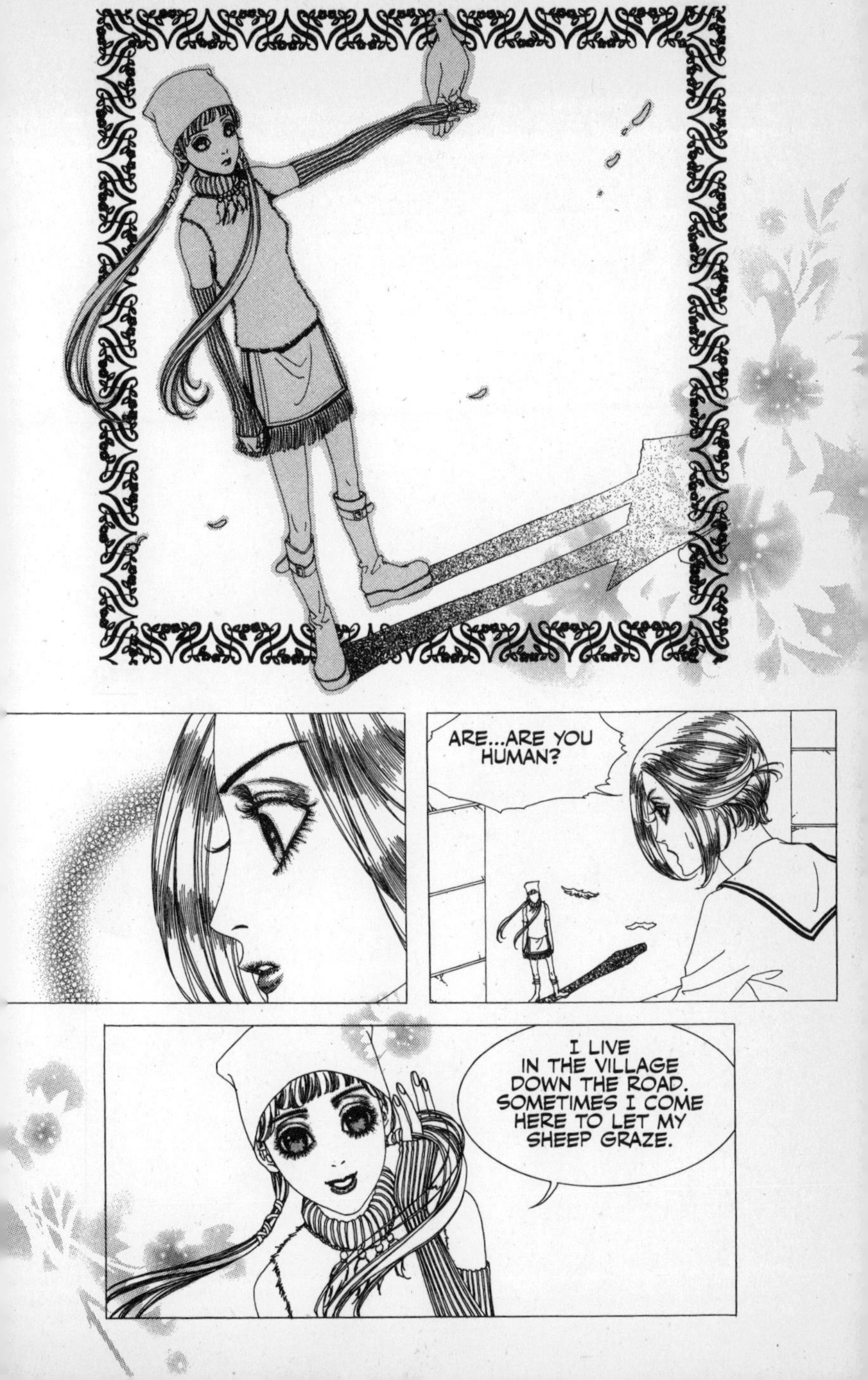
ARE...ARE YOU HUMAN?
I LIVE IN THE VILLAGE DOWN THE ROAD. SOMETIMES I COME HERE TO LET MY SHEEP GRAZE.

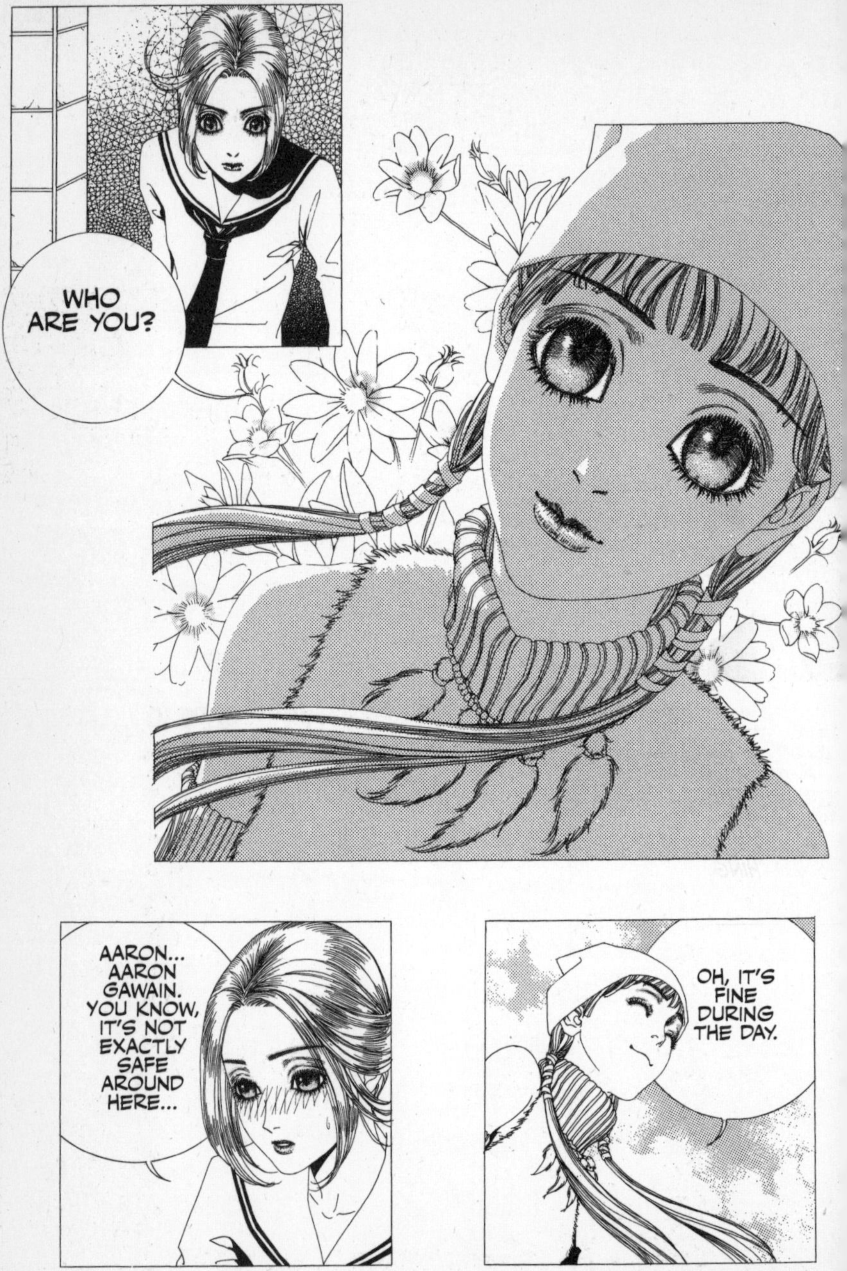
WHO ARE YOU?
AARON... AARON GAWAIN. YOU KNOW, IT'S NOT EXACTLY SAFE AROUND HERE...
OH, IT'S FINE DURING THE DAY.

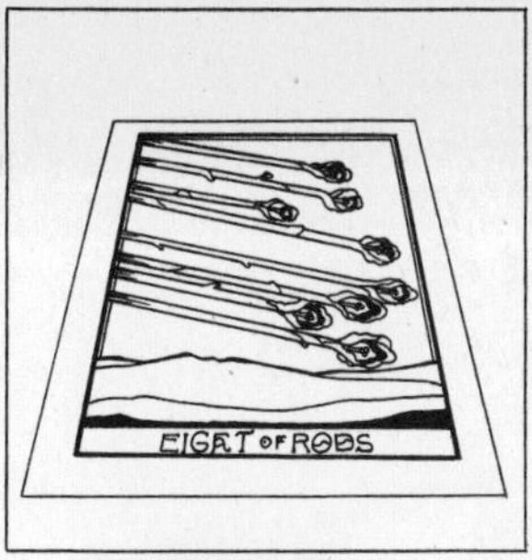
EIGHT OF RODS

*Eight of Wands: This card represents putting one's plans into action; preparing to move on. It also signifies finding a resolution and discovering the truth. It may indicate haste in one's actions and the arrow of love.

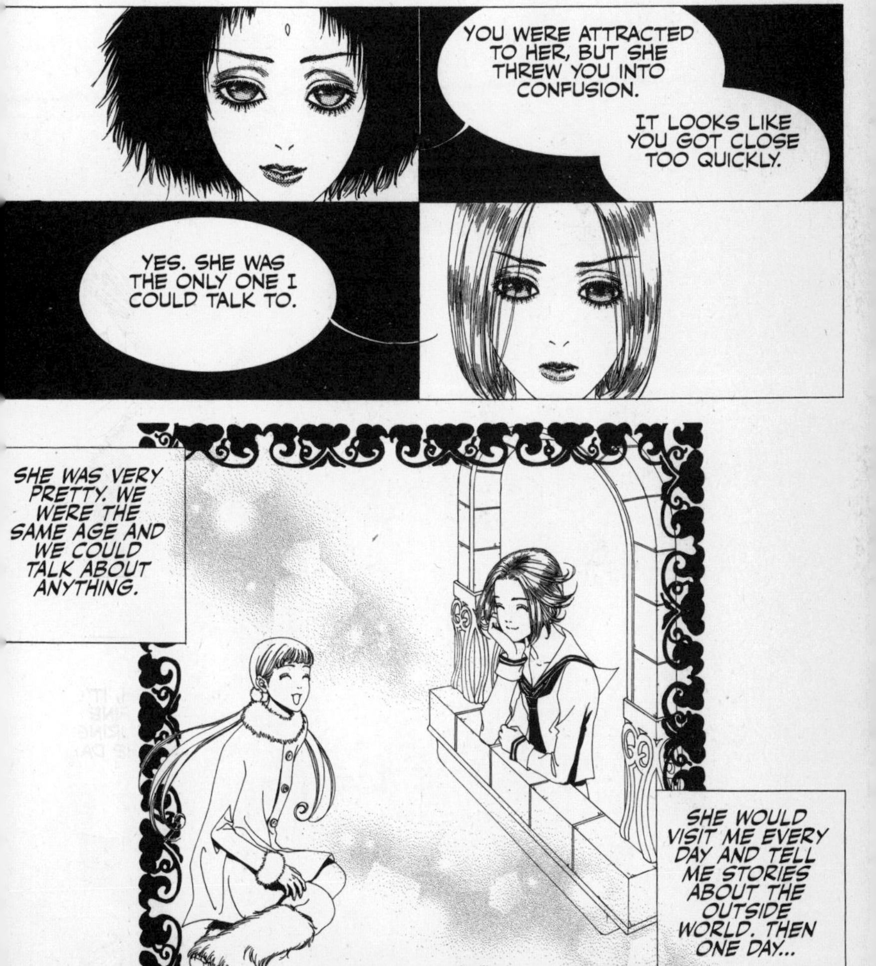
YOU WERE ATTRACTED TO HER, BUT SHE THREW YOU INTO CONFUSION.
IT LOOKS LIKE YOU GOT CLOSE TOO QUICKLY.
YES. SHE WAS THE ONLY ONE I COULD TALK TO.
SHE WAS VERY PRETTY. WE WERE THE SAME AGE AND WE COULD TALK ABOUT ANYTHING.
SHE WOULD VISIT ME EVERY DAY AND TELL ME STORIES ABOUT THE OUTSIDE WORLD. THEN ONE DAY...

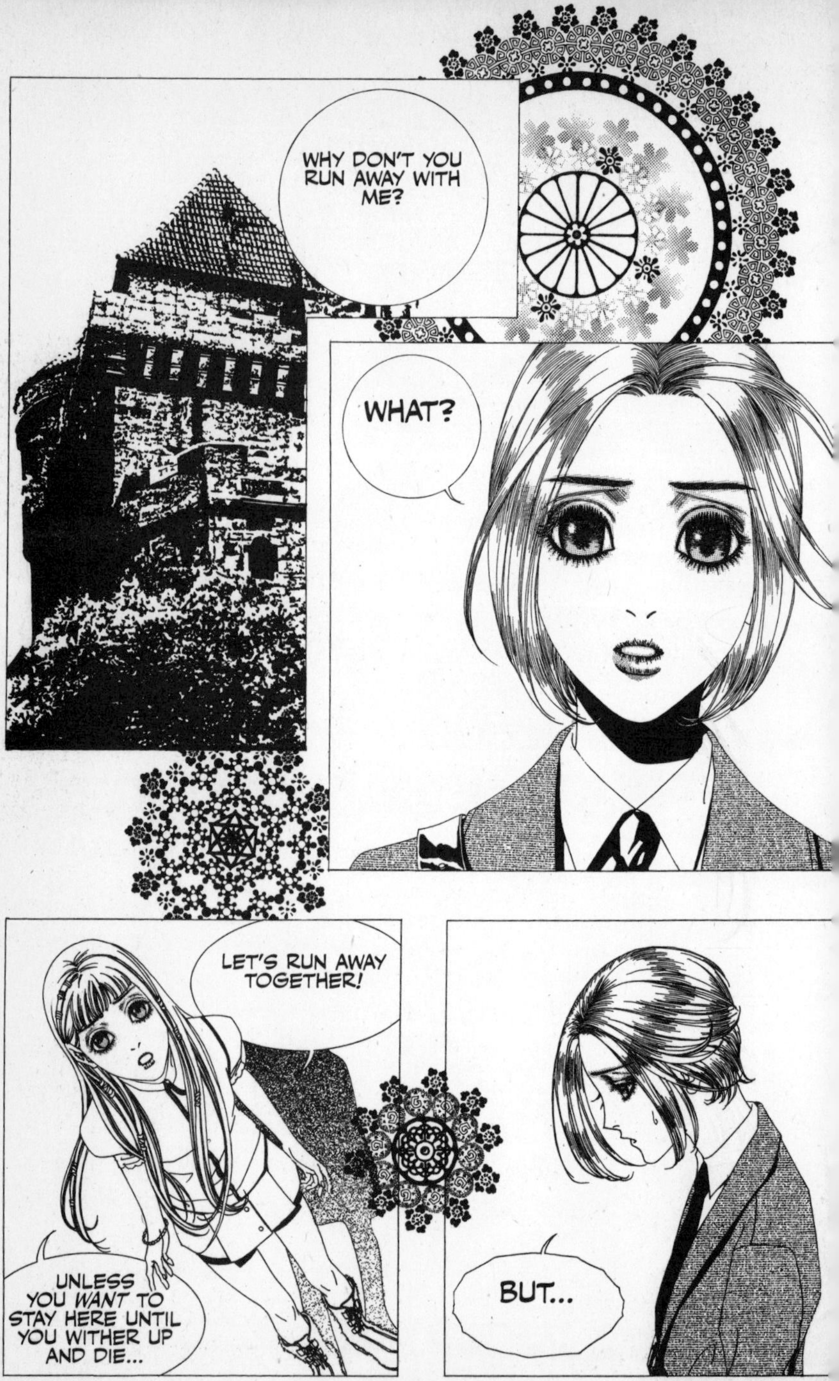
WHY DON'T YOU RUN AWAY WITH ME?
WHAT?
LET'S RUN AWAY TOGETHER!
UNLESS YOU *WANT* TO STAY HERE UNTIL YOU WITHER UP AND DIE...
BUT...

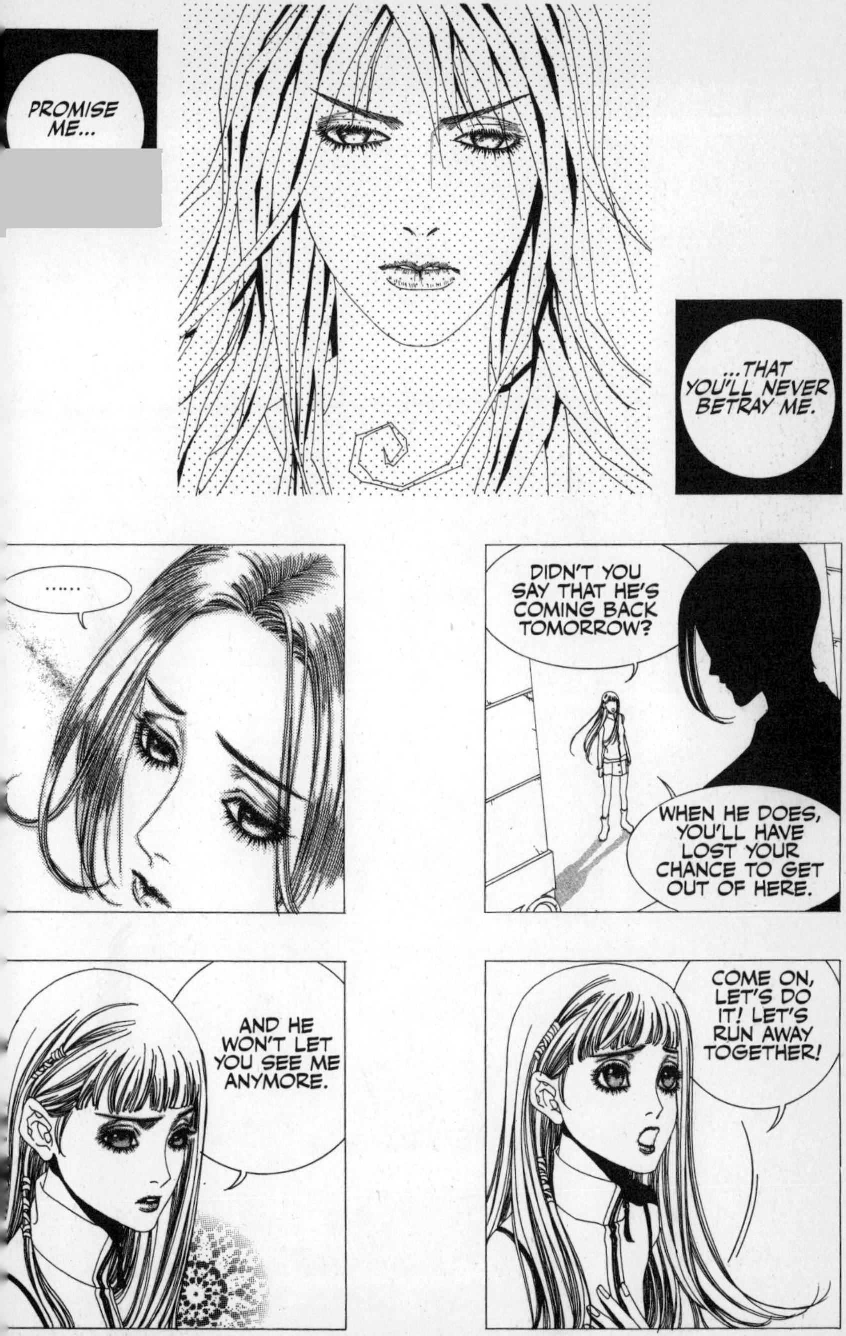
PROMISE ME...
...THAT YOU'LL NEVER BETRAY ME.
......
DIDN'T YOU SAY THAT HE'S COMING BACK TOMORROW?
WHEN HE DOES, YOU'LL HAVE LOST YOUR CHANCE TO GET OUT OF HERE.
AND HE WON'T LET YOU SEE ME ANYMORE.
COME ON, LET'S DO IT! LET'S RUN AWAY TOGETHER!

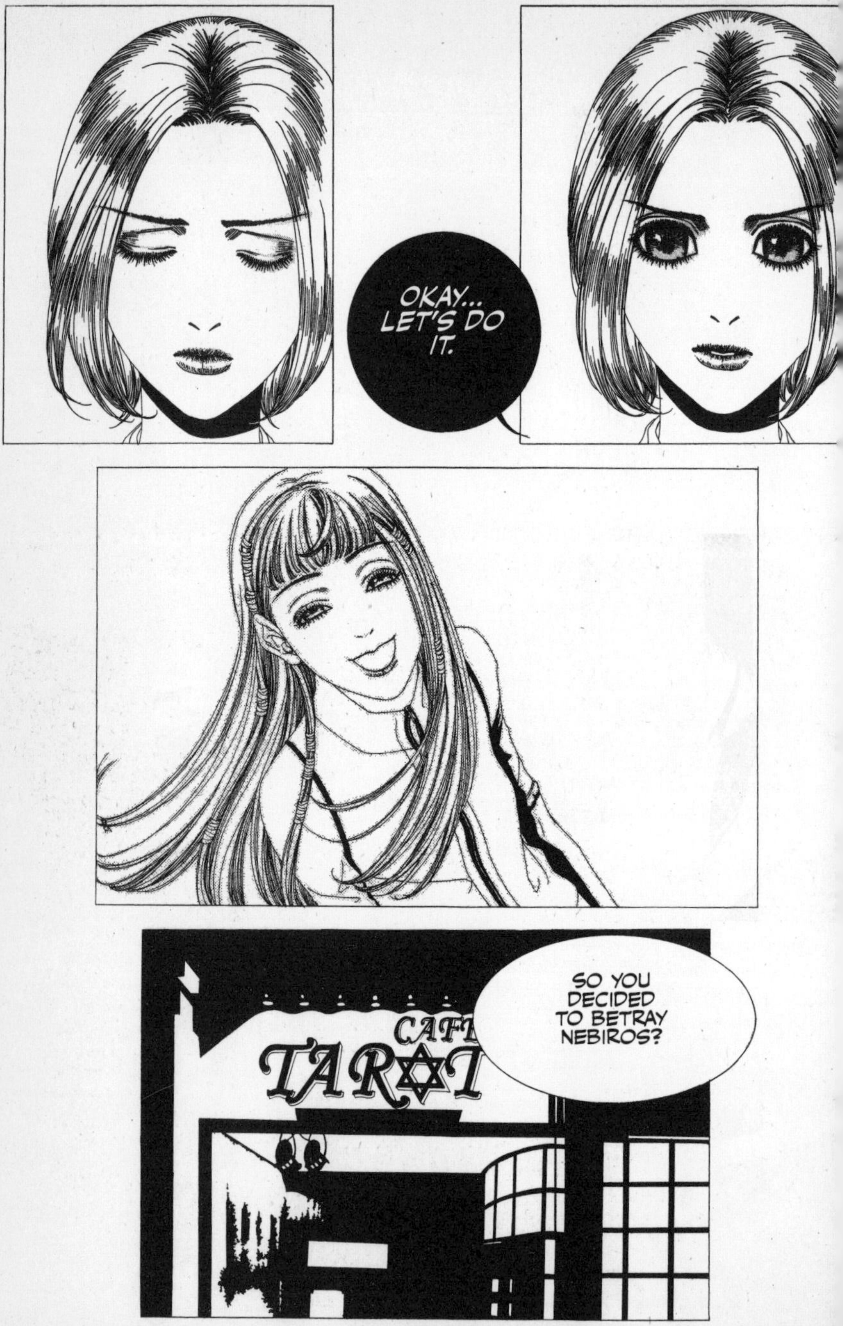
OKAY... LET'S DO IT.
SO YOU DECIDED TO BETRAY NEBIROS?
CAFE
TAROT

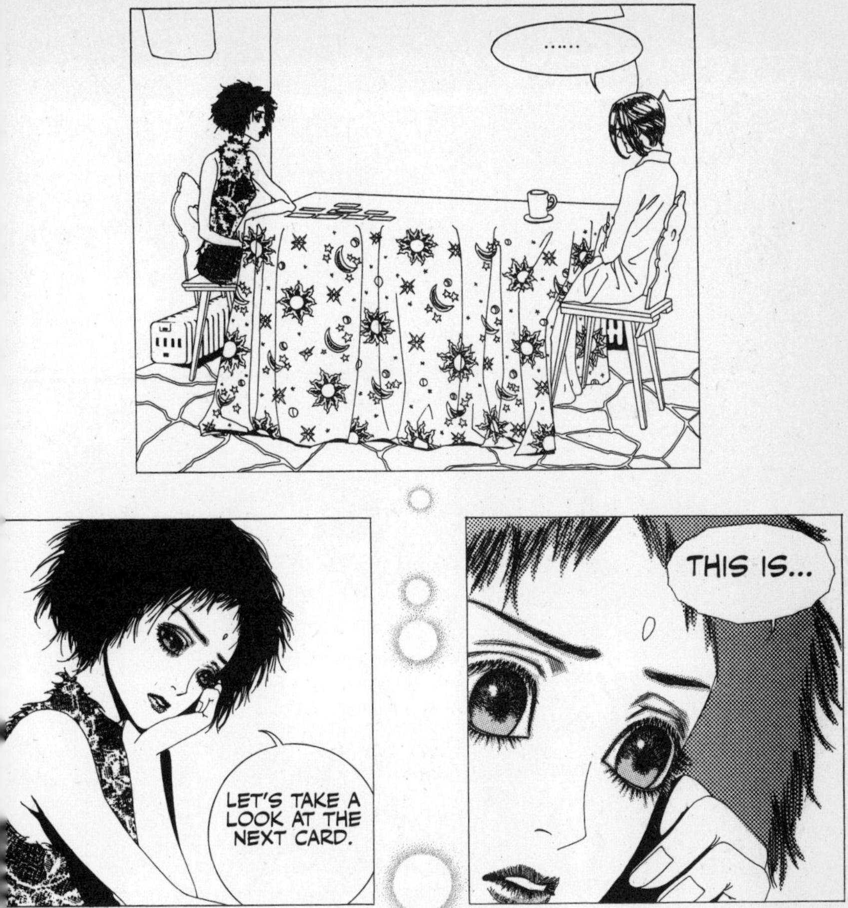
……
LET'S TAKE A LOOK AT THE NEXT CARD.
THIS IS...

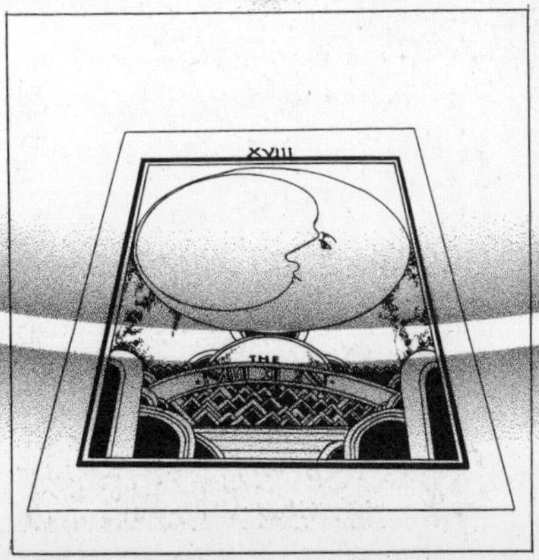

*The Moon: This card represents the acceptance of a false picture, entertaining unusual thoughts, and feeling bewildered. It may also hint at unexpected danger and a risky situation involving loved ones.

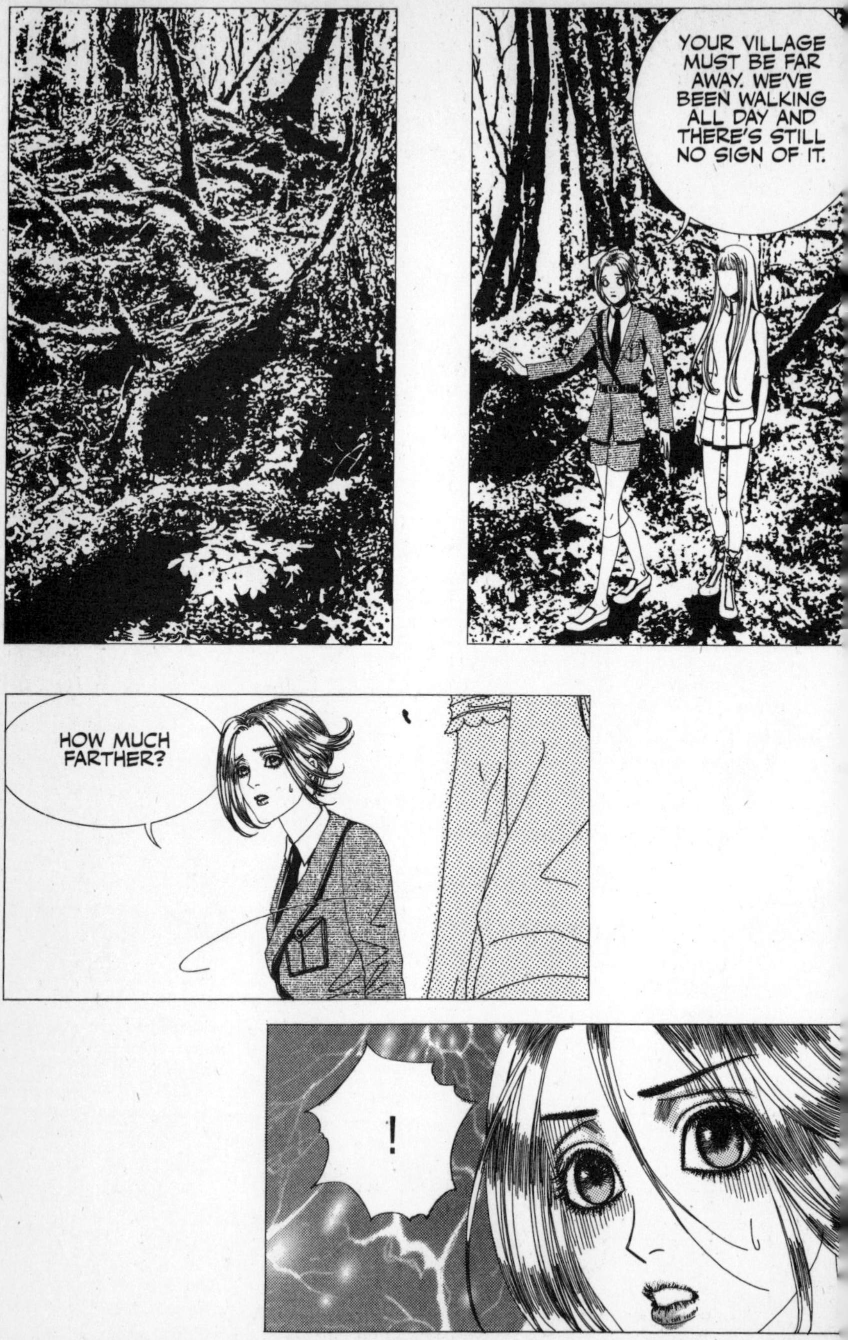
YOUR VILLAGE MUST BE FAR AWAY. WE'VE BEEN WALKING ALL DAY AND THERE'S STILL NO SIGN OF IT.
HOW MUCH FARTHER?
!

ILLUSTRATION FROM HALLOWEEN TAROT

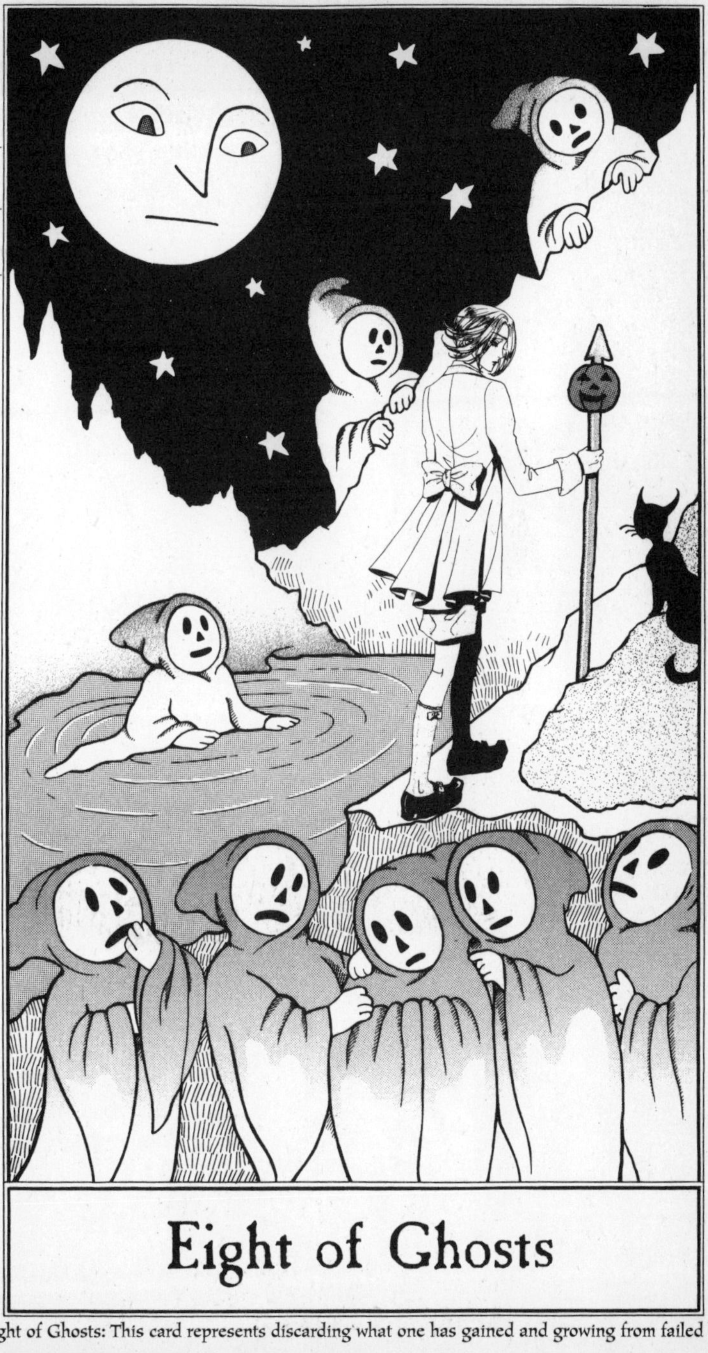
Eight of Ghosts

* Eight of Ghosts: This card represents discarding what one has gained and growing from failed love.

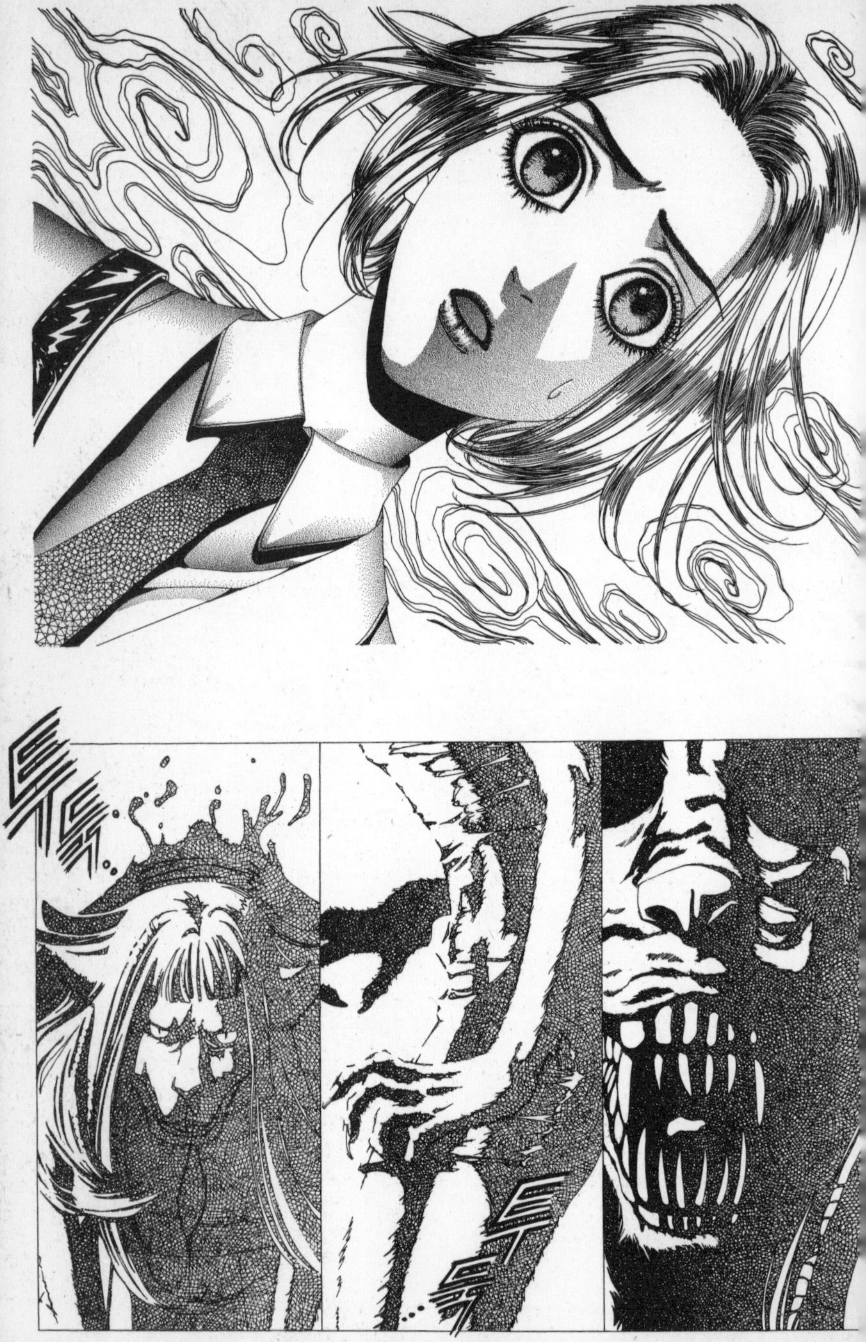

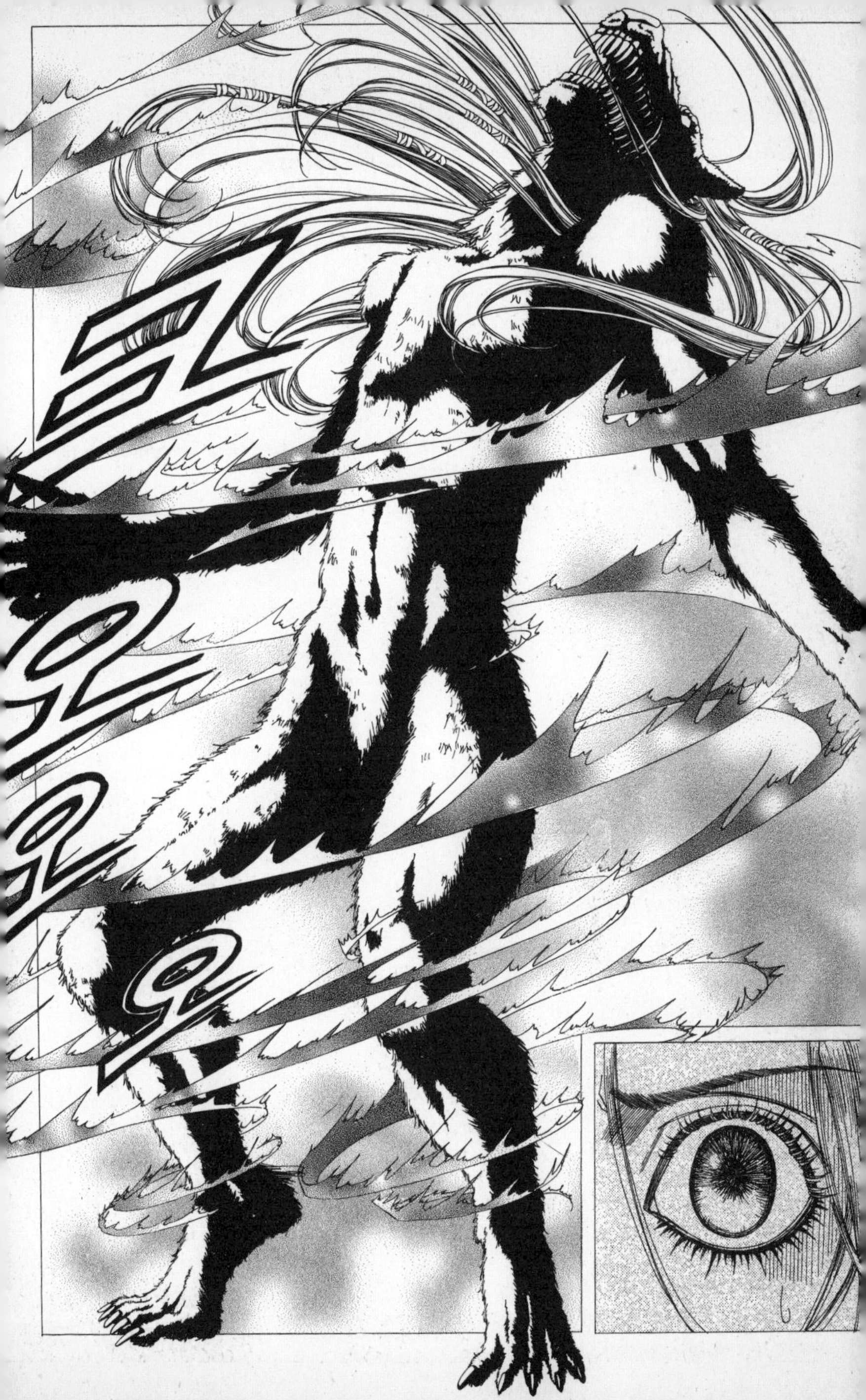

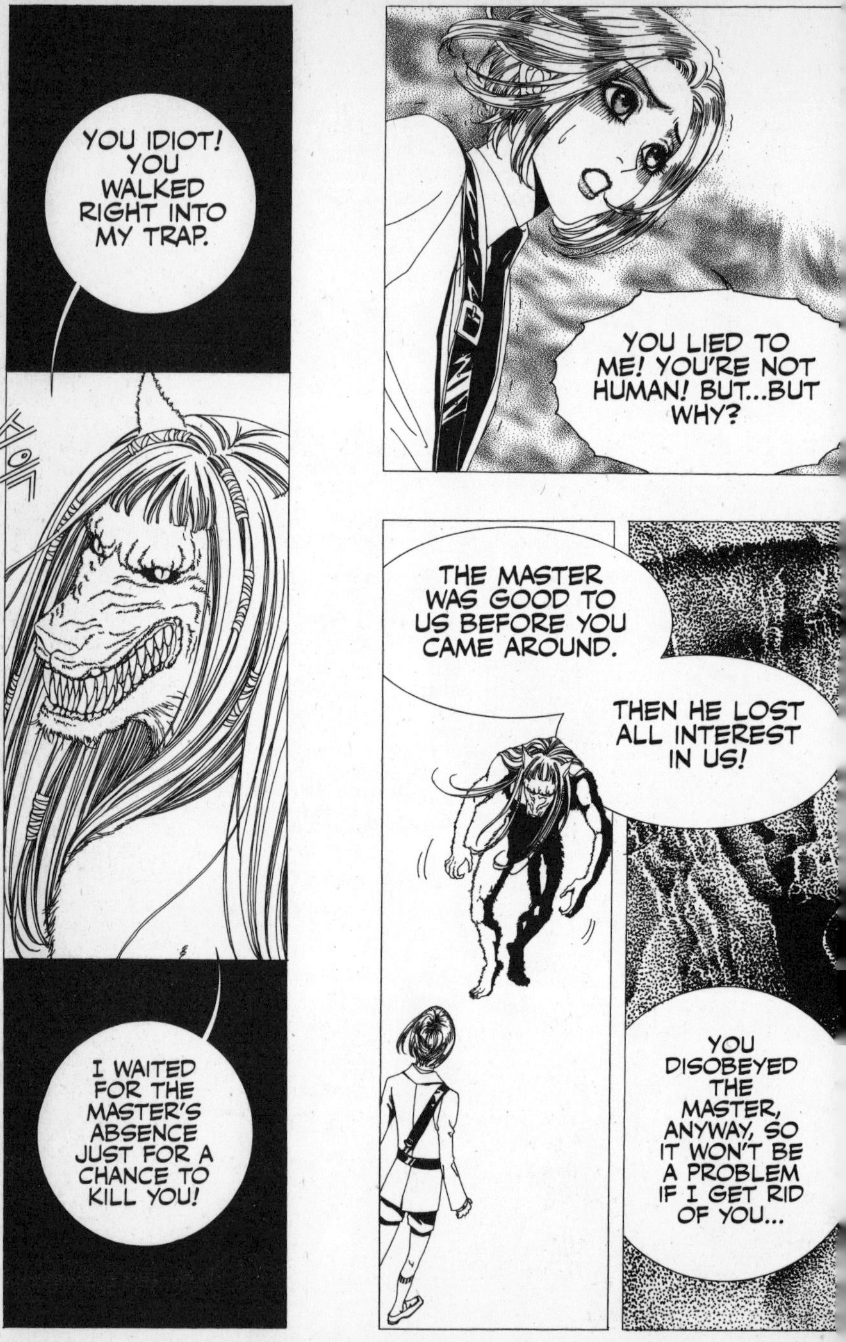
YOU IDIOT! YOU WALKED RIGHT INTO MY TRAP.
I WAITED FOR THE MASTER'S ABSENCE JUST FOR A CHANCE TO KILL YOU!
YOU LIED TO ME! YOU'RE NOT HUMAN! BUT...BUT WHY?
THE MASTER WAS GOOD TO US BEFORE YOU CAME AROUND.
THEN HE LOST ALL INTEREST IN US!
YOU DISOBEYED THE MASTER, ANYWAY, SO IT WON'T BE A PROBLEM IF I GET RID OF YOU...

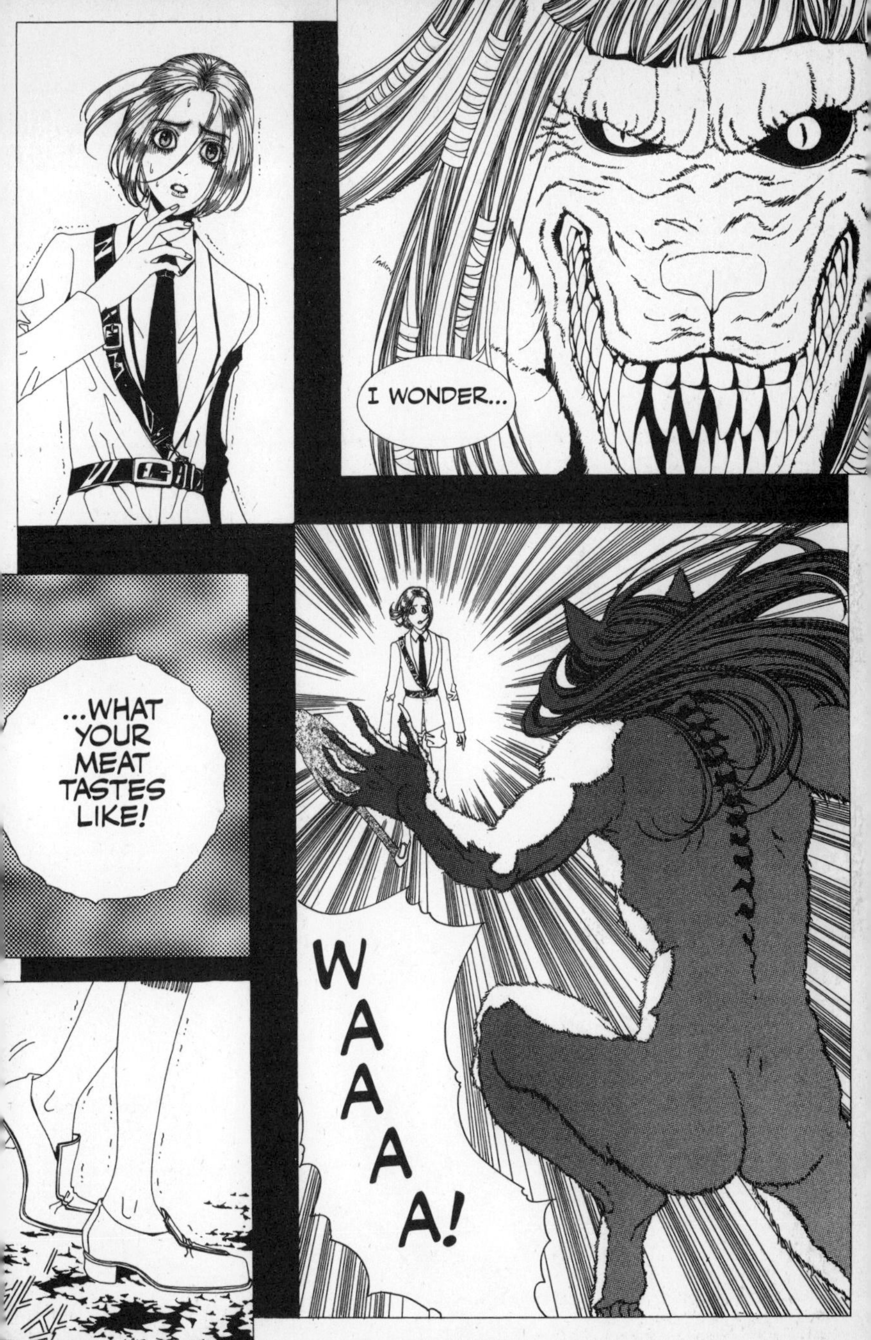
I WONDER...
...WHAT YOUR MEAT TASTES LIKE!
WAAAAA!

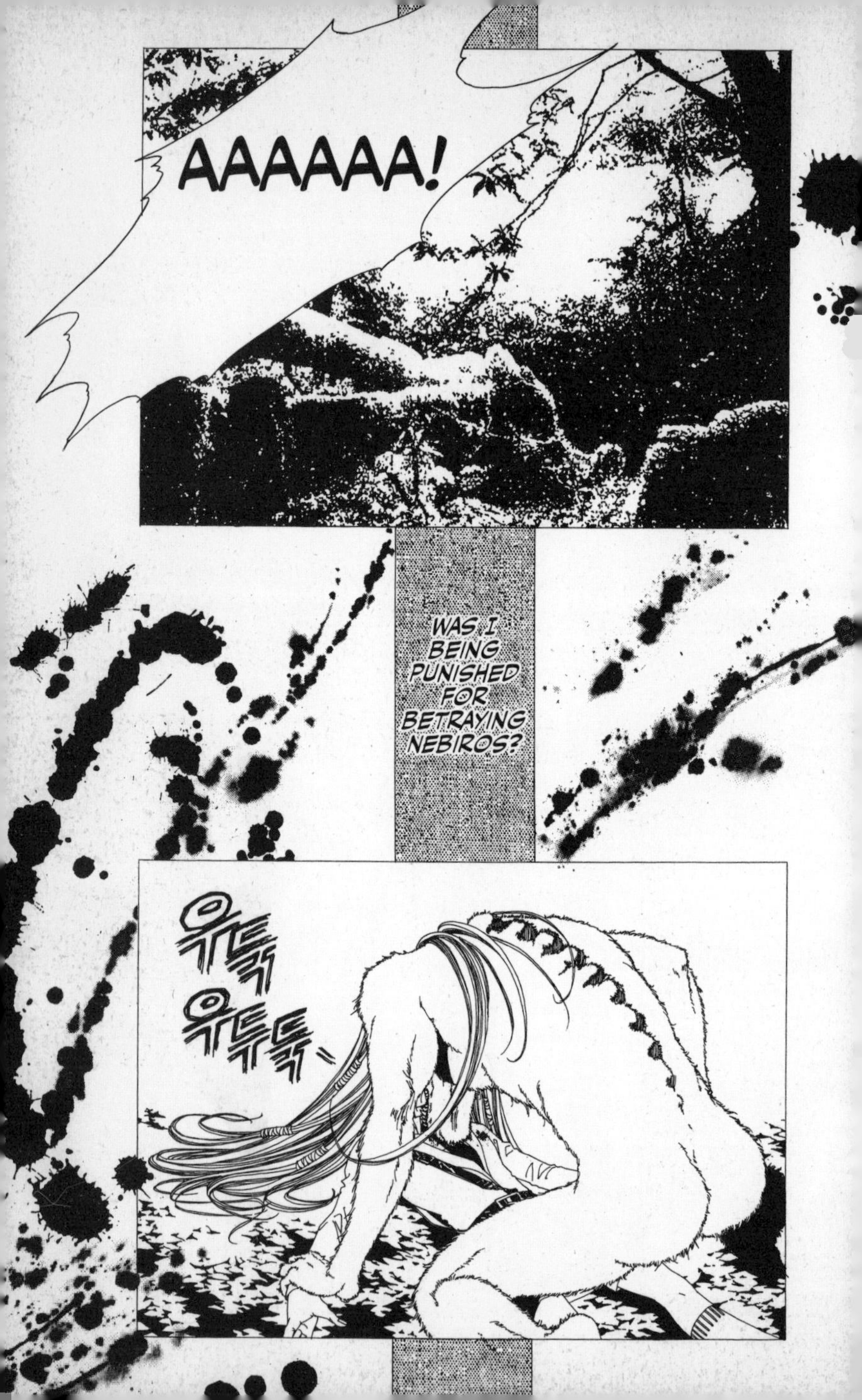
AAAAAA!
WAS I BEING PUNISHED FOR BETRAYING NEBIROS?
우둑
우두둑

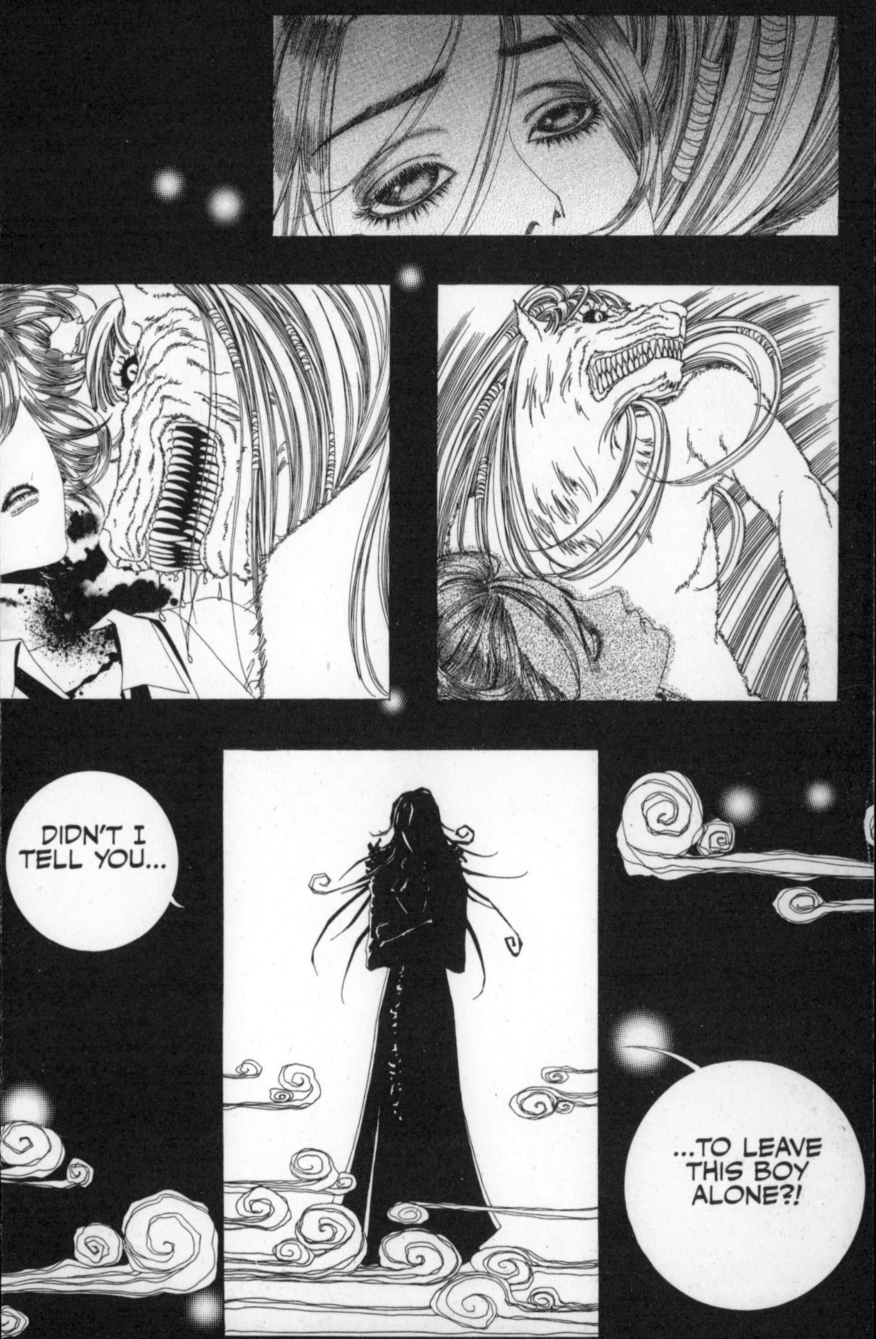
DIDN'T I TELL YOU...
...TO LEAVE THIS BOY ALONE?!

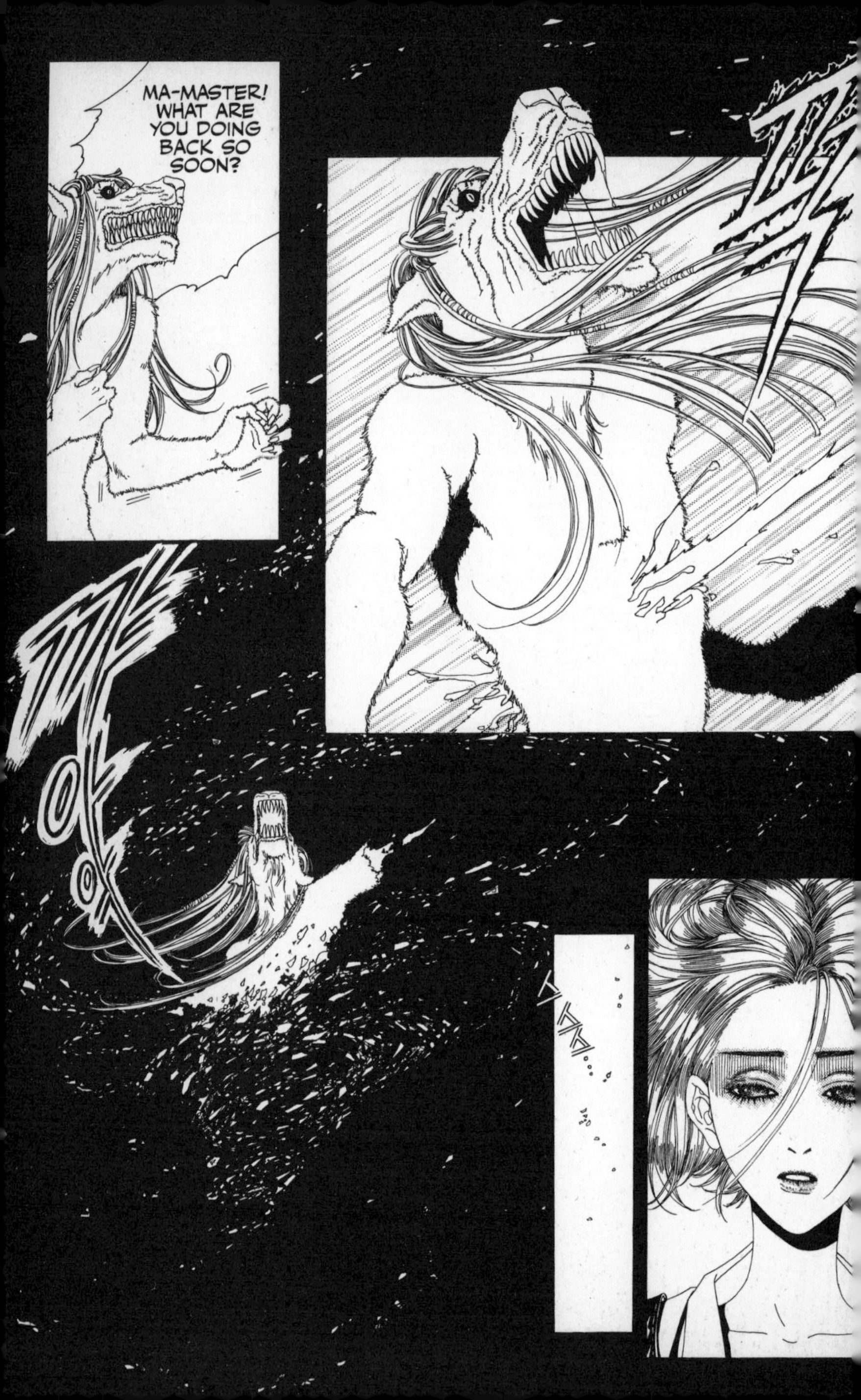
MA-MASTER! WHAT ARE YOU DOING BACK SO SOON?

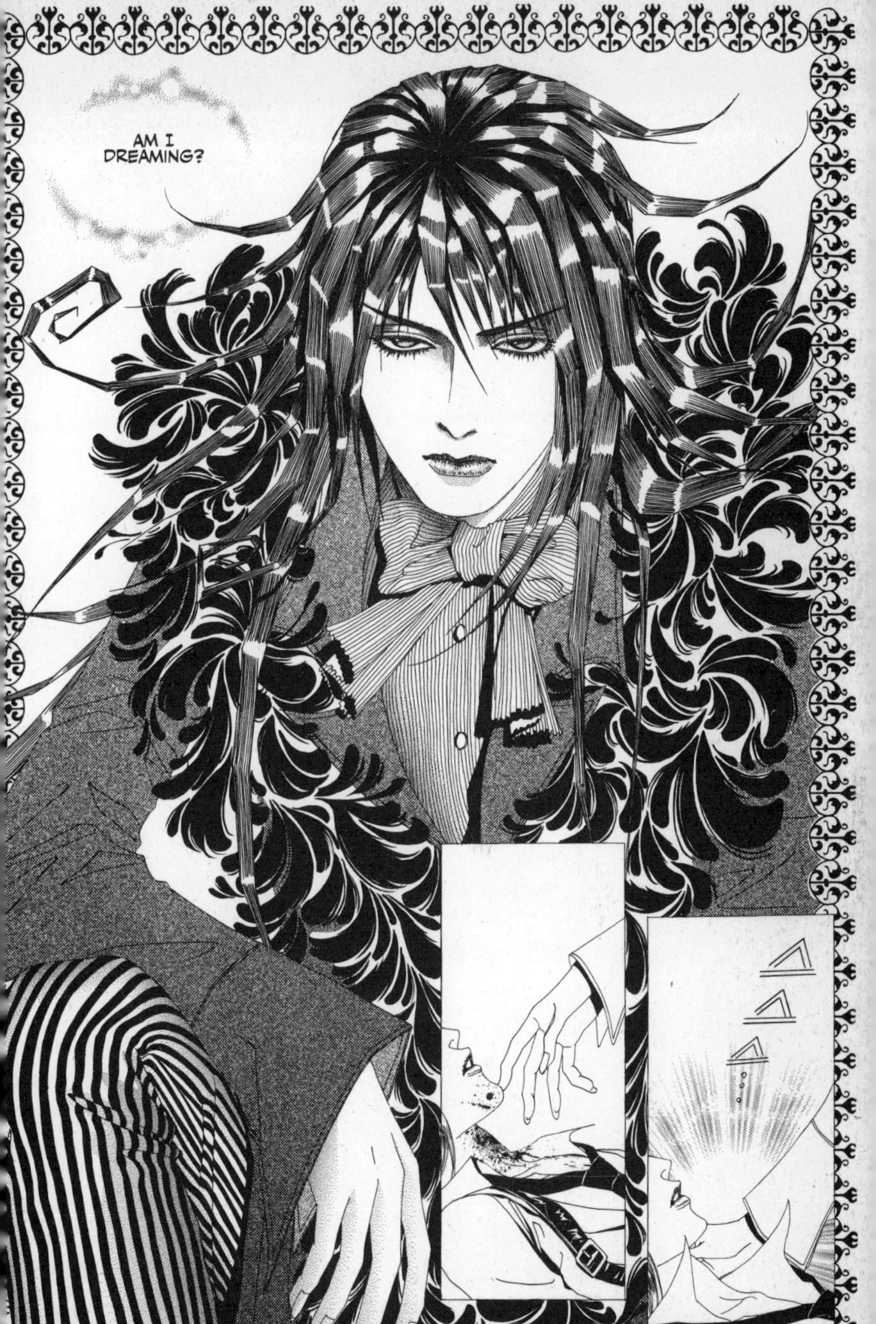
AM I DREAMING?

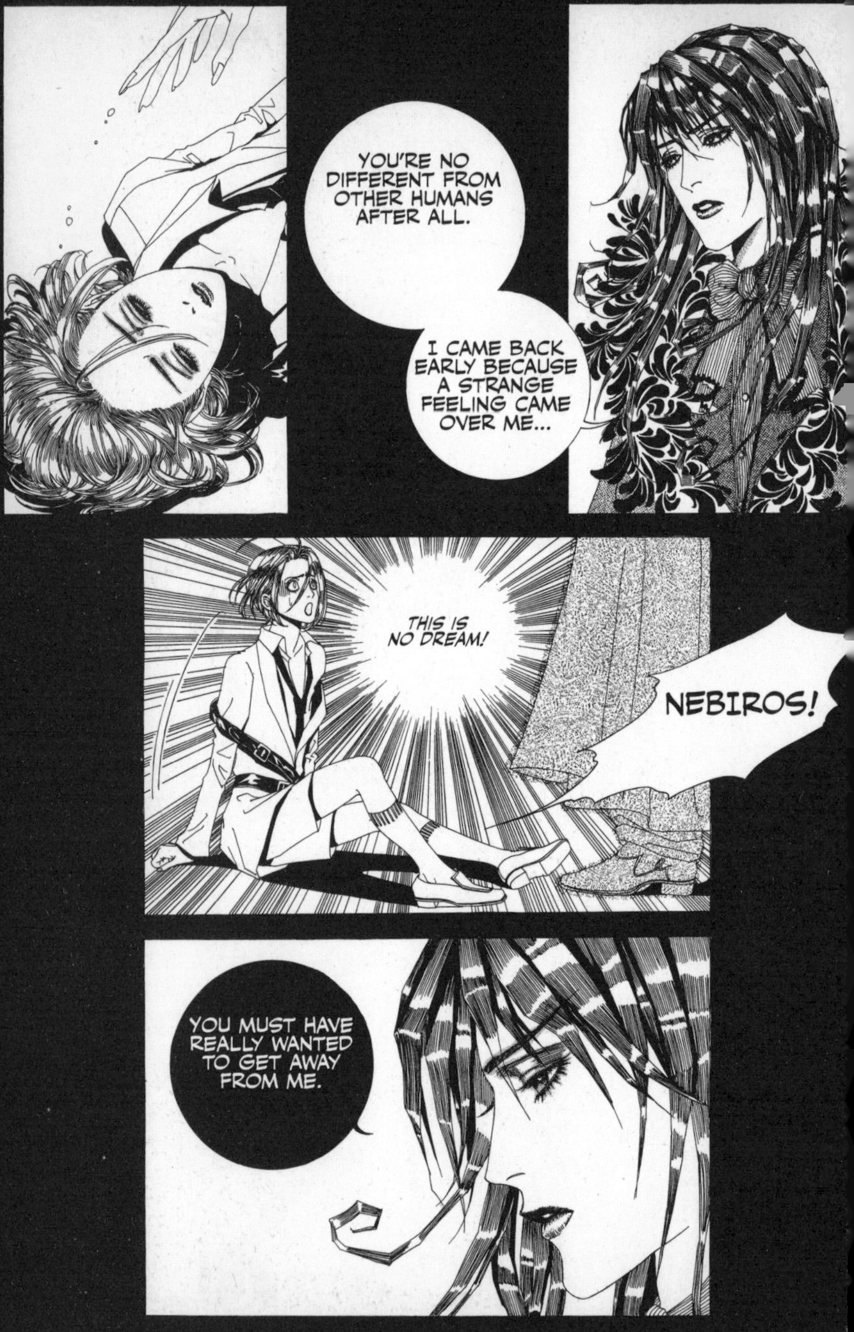
YOU'RE NO DIFFERENT FROM OTHER HUMANS AFTER ALL.
I CAME BACK EARLY BECAUSE A STRANGE FEELING CAME OVER ME...
THIS IS NO DREAM!
NEBIROS!
YOU MUST HAVE REALLY WANTED TO GET AWAY FROM ME.

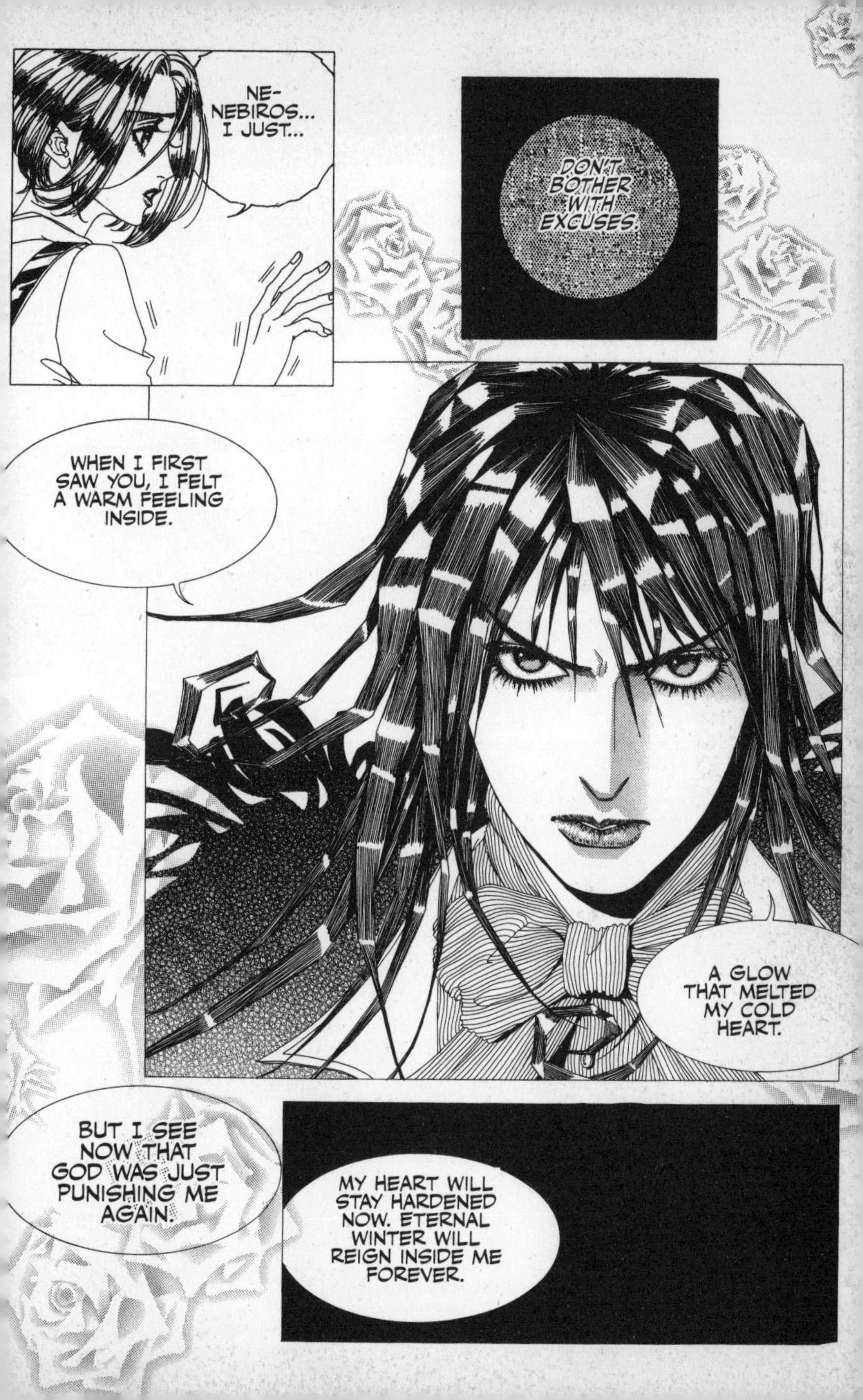
NE- NEBIROS... I JUST...
DON'T BOTHER WITH EXCUSES.
WHEN I FIRST SAW YOU, I FELT A WARM FEELING INSIDE.
A GLOW THAT MELTED MY COLD HEART.
BUT I SEE NOW THAT GOD WAS JUST PUNISHING ME AGAIN.
MY HEART WILL STAY HARDENED NOW. ETERNAL WINTER WILL REIGN INSIDE ME FOREVER.

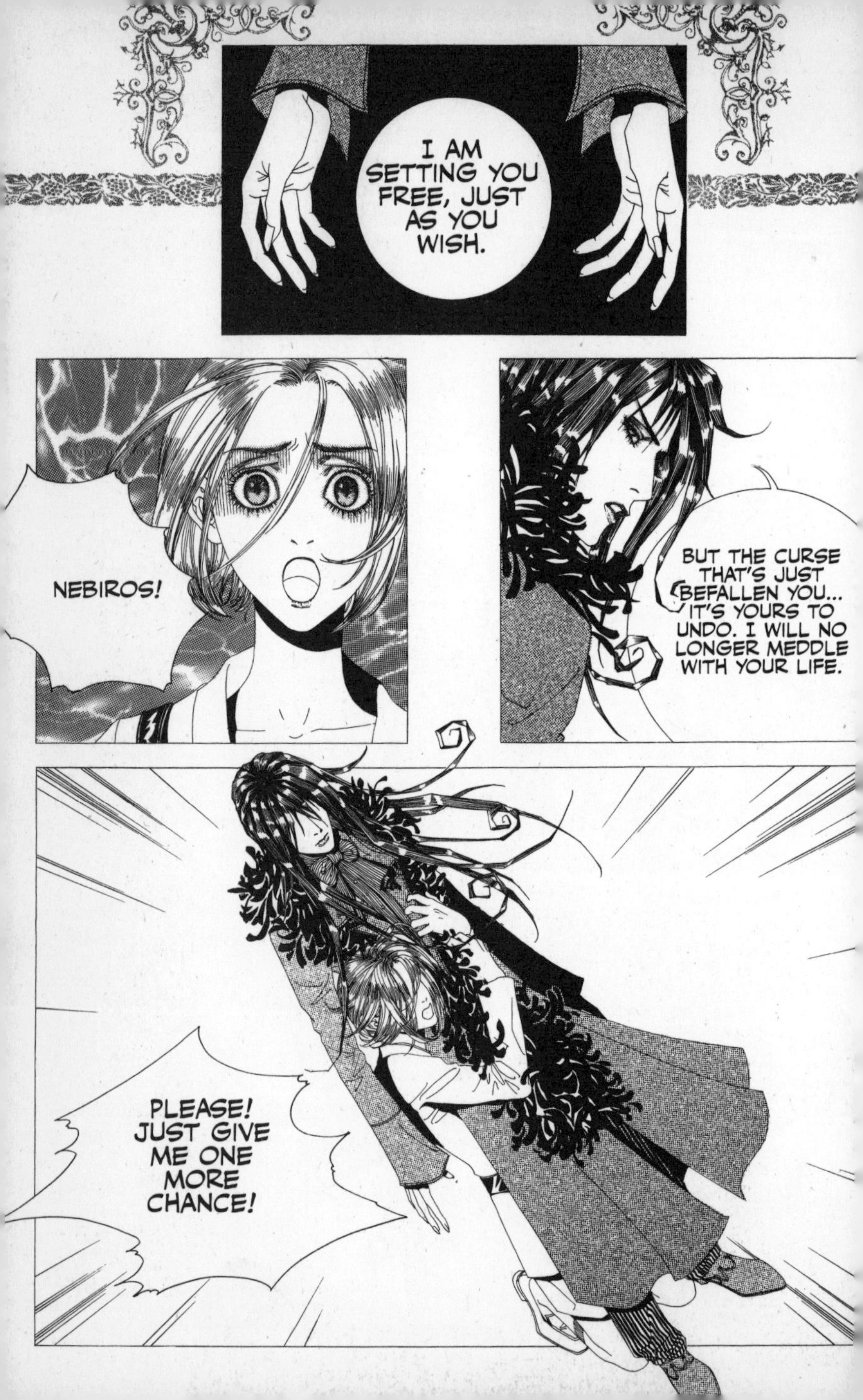
I AM SETTING YOU FREE, JUST AS YOU WISH.
NEBIROS!
BUT THE CURSE THAT'S JUST BEFALLEN YOU... IT'S YOURS TO UNDO. I WILL NO LONGER MEDDLE WITH YOUR LIFE.
PLEASE! JUST GIVE ME ONE MORE CHANCE!

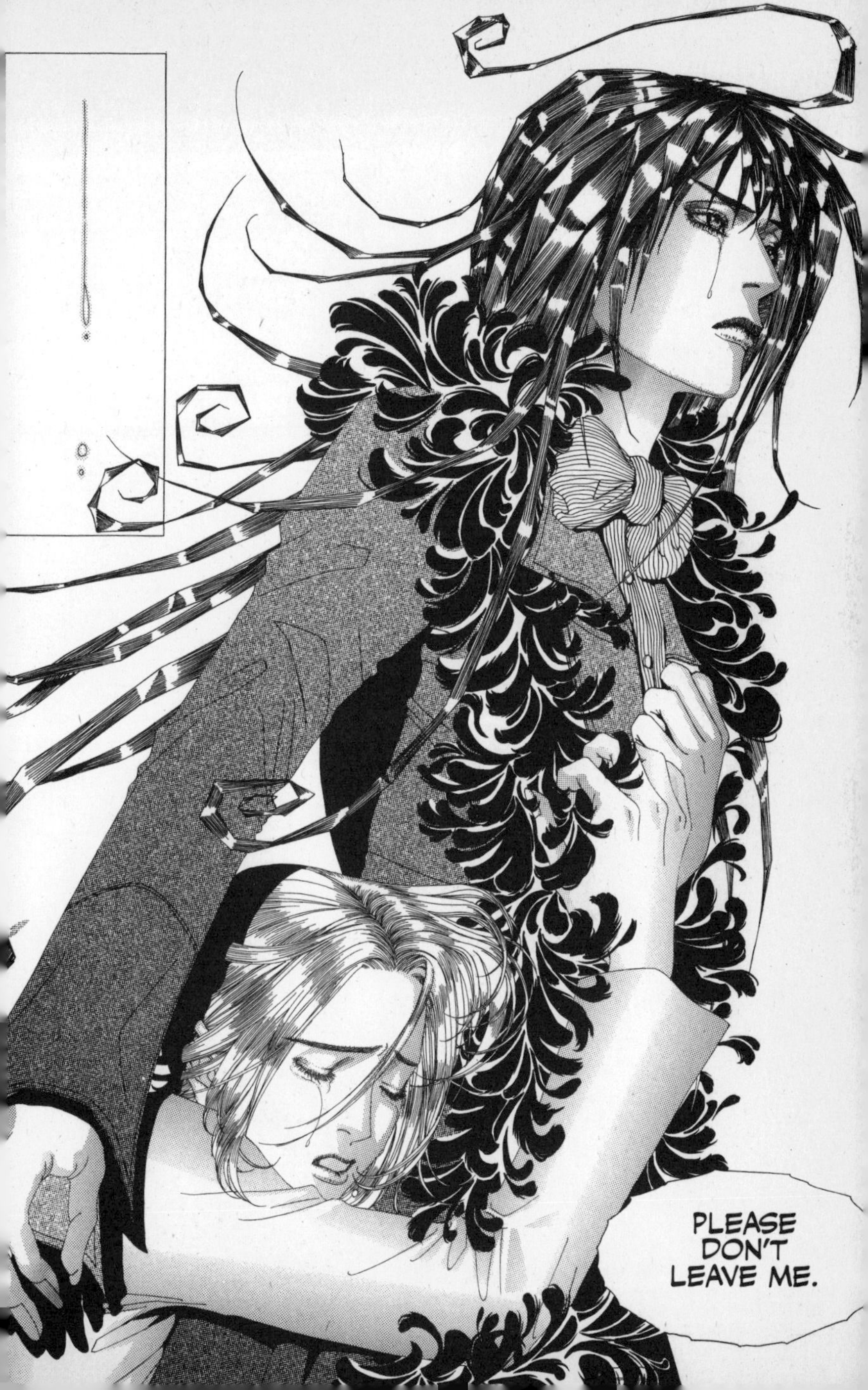
PLEASE DON'T LEAVE ME.

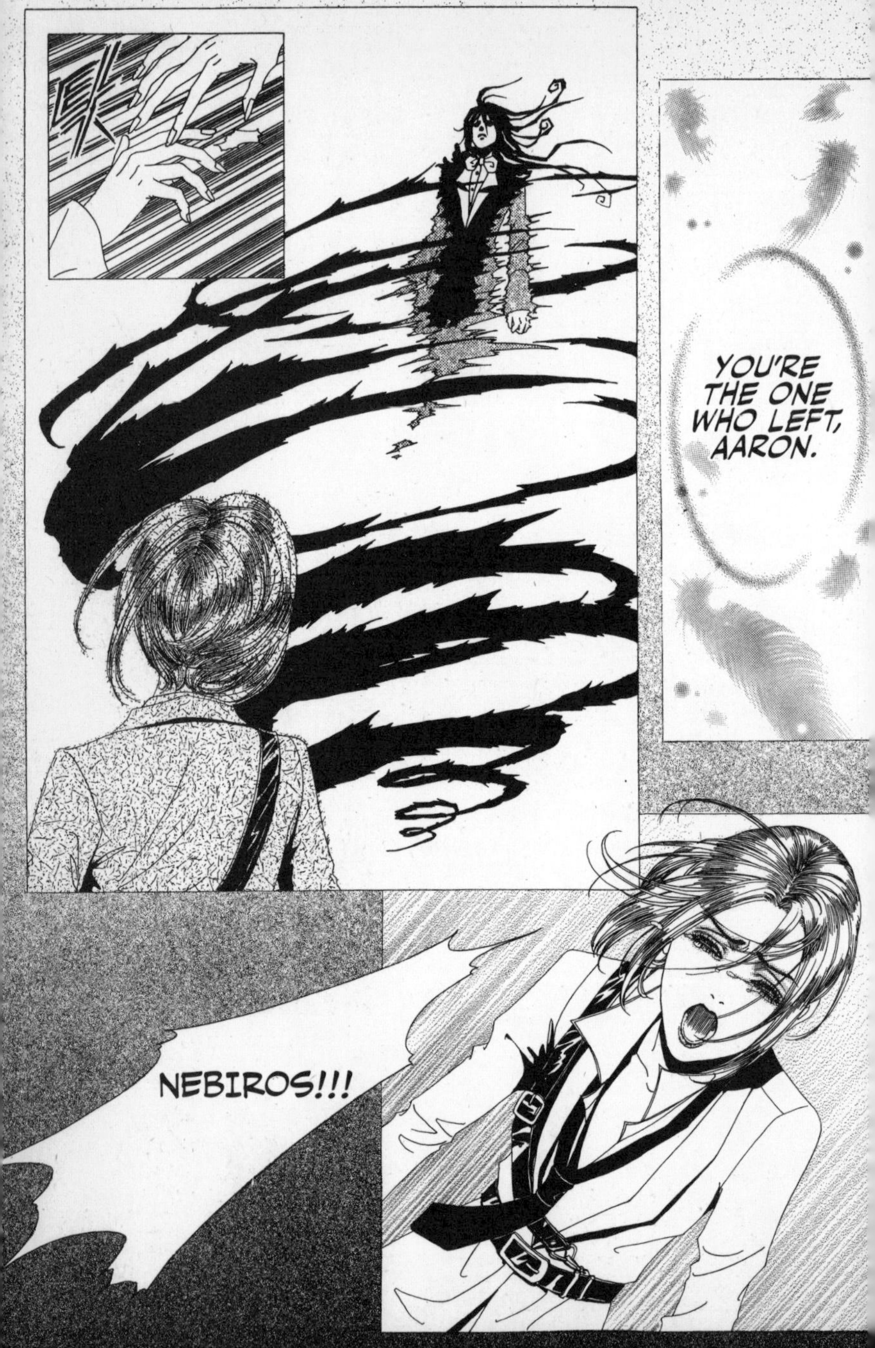
YOU'RE THE ONE WHO LEFT, AARON.
NEBIROS!!!

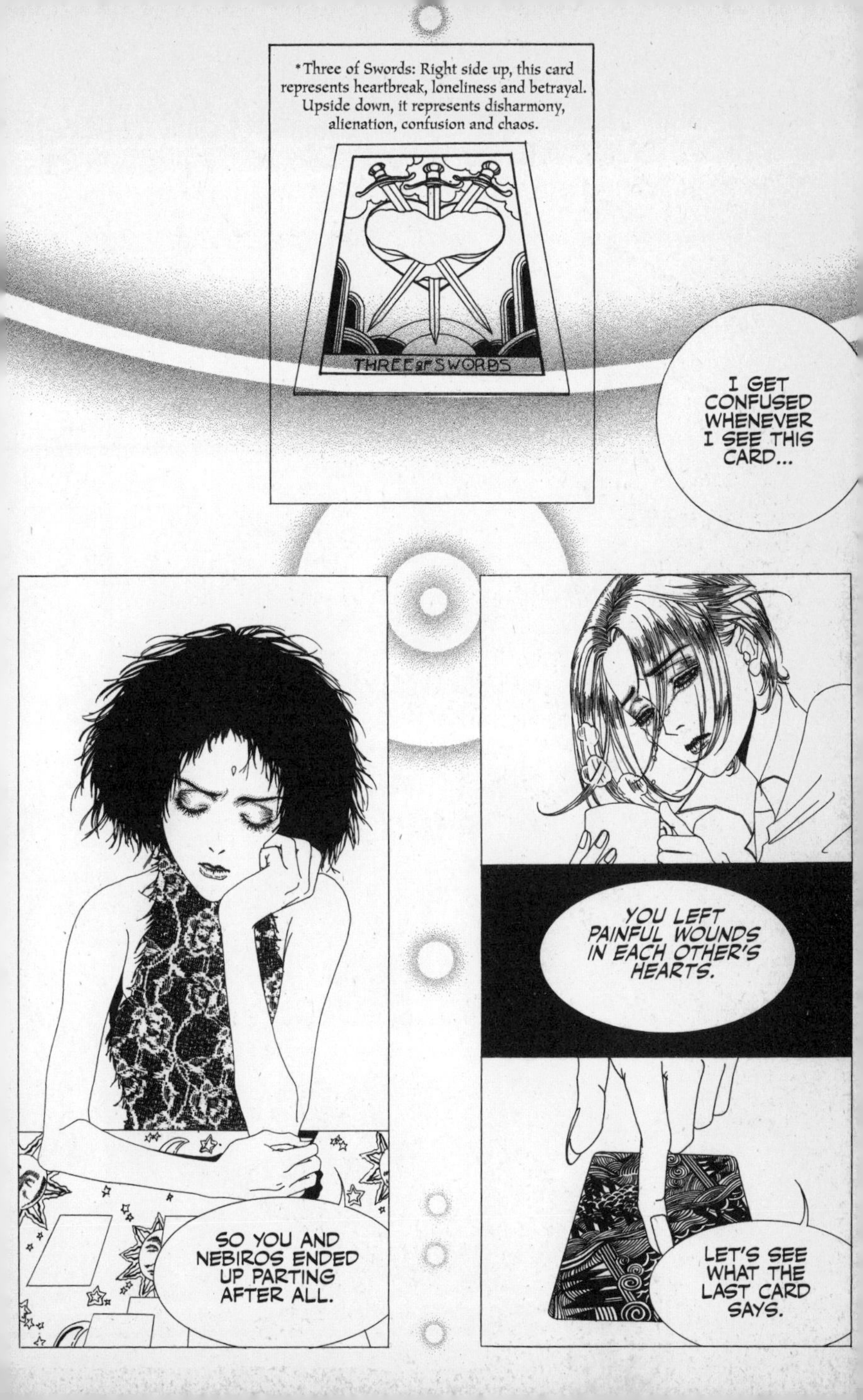
*Three of Swords: Right side up, this card represents heartbreak, loneliness and betrayal. Upside down, it represents disharmony, alienation, confusion and chaos.
THREE of SWORDS
I GET CONFUSED WHENEVER I SEE THIS CARD...
SO YOU AND NEBIROS ENDED UP PARTING AFTER ALL.
YOU LEFT PAINFUL WOUNDS IN EACH OTHER'S HEARTS.
LET'S SEE WHAT THE LAST CARD SAYS.

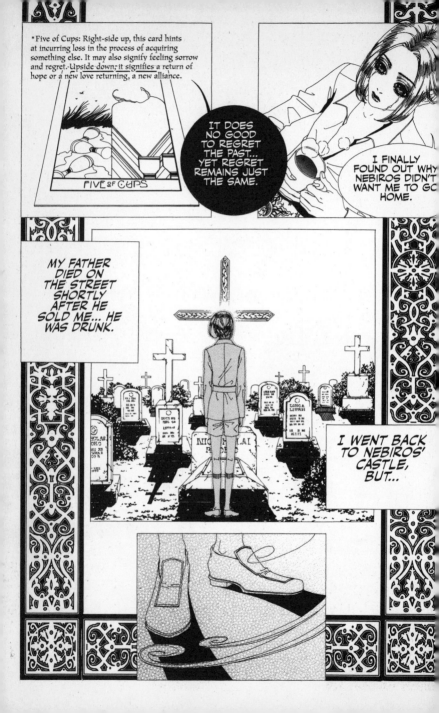

*Five of Cups: Right-side up, this card hints at incurring loss in the process of acquiring something else. It may also signify feeling sorrow and regret. Upside down, it signifies a return of hope or a new love returning, a new alliance.

FIVE OF CUPS

IT DOES NO GOOD TO REGRET THE PAST... YET REGRET REMAINS JUST THE SAME.

I FINALLY FOUND OUT WHY NEBIROS DIDN'T WANT ME TO GO HOME.

MY FATHER DIED ON THE STREET SHORTLY AFTER HE SOLD ME... HE WAS DRUNK.

I WENT BACK TO NEBIROS' CASTLE, BUT...

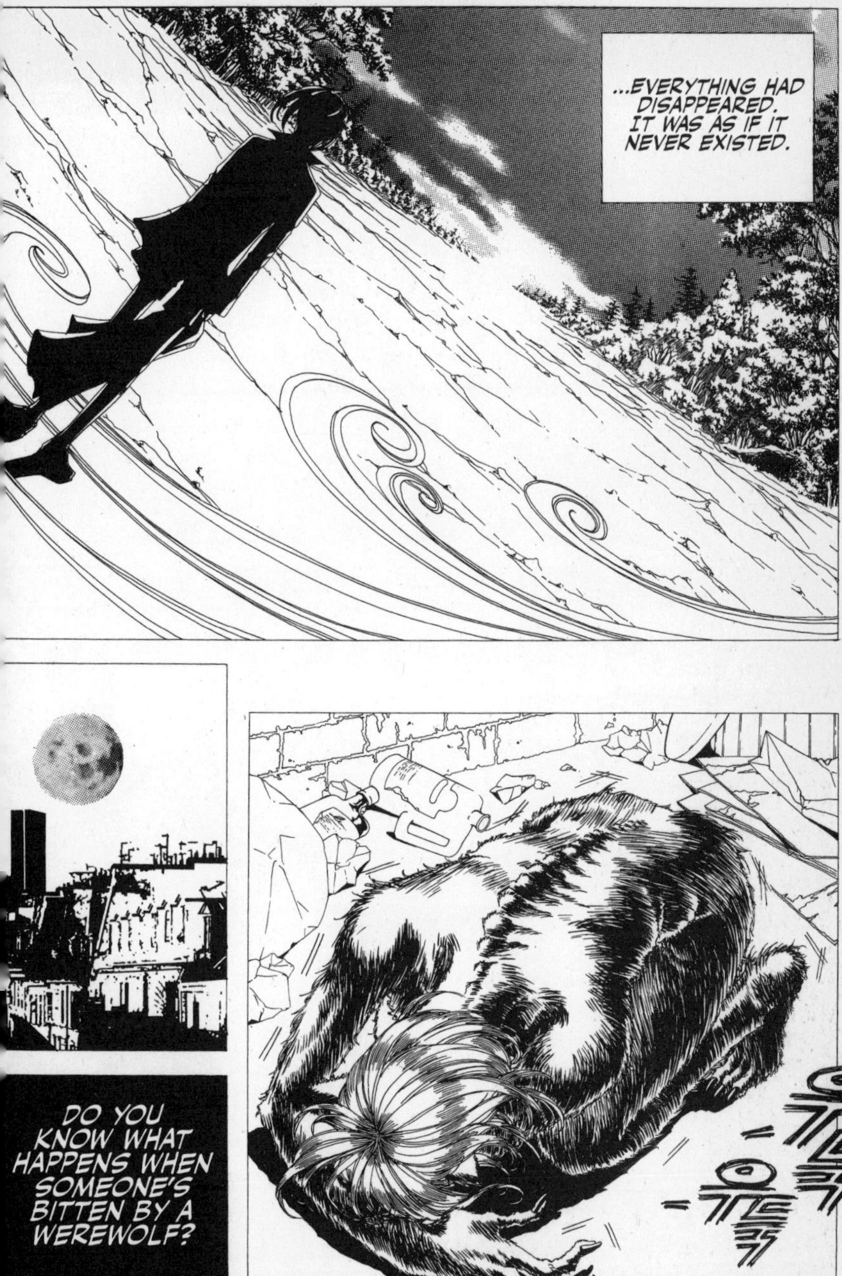
...EVERYTHING HAD DISAPPEARED. IT WAS AS IF IT NEVER EXISTED.
DO YOU KNOW WHAT HAPPENS WHEN SOMEONE'S BITTEN BY A WEREWOLF?

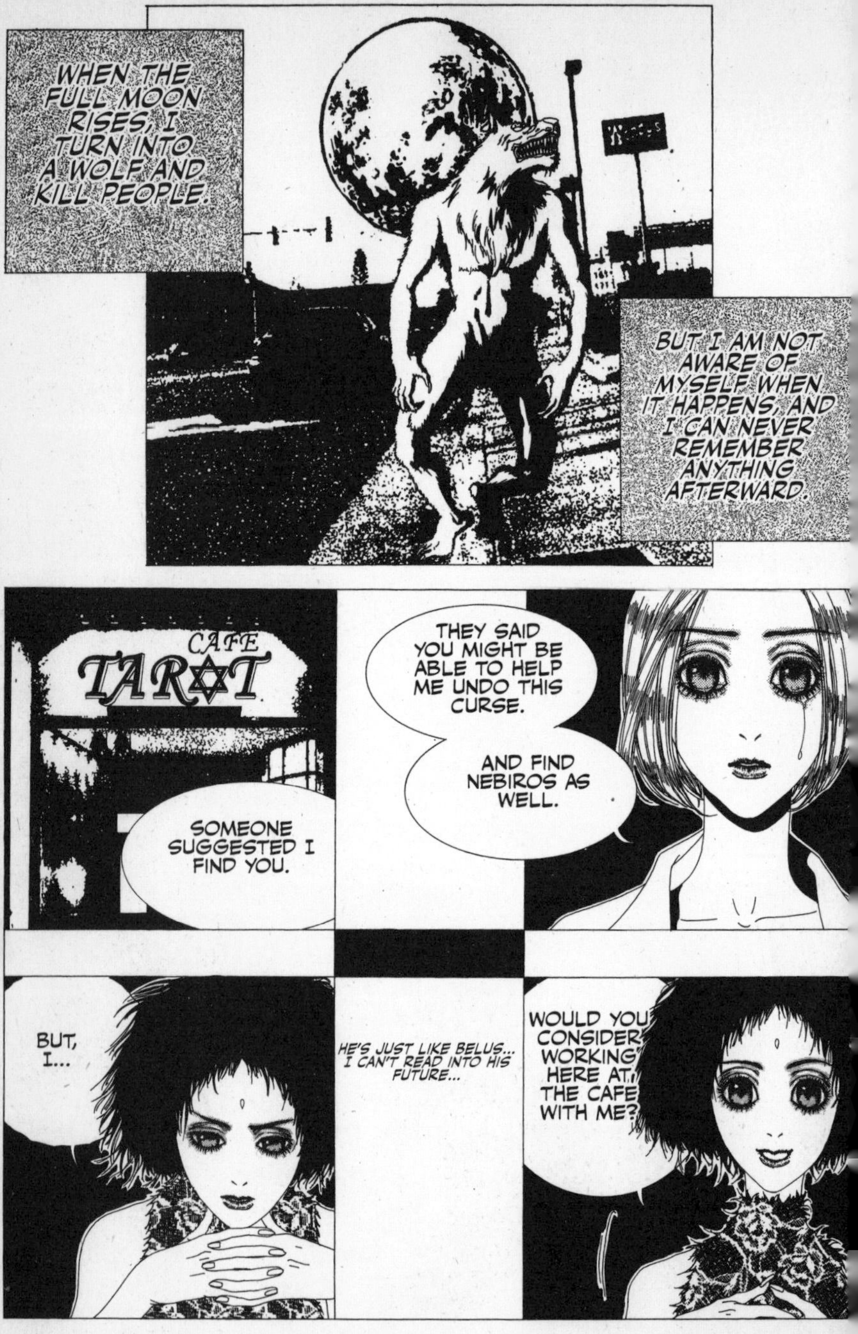
WHEN THE FULL MOON RISES, I TURN INTO A WOLF AND KILL PEOPLE.
BUT I AM NOT AWARE OF MYSELF WHEN IT HAPPENS, AND I CAN NEVER REMEMBER ANYTHING AFTERWARD.
CAFE TAROT
SOMEONE SUGGESTED I FIND YOU.
THEY SAID YOU MIGHT BE ABLE TO HELP ME UNDO THIS CURSE.
AND FIND NEBIROS AS WELL.
BUT, I...
HE'S JUST LIKE BELUS... I CAN'T READ INTO HIS FUTURE...
WOULD YOU CONSIDER WORKING HERE AT THE CAFE WITH ME?

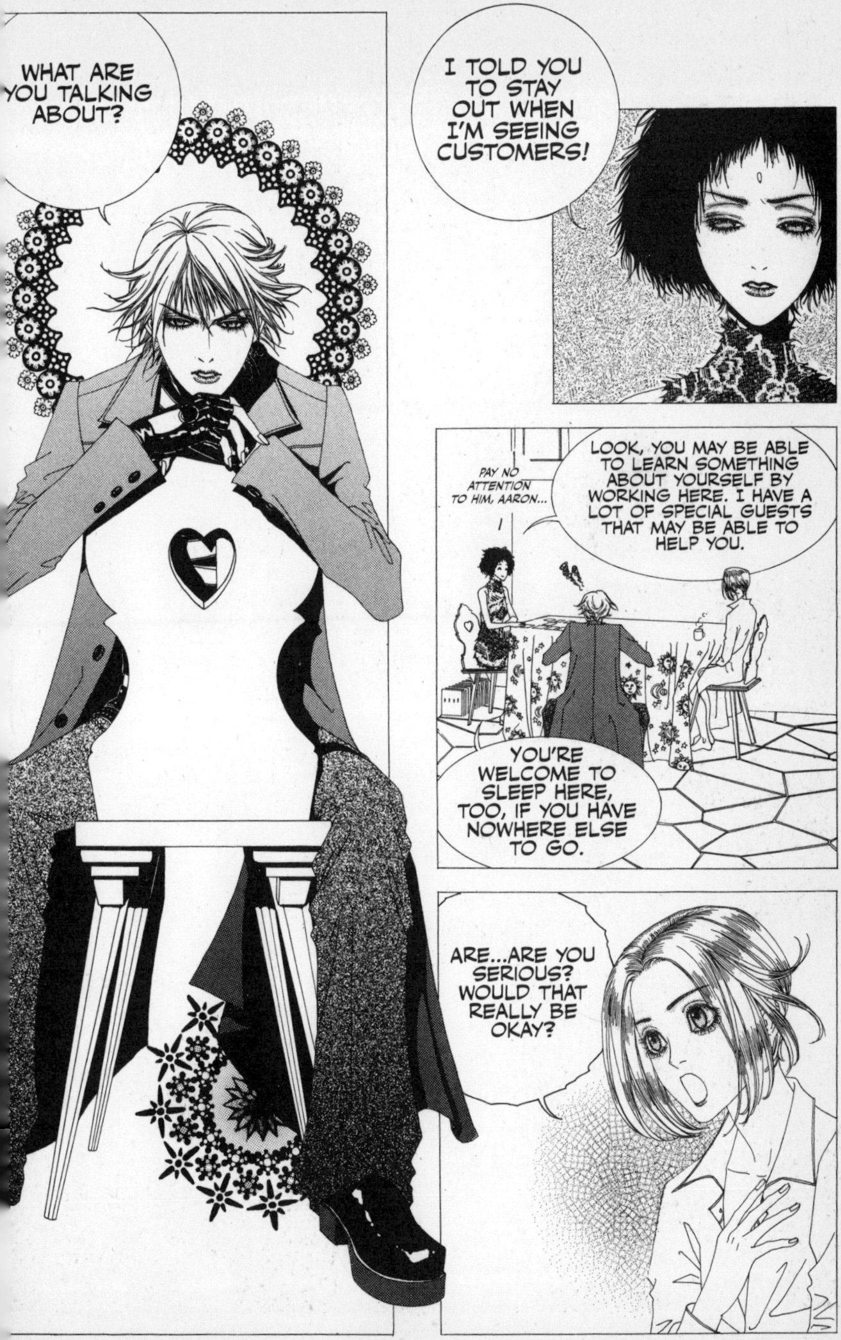
WHAT ARE YOU TALKING ABOUT?
I TOLD YOU TO STAY OUT WHEN I'M SEEING CUSTOMERS!
PAY NO ATTENTION TO HIM, AARON...
LOOK, YOU MAY BE ABLE TO LEARN SOMETHING ABOUT YOURSELF BY WORKING HERE. I HAVE A LOT OF SPECIAL GUESTS THAT MAY BE ABLE TO HELP YOU.
YOU'RE WELCOME TO SLEEP HERE, TOO, IF YOU HAVE NOWHERE ELSE TO GO.
ARE...ARE YOU SERIOUS? WOULD THAT REALLY BE OKAY?

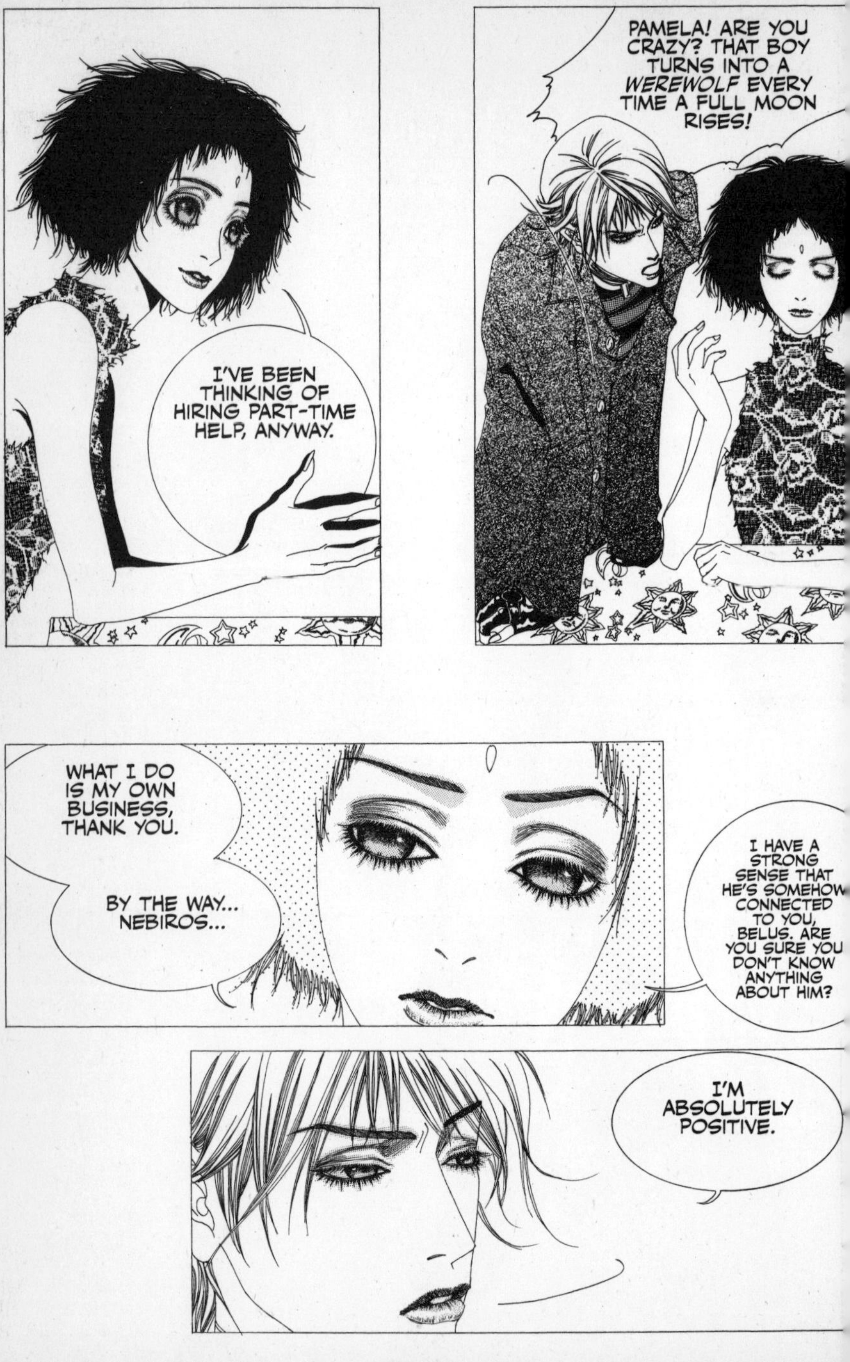
I'VE BEEN THINKING OF HIRING PART-TIME HELP, ANYWAY.
PAMELA! ARE YOU CRAZY? THAT BOY TURNS INTO A *WEREWOLF* EVERY TIME A FULL MOON RISES!
WHAT I DO IS MY OWN BUSINESS, THANK YOU.
BY THE WAY... NEBIROS...
I HAVE A STRONG SENSE THAT HE'S SOMEHOW CONNECTED TO YOU, BELUS. ARE YOU SURE YOU DON'T KNOW ANYTHING ABOUT HIM?
I'M ABSOLUTELY POSITIVE.

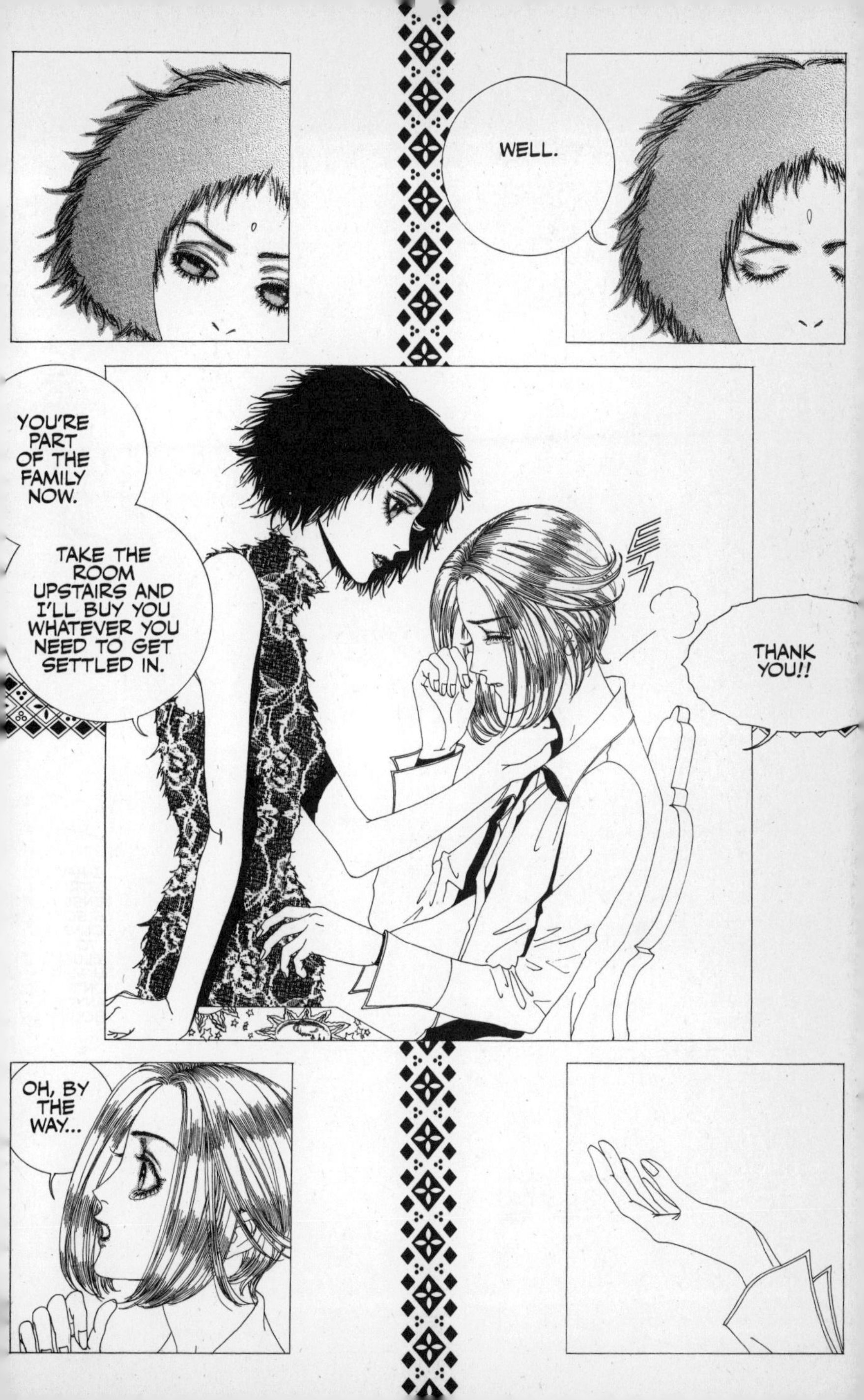
WELL.
YOU'RE PART OF THE FAMILY NOW.
TAKE THE ROOM UPSTAIRS AND I'LL BUY YOU WHATEVER YOU NEED TO GET SETTLED IN.
THANK YOU!!
OH, BY THE WAY...

NEBIROS GAVE THIS TO ME.

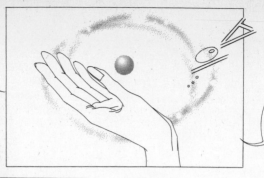

BUT I THINK YOU'LL NEED IT MORE THAN I.

HMM... THANK YOU.

SO I STARTED WORKING AT THE CAFE WITH PAMELA. I HOPE TO UNDO THIS CURSE AND SOMEDAY MEET NEBIROS ONCE AGAIN.

THERE IS A LOT I WANT TO SAY TO HIM WHEN I SEE HIM.

BUT THAT'S A SECRET...

......

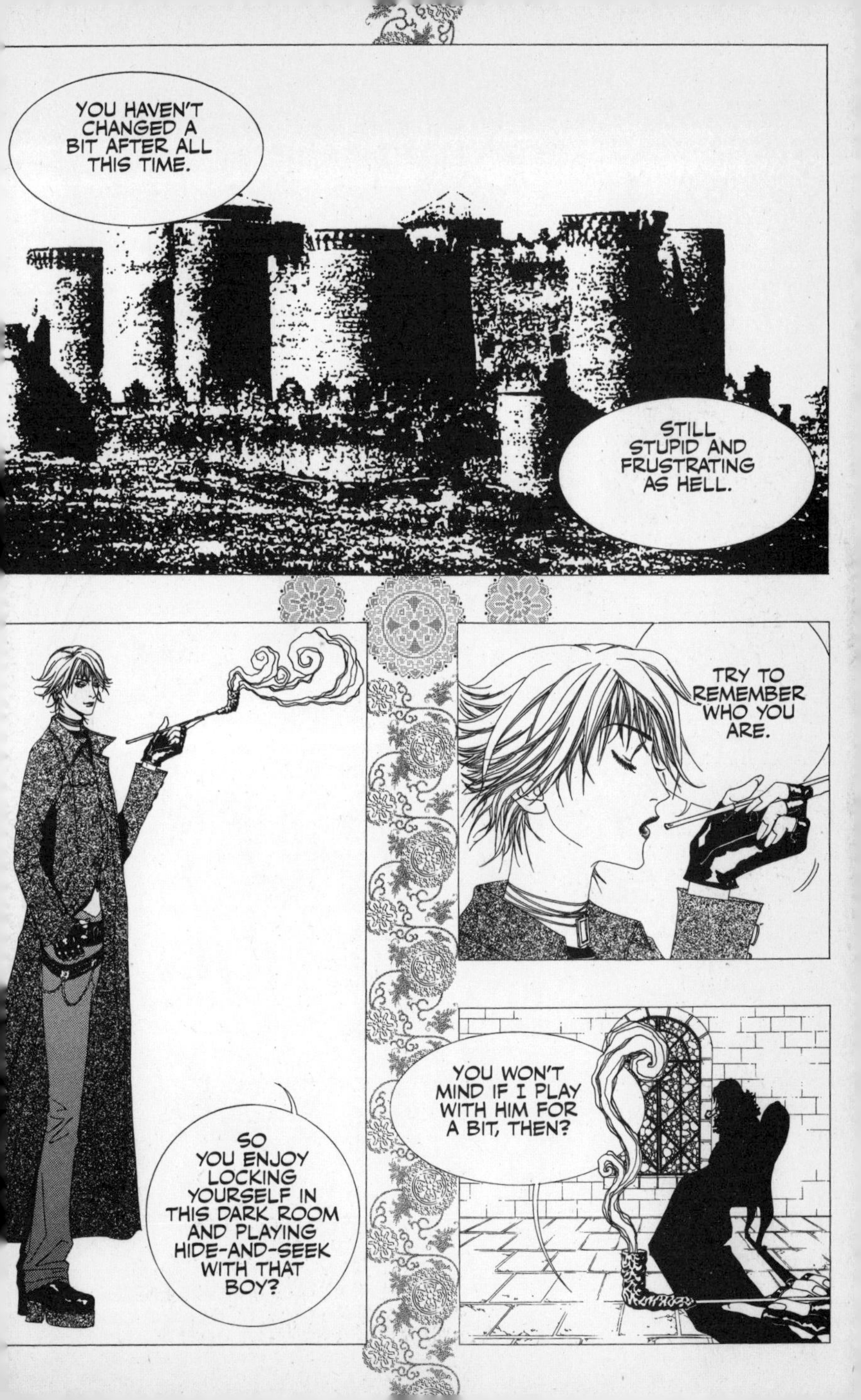
YOU HAVEN'T CHANGED A BIT AFTER ALL THIS TIME.
STILL STUPID AND FRUSTRATING AS HELL.
SO YOU ENJOY LOCKING YOURSELF IN THIS DARK ROOM AND PLAYING HIDE-AND-SEEK WITH THAT BOY?
TRY TO REMEMBER WHO YOU ARE.
YOU WON'T MIND IF I PLAY WITH HIM FOR A BIT, THEN?

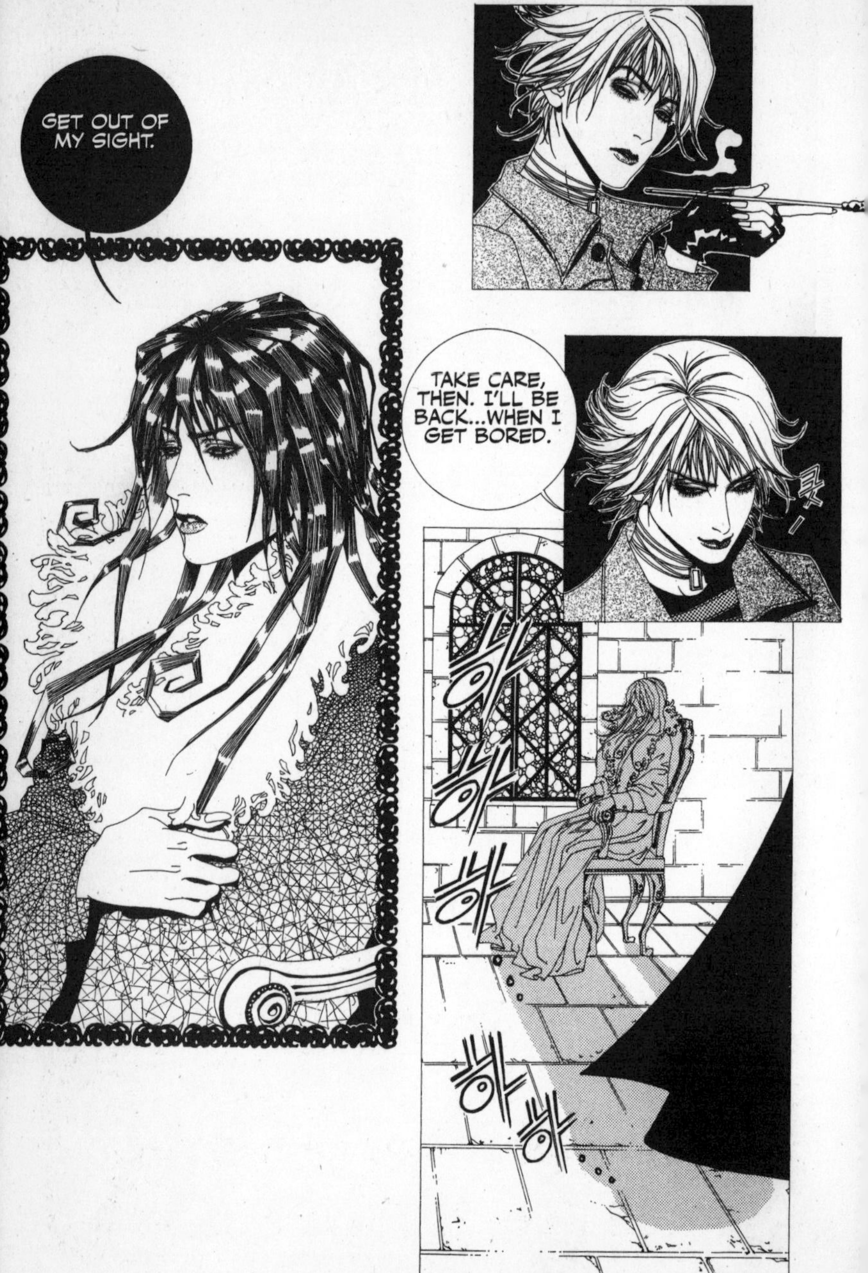
GET OUT OF MY SIGHT.
TAKE CARE, THEN. I'LL BE BACK...WHEN I GET BORED.

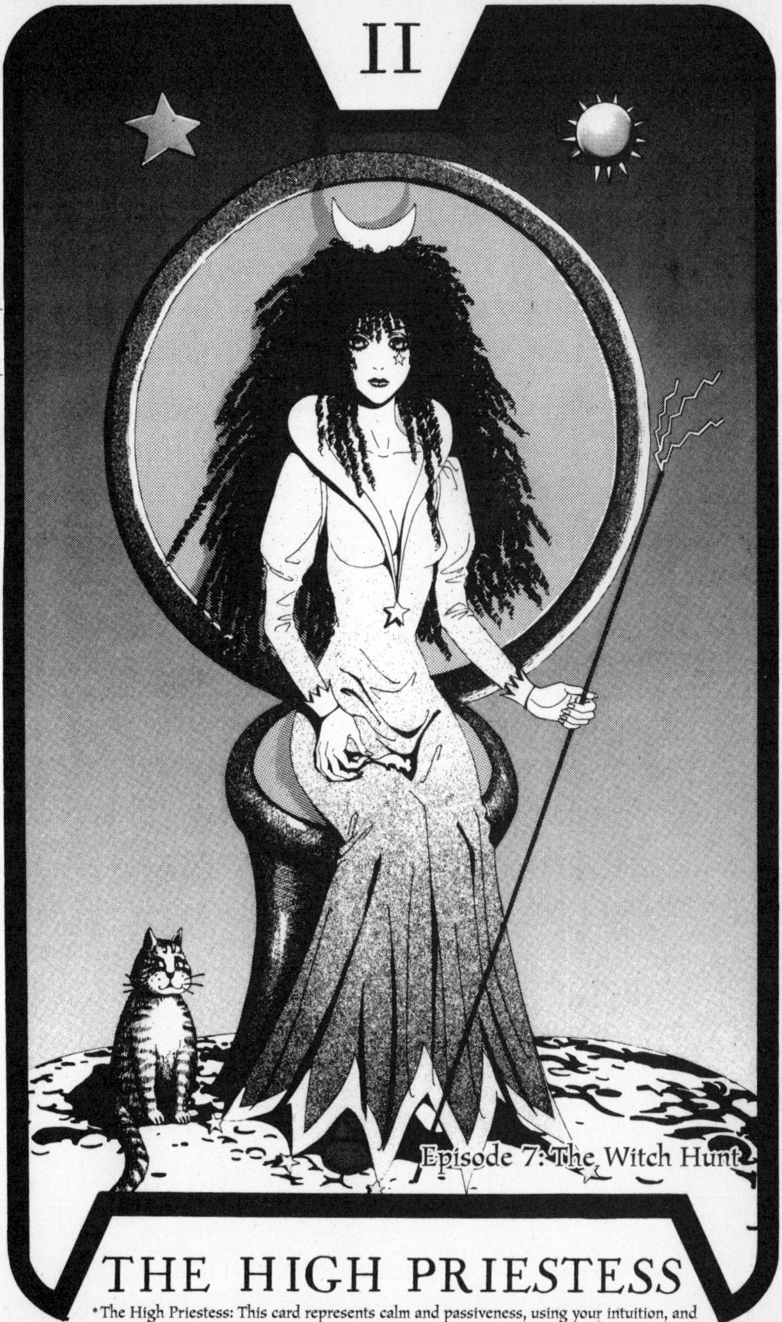
II
Episode 7: The Witch Hunt
THE HIGH PRIESTESS
*The High Priestess: This card represents calm and passiveness, using your intuition, and being open to new possibilities; seeking what is concealed.

ILLUSTRATION FROM TAROT OF THE WOLVES

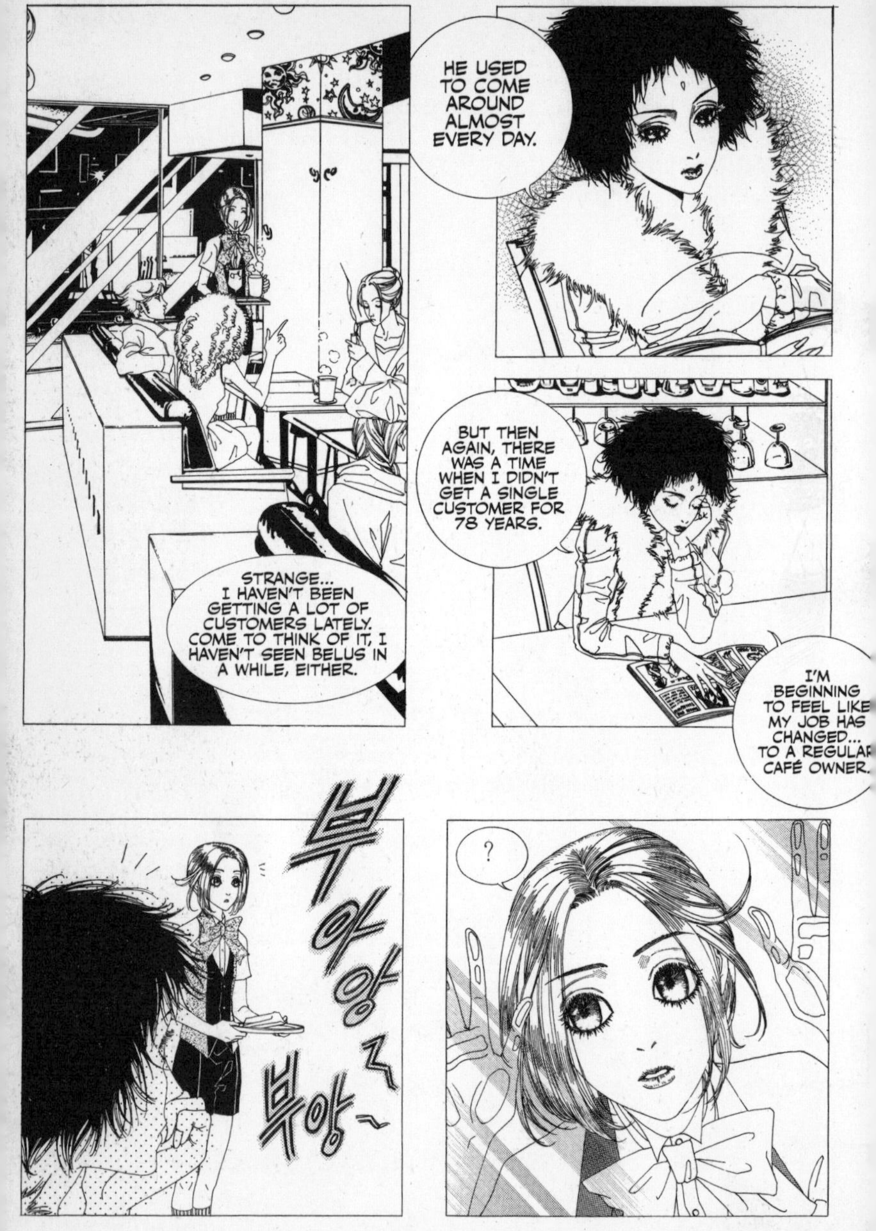
STRANGE... I HAVEN'T BEEN GETTING A LOT OF CUSTOMERS LATELY. COME TO THINK OF IT, I HAVEN'T SEEN BELUS IN A WHILE, EITHER.
HE USED TO COME AROUND ALMOST EVERY DAY.
BUT THEN AGAIN, THERE WAS A TIME WHEN I DIDN'T GET A SINGLE CUSTOMER FOR 78 YEARS.
I'M BEGINNING TO FEEL LIKE MY JOB HAS CHANGED... TO A REGULA CAFÉ OWNER.
부야양~
부양~
?

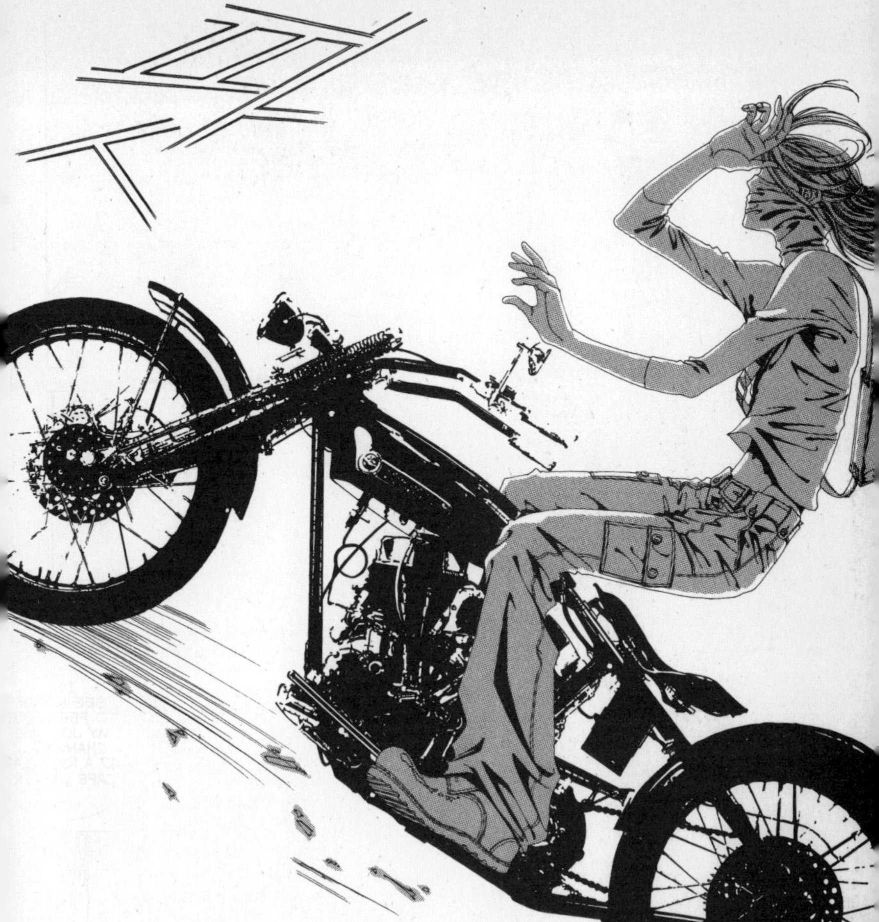

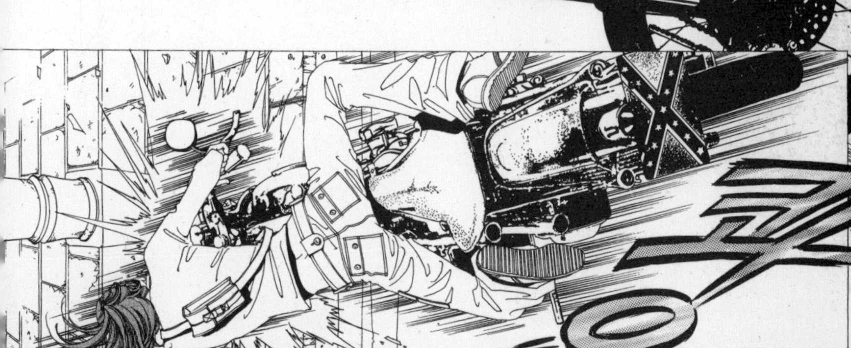

OH MY GOD!

THERE'S A DEAD GUY IN FRONT OF THE CAFE!

SOMEONE'S DEAD OUT THERE!

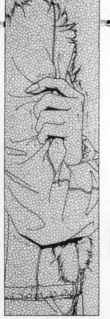

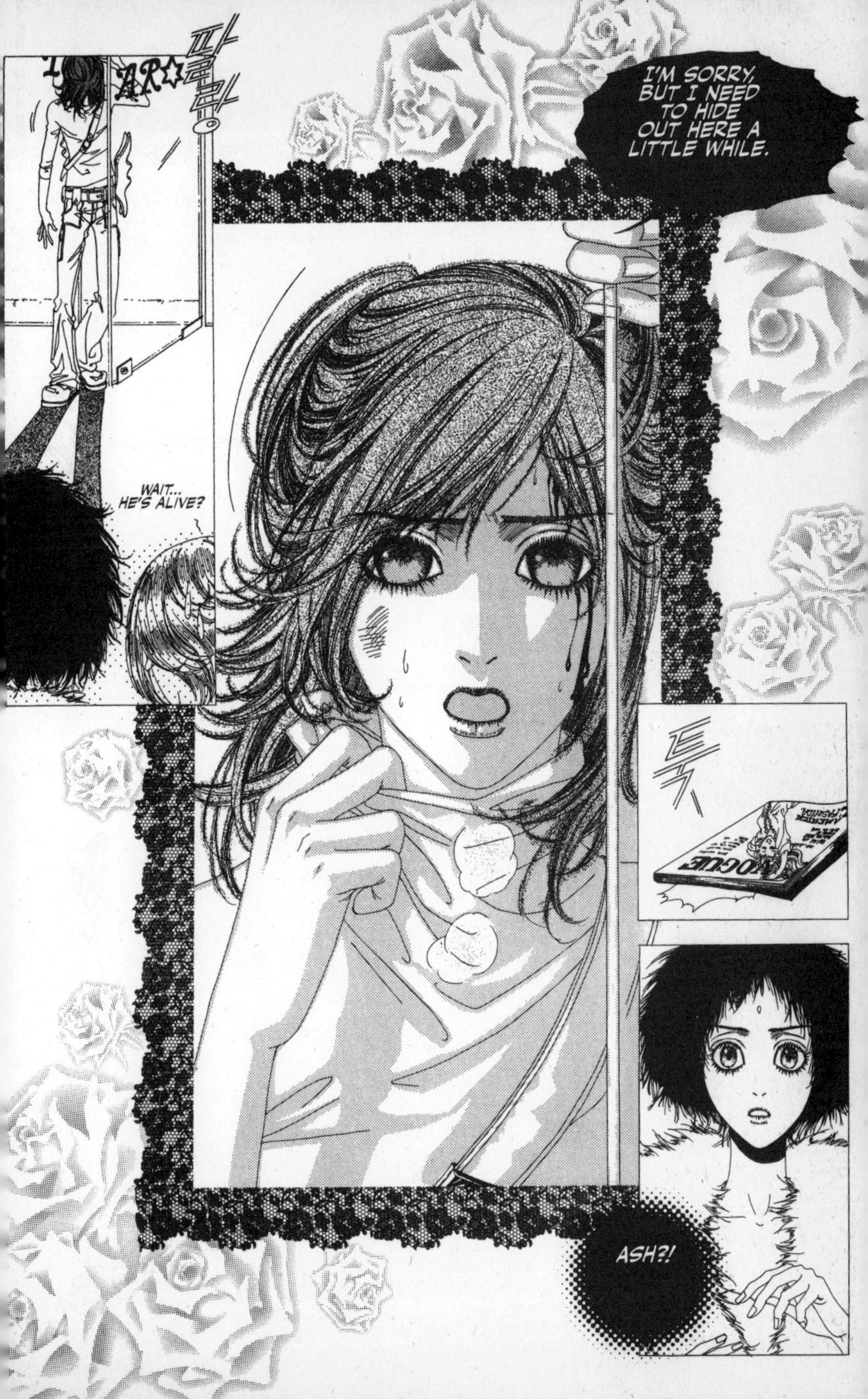
WAIT... HE'S ALIVE?
I'M SORRY, BUT I NEED TO HIDE OUT HERE A LITTLE WHILE.
ASH?!

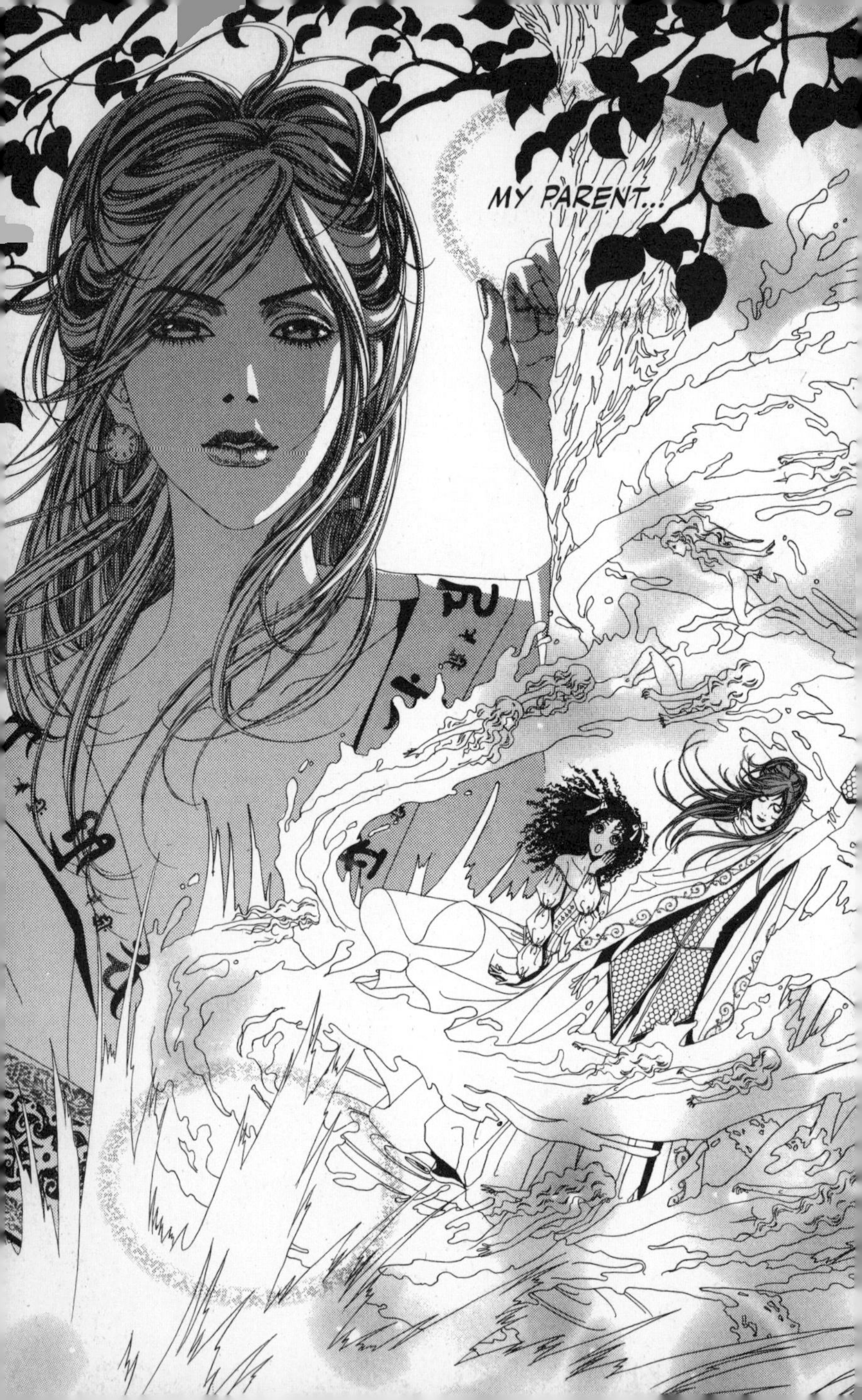
MY PARENT...

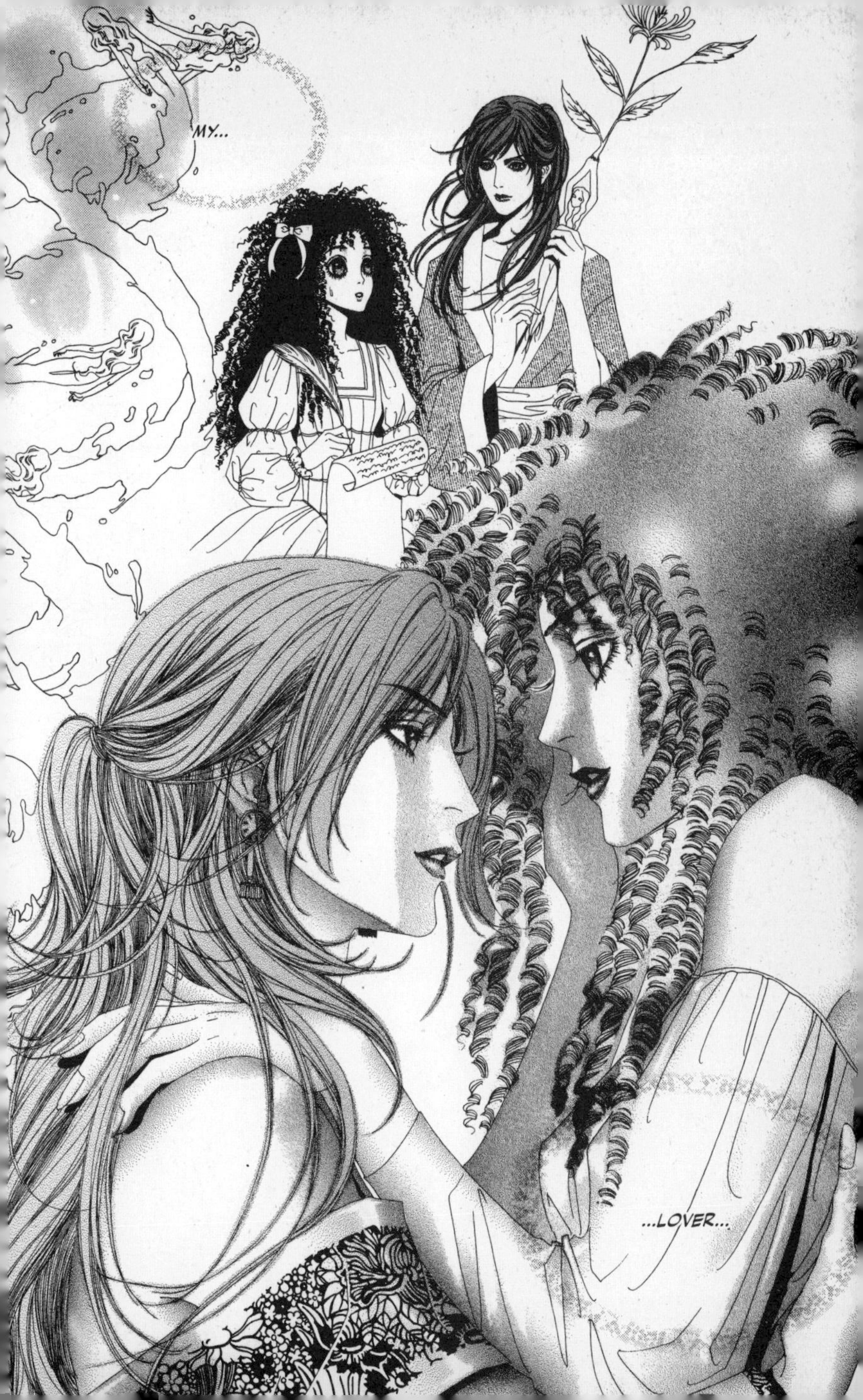
MY...
...LOVER...

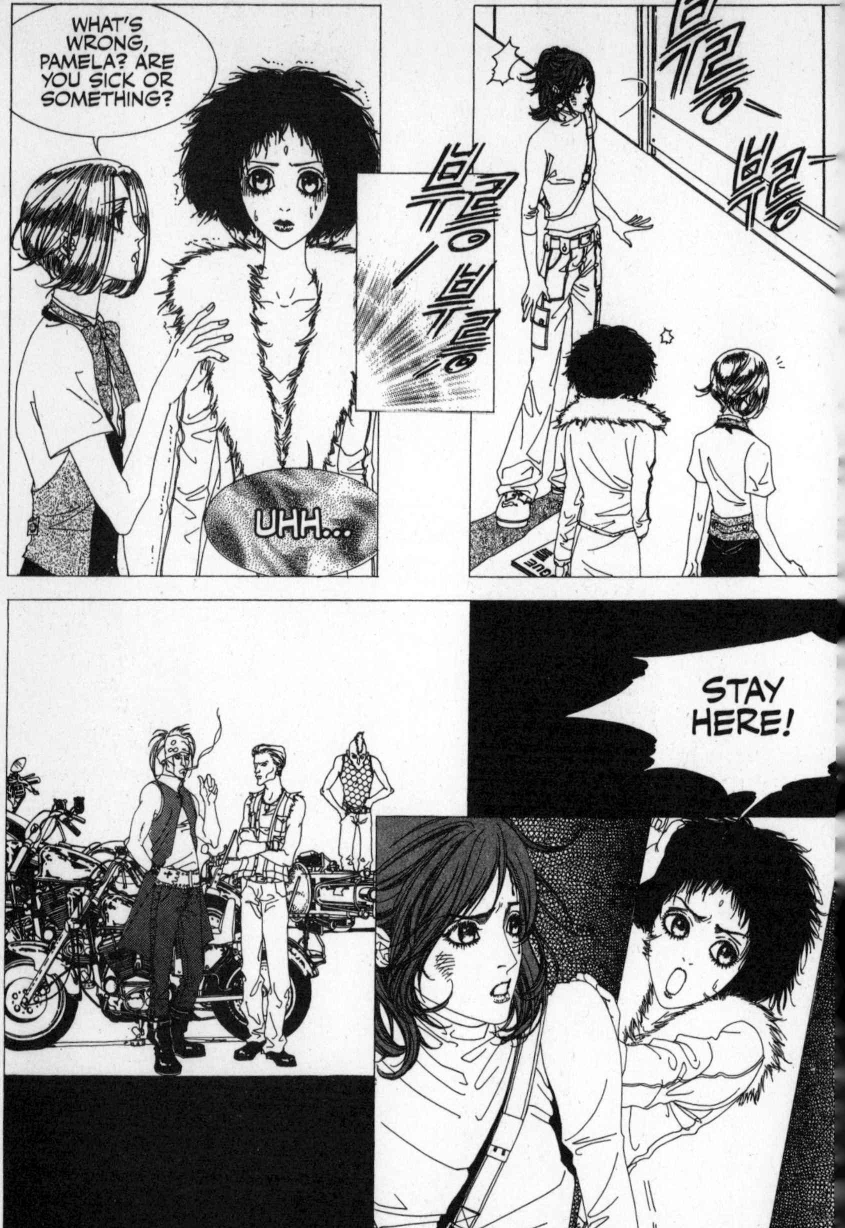
WHAT'S WRONG, PAMELA? ARE YOU SICK OR SOMETHING?
UHH...
부릉- 부릉
부릉- 부릉-
STAY HERE!

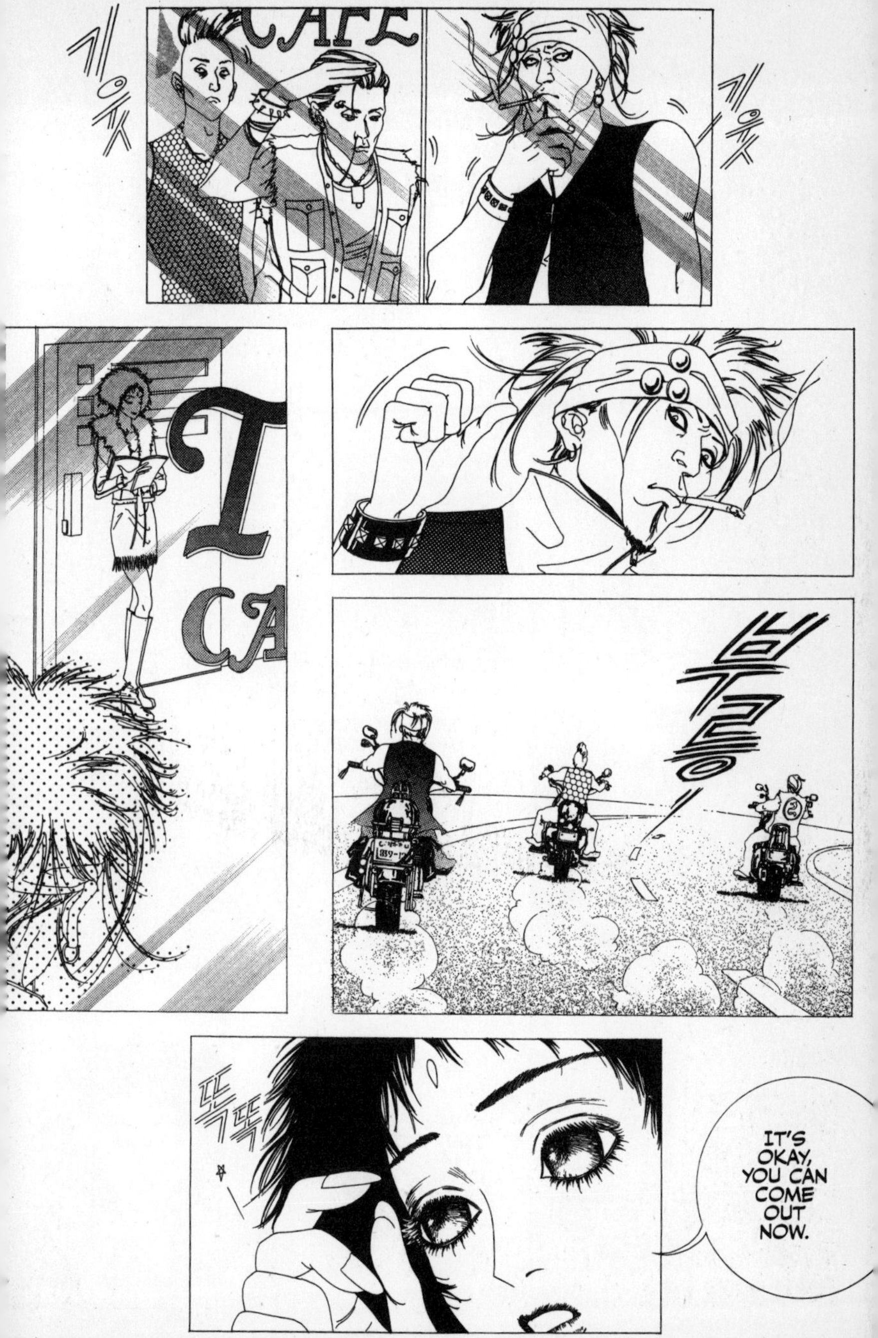
부르릉
또각또각
IT'S OKAY, YOU CAN COME OUT NOW.

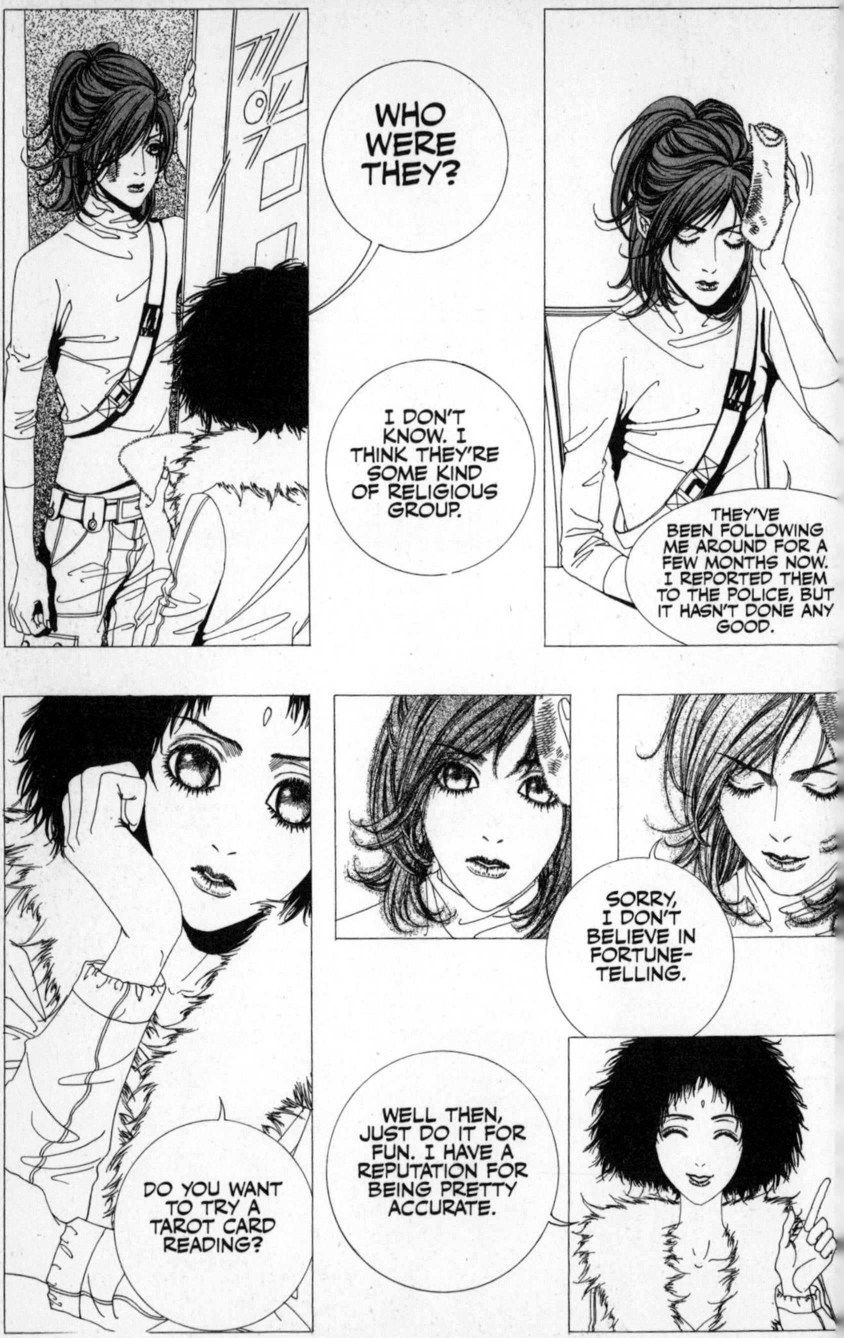
WHO WERE THEY?
I DON'T KNOW. I THINK THEY'RE SOME KIND OF RELIGIOUS GROUP.
THEY'VE BEEN FOLLOWING ME AROUND FOR A FEW MONTHS NOW. I REPORTED THEM TO THE POLICE, BUT IT HASN'T DONE ANY GOOD.
DO YOU WANT TO TRY A TAROT CARD READING?
SORRY, I DON'T BELIEVE IN FORTUNE-TELLING.
WELL THEN, JUST DO IT FOR FUN. I HAVE A REPUTATION FOR BEING PRETTY ACCURATE.

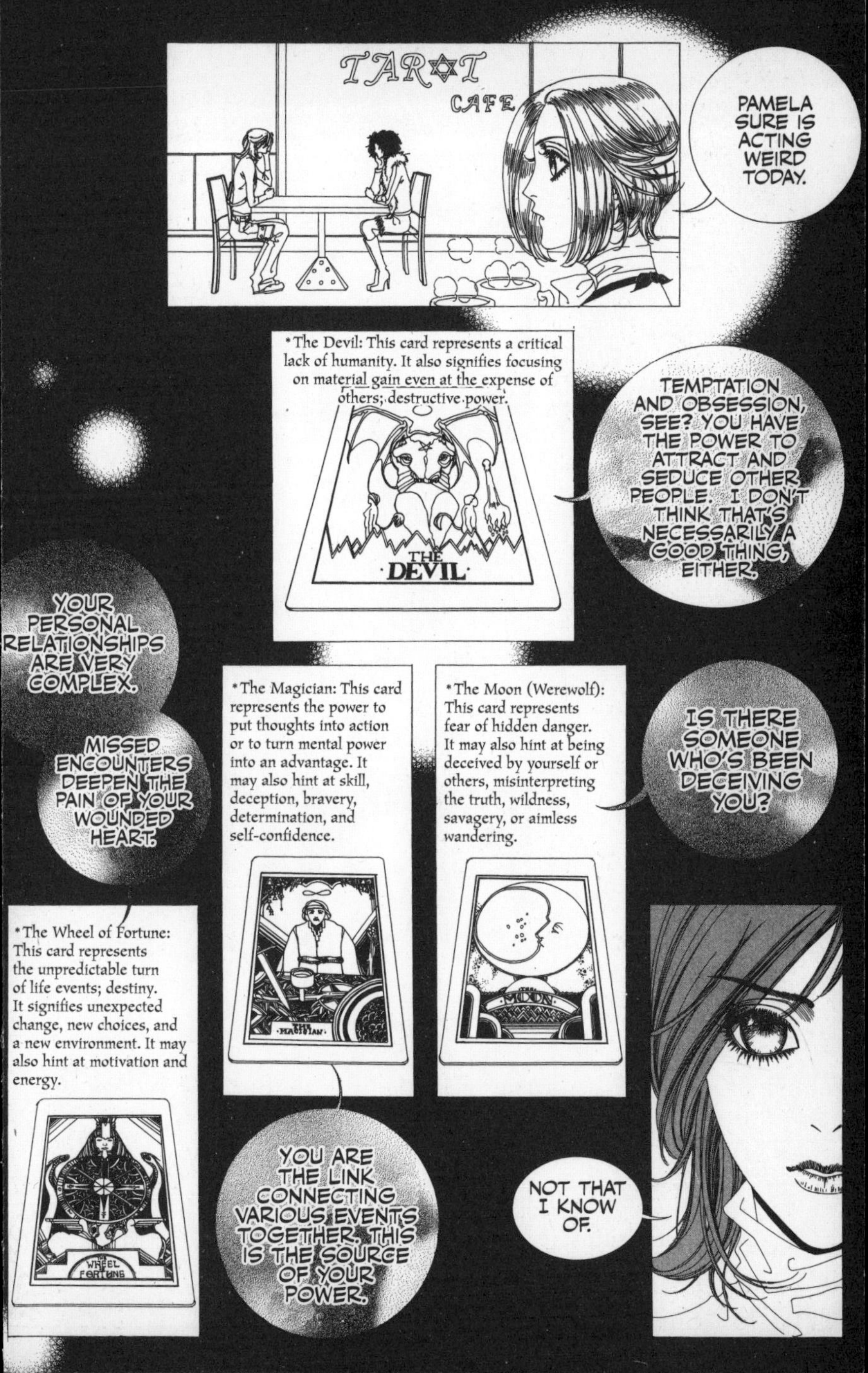

TAROT
CAFE
PAMELA SURE IS ACTING WEIRD TODAY.
TEMPTATION AND OBSESSION, SEE? YOU HAVE THE POWER TO ATTRACT AND SEDUCE OTHER PEOPLE. I DON'T THINK THAT'S NECESSARILY A GOOD THING, EITHER.
*The Devil: This card represents a critical lack of humanity. It also signifies focusing on material gain even at the expense of others; destructive power.
THE DEVIL
IS THERE SOMEONE WHO'S BEEN DECEIVING YOU?
*The Moon (Werewolf): This card represents fear of hidden danger. It may also hint at being deceived by yourself or others, misinterpreting the truth, wildness, savagery, or aimless wandering.
*The Magician: This card represents the power to put thoughts into action or to turn mental power into an advantage. It may also hint at skill, deception, bravery, determination, and self-confidence.
YOUR PERSONAL RELATIONSHIPS ARE VERY COMPLEX.
MISSED ENCOUNTERS DEEPEN THE PAIN OF YOUR WOUNDED HEART.
NOT THAT I KNOW OF.
YOU ARE THE LINK CONNECTING VARIOUS EVENTS TOGETHER. THIS IS THE SOURCE OF YOUR POWER.
*The Wheel of Fortune: This card represents the unpredictable turn of life events; destiny. It signifies unexpected change, new choices, and a new environment. It may also hint at motivation and energy.

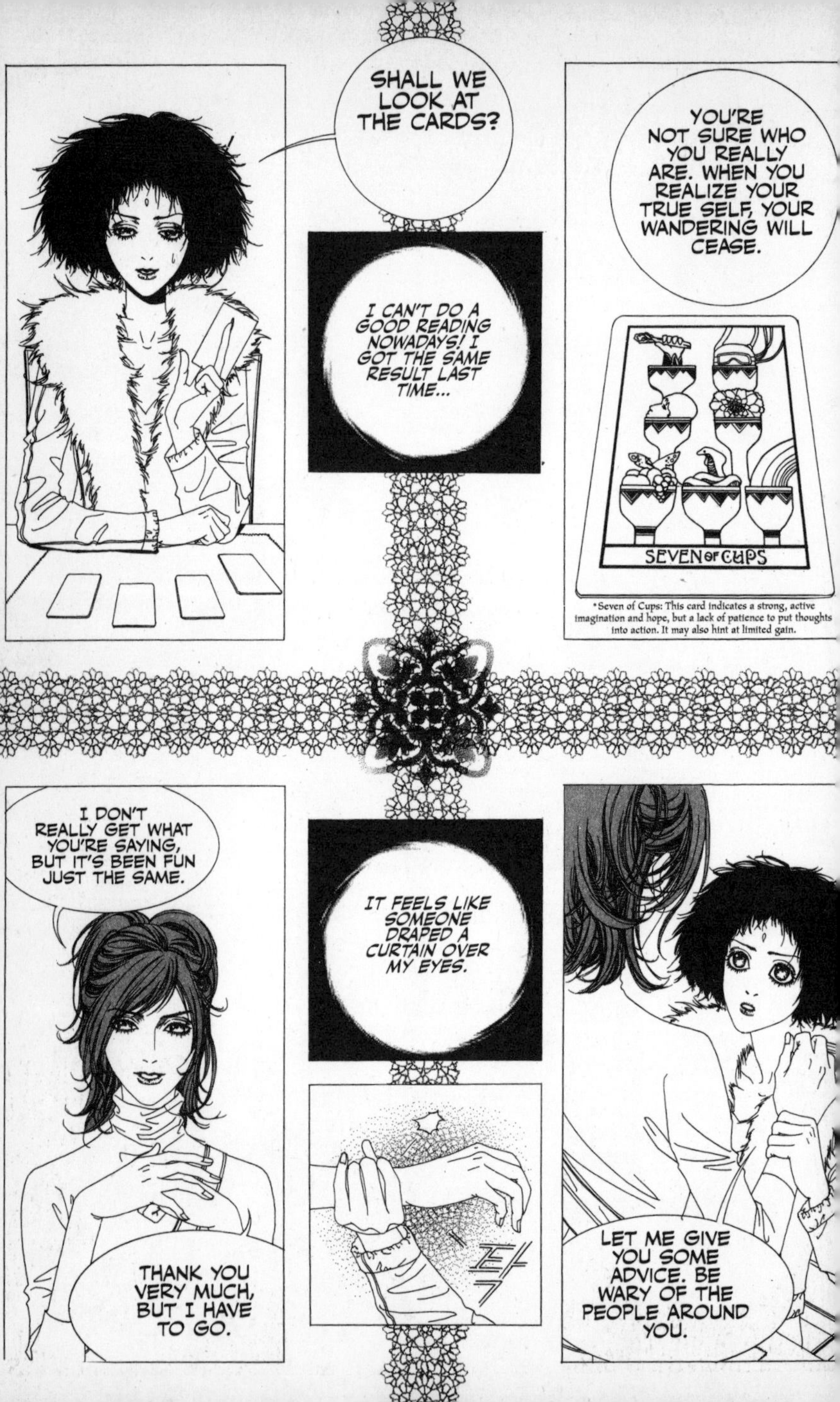
SHALL WE LOOK AT THE CARDS?
I CAN'T DO A GOOD READING NOWADAYS! I GOT THE SAME RESULT LAST TIME...
YOU'RE NOT SURE WHO YOU REALLY ARE. WHEN YOU REALIZE YOUR TRUE SELF, YOUR WANDERING WILL CEASE.
SEVEN of CUPS
*Seven of Cups: This card indicates a strong, active imagination and hope, but a lack of patience to put thoughts into action. It may also hint at limited gain.
I DON'T REALLY GET WHAT YOU'RE SAYING, BUT IT'S BEEN FUN JUST THE SAME.
THANK YOU VERY MUCH, BUT I HAVE TO GO.
IT FEELS LIKE SOMEONE DRAPED A CURTAIN OVER MY EYES.
LET ME GIVE YOU SOME ADVICE. BE WARY OF THE PEOPLE AROUND YOU.

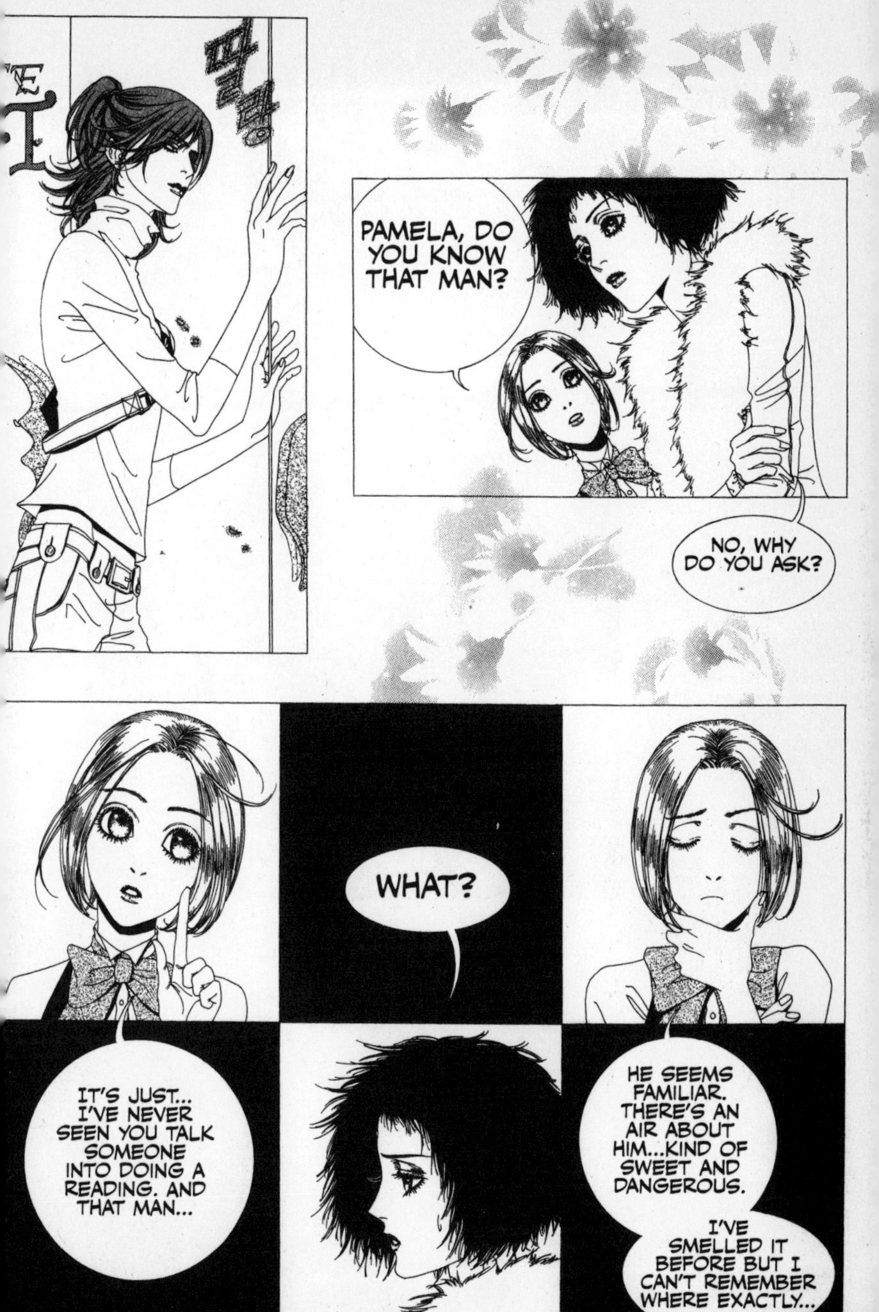
PAMELA, DO YOU KNOW THAT MAN?
NO, WHY DO YOU ASK?
WHAT?
IT'S JUST... I'VE NEVER SEEN YOU TALK SOMEONE INTO DOING A READING. AND THAT MAN...
HE SEEMS FAMILIAR. THERE'S AN AIR ABOUT HIM...KIND OF SWEET AND DANGEROUS.
I'VE SMELLED IT BEFORE BUT I CAN'T REMEMBER WHERE EXACTLY...

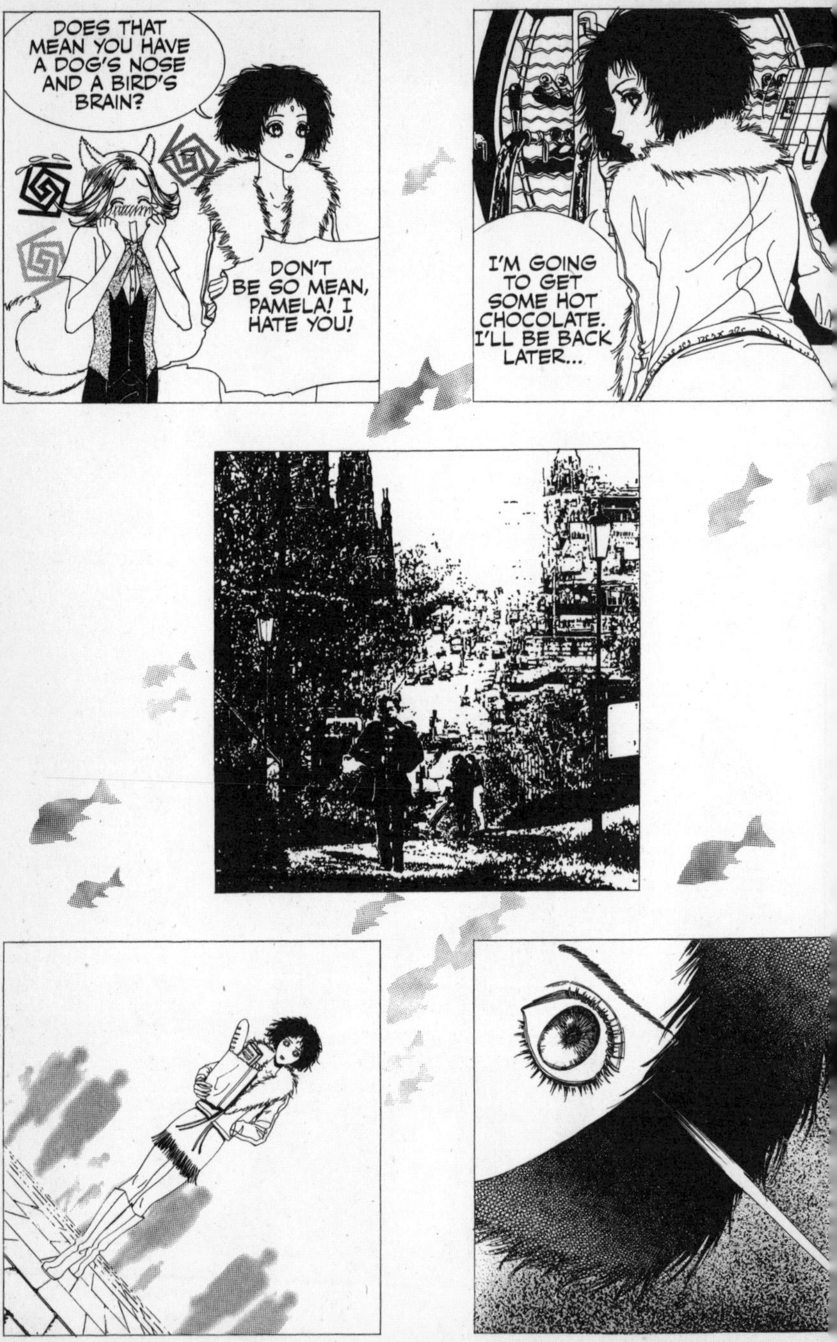
DOES THAT MEAN YOU HAVE A DOG'S NOSE AND A BIRD'S BRAIN?
DON'T BE SO MEAN, PAMELA! I HATE YOU!
I'M GOING TO GET SOME HOT CHOCOLATE. I'LL BE BACK LATER...

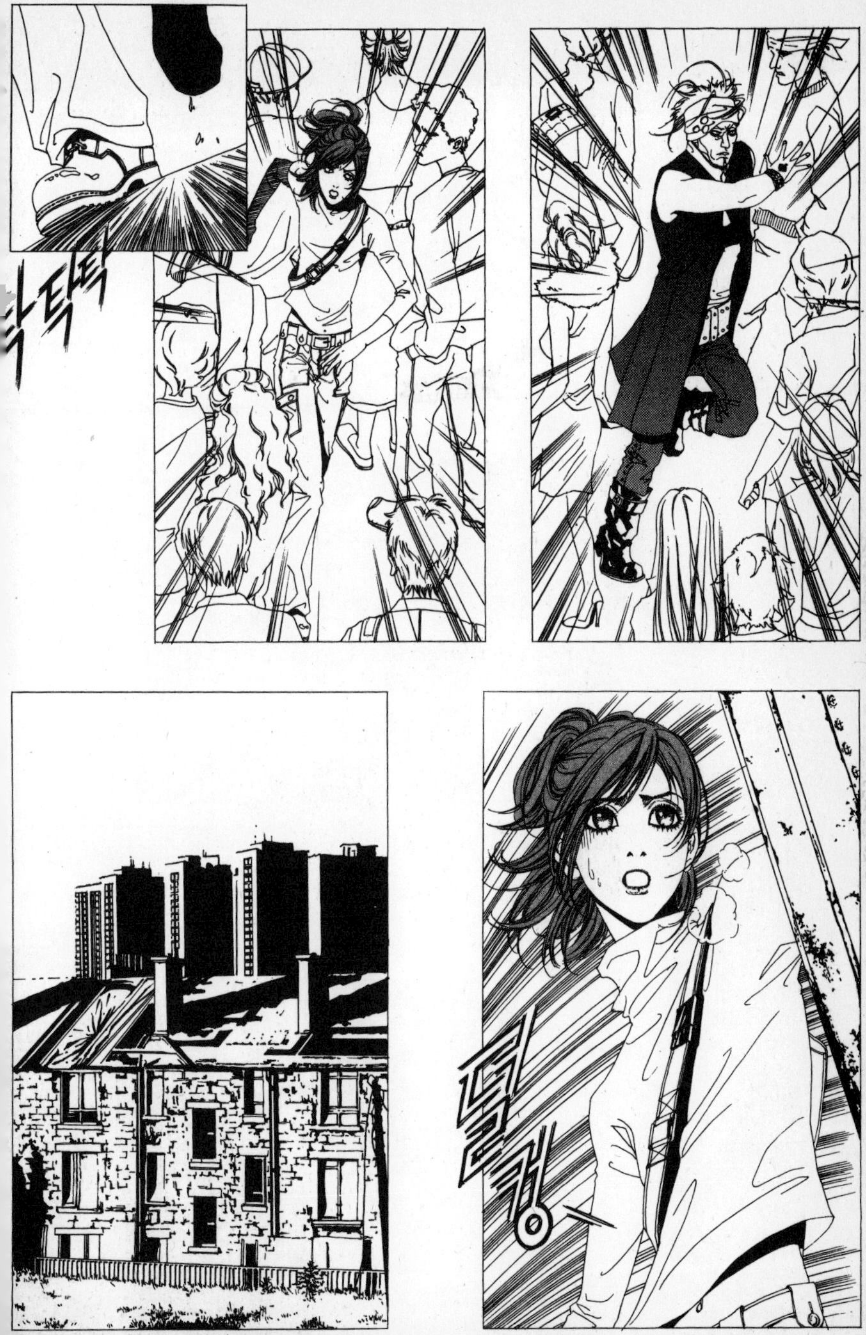

탁탁
덜컹

COME OUT LITTLE KITTY. I KNOW YOU'RE HERE SOMEWHERE.

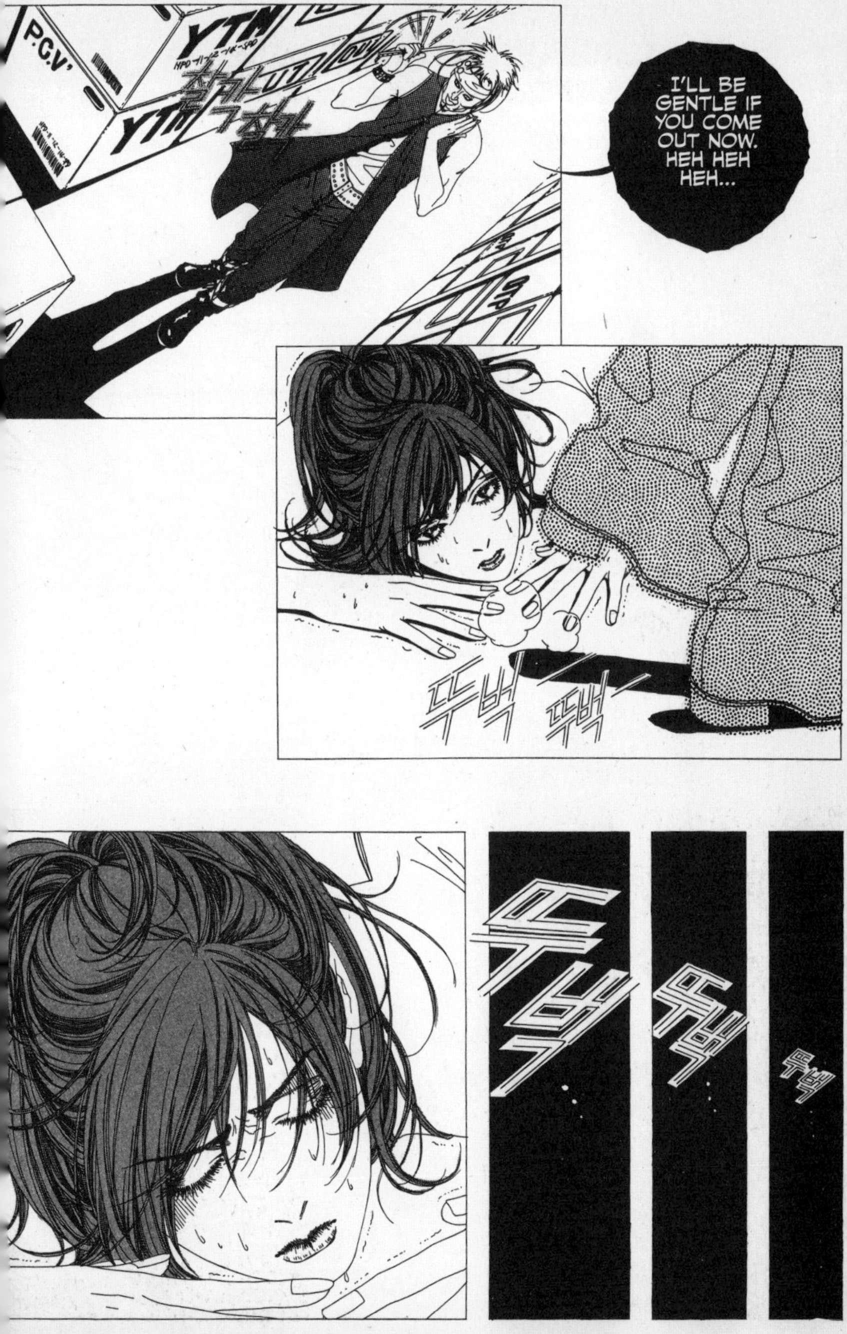
I'LL BE GENTLE IF YOU COME OUT NOW. HEH HEH HEH...
뚜벅 뚜벅
뚜벅 뚜벅 뚜벅

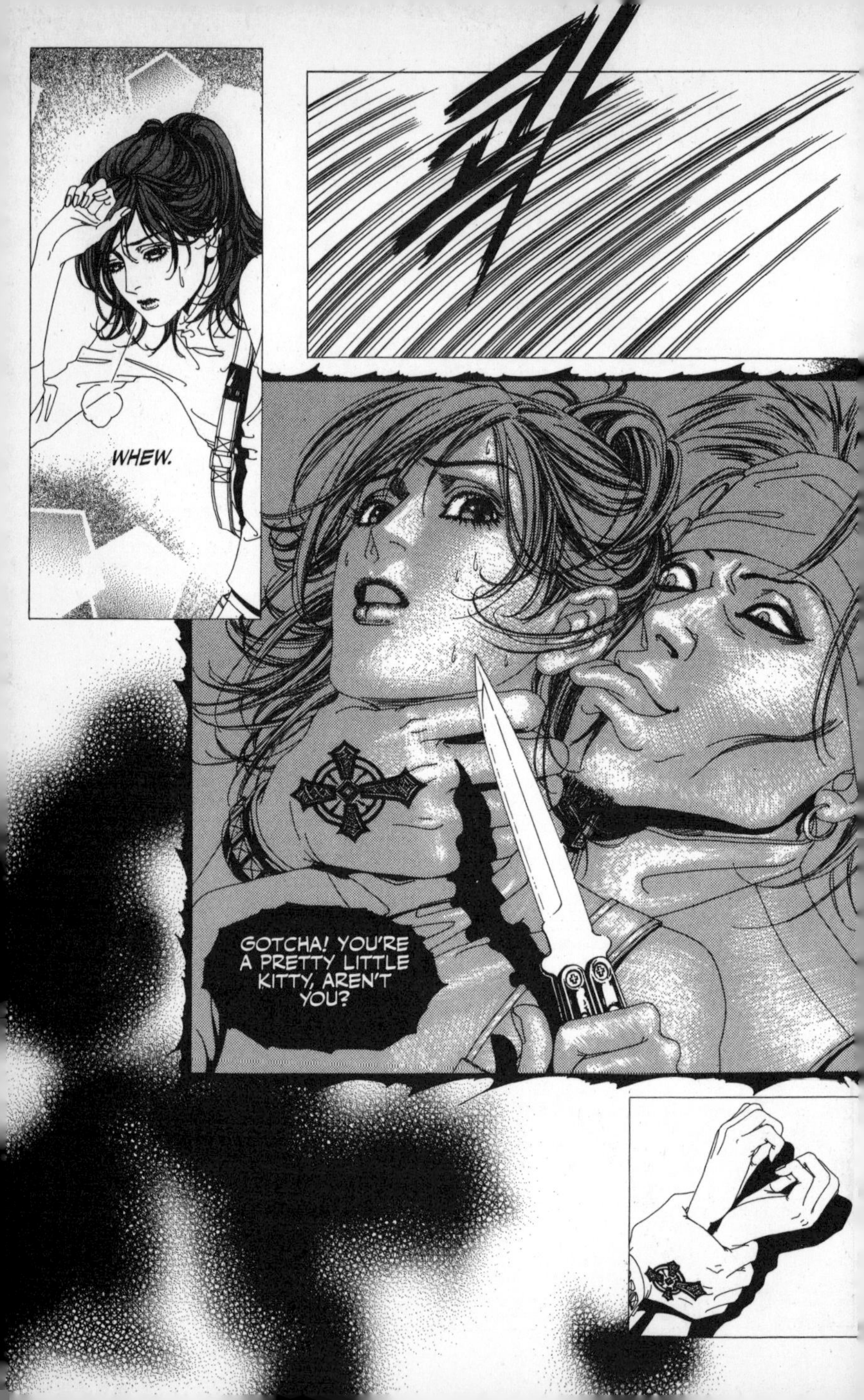
WHEW.
GOTCHA! YOU'RE A PRETTY LITTLE KITTY, AREN'T YOU?

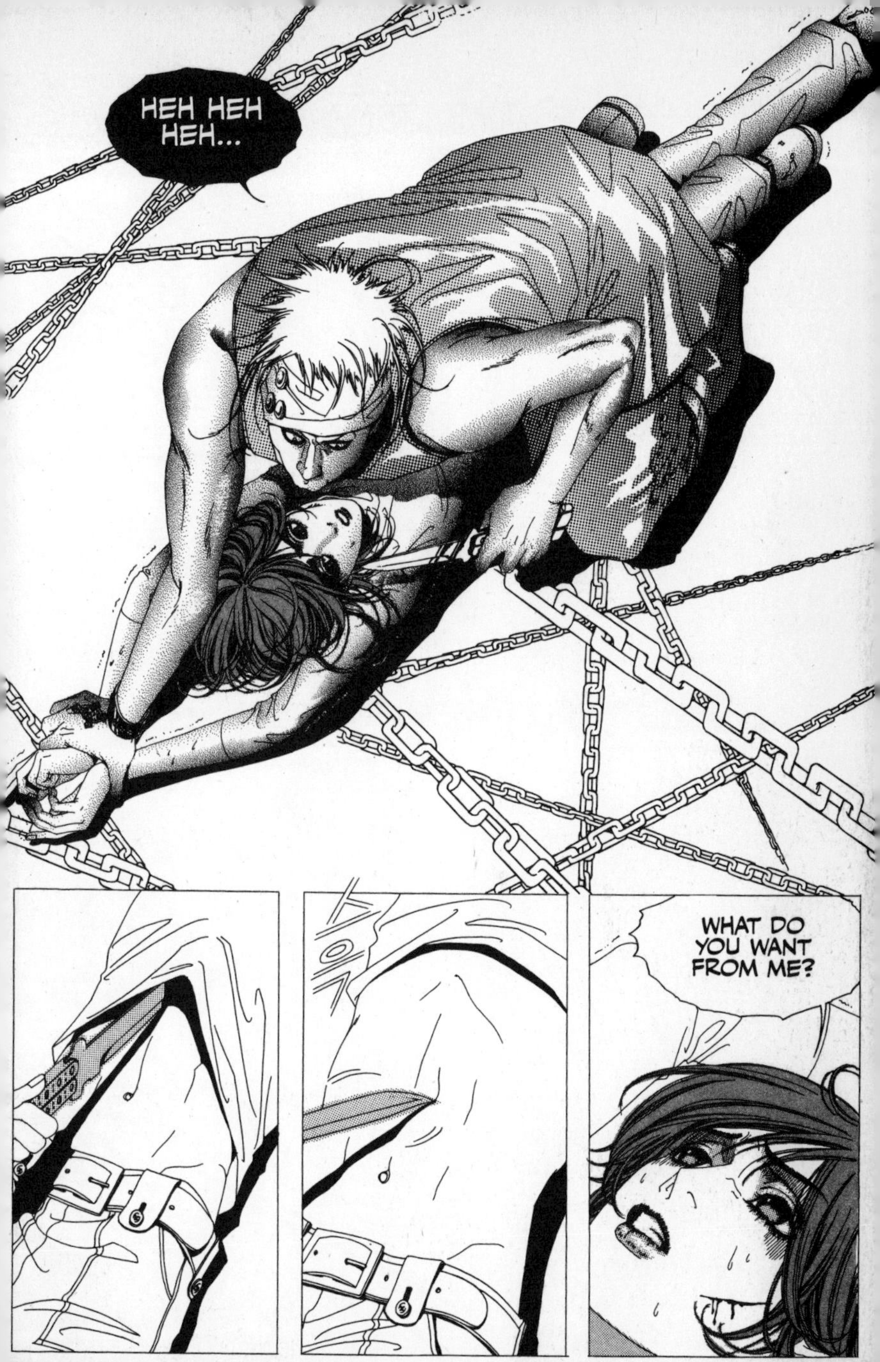
HEH HEH HEH...
WHAT DO YOU WANT FROM ME?

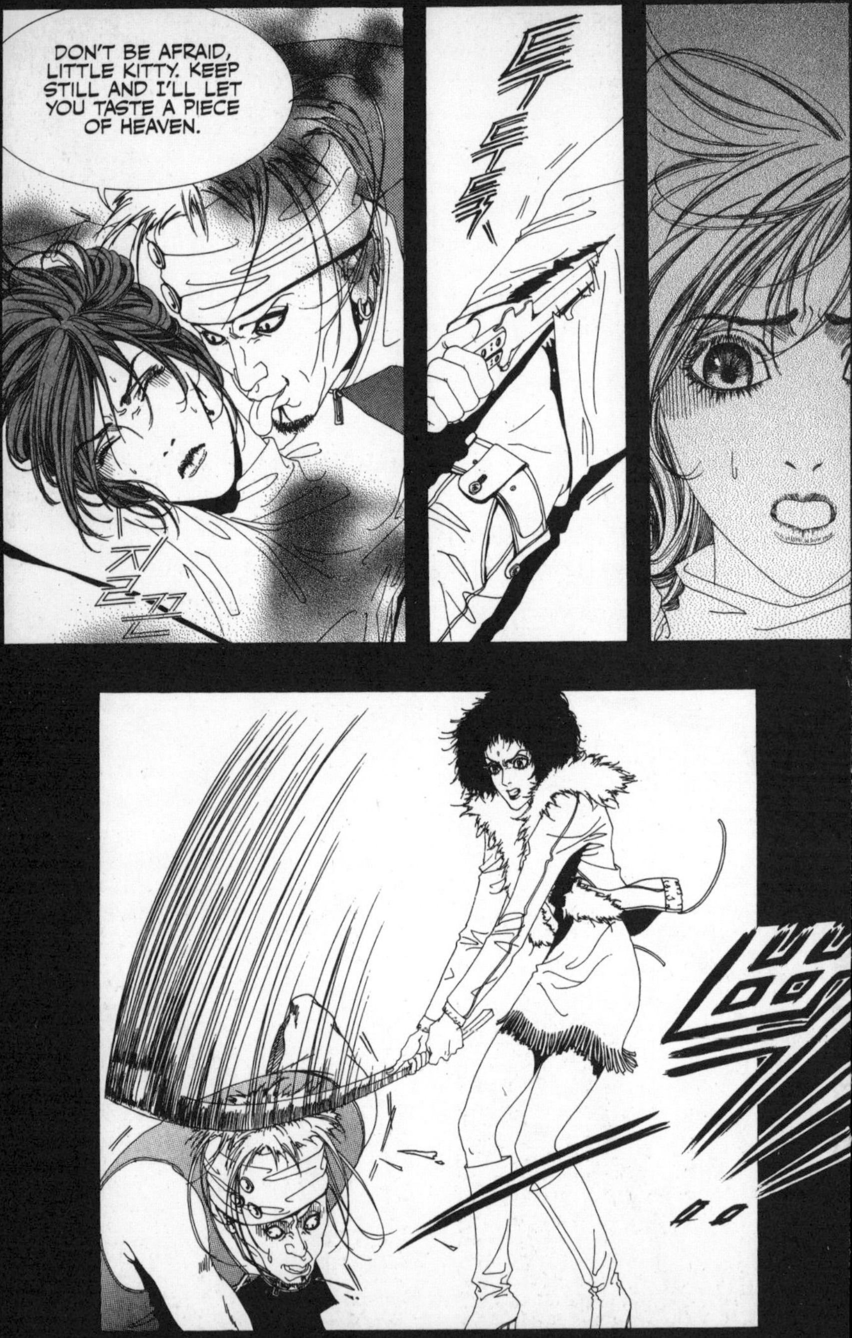
DON'T BE AFRAID, LITTLE KITTY. KEEP STILL AND I'LL LET YOU TASTE A PIECE OF HEAVEN.

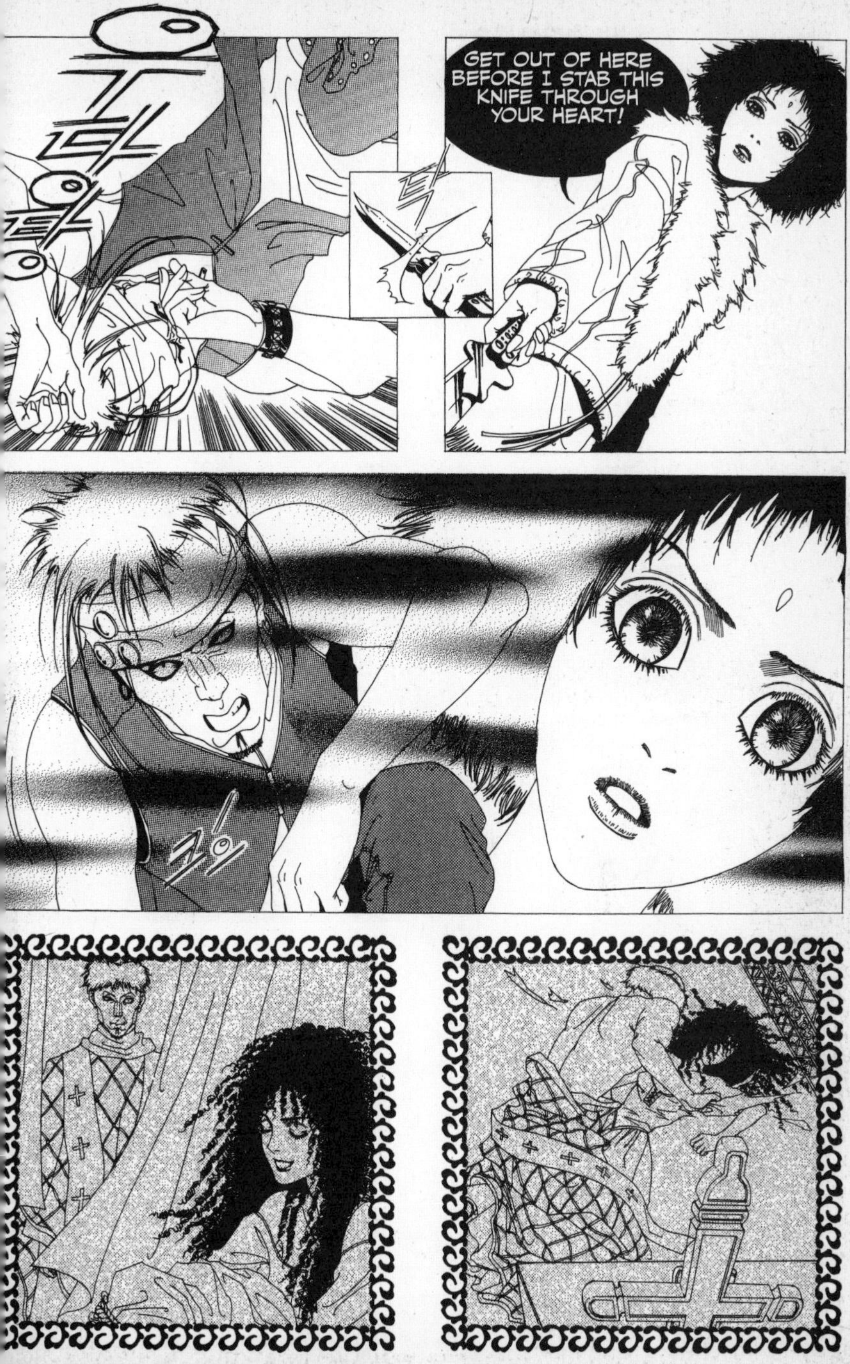
GET OUT OF HERE BEFORE I STAB THIS KNIFE THROUGH YOUR HEART!

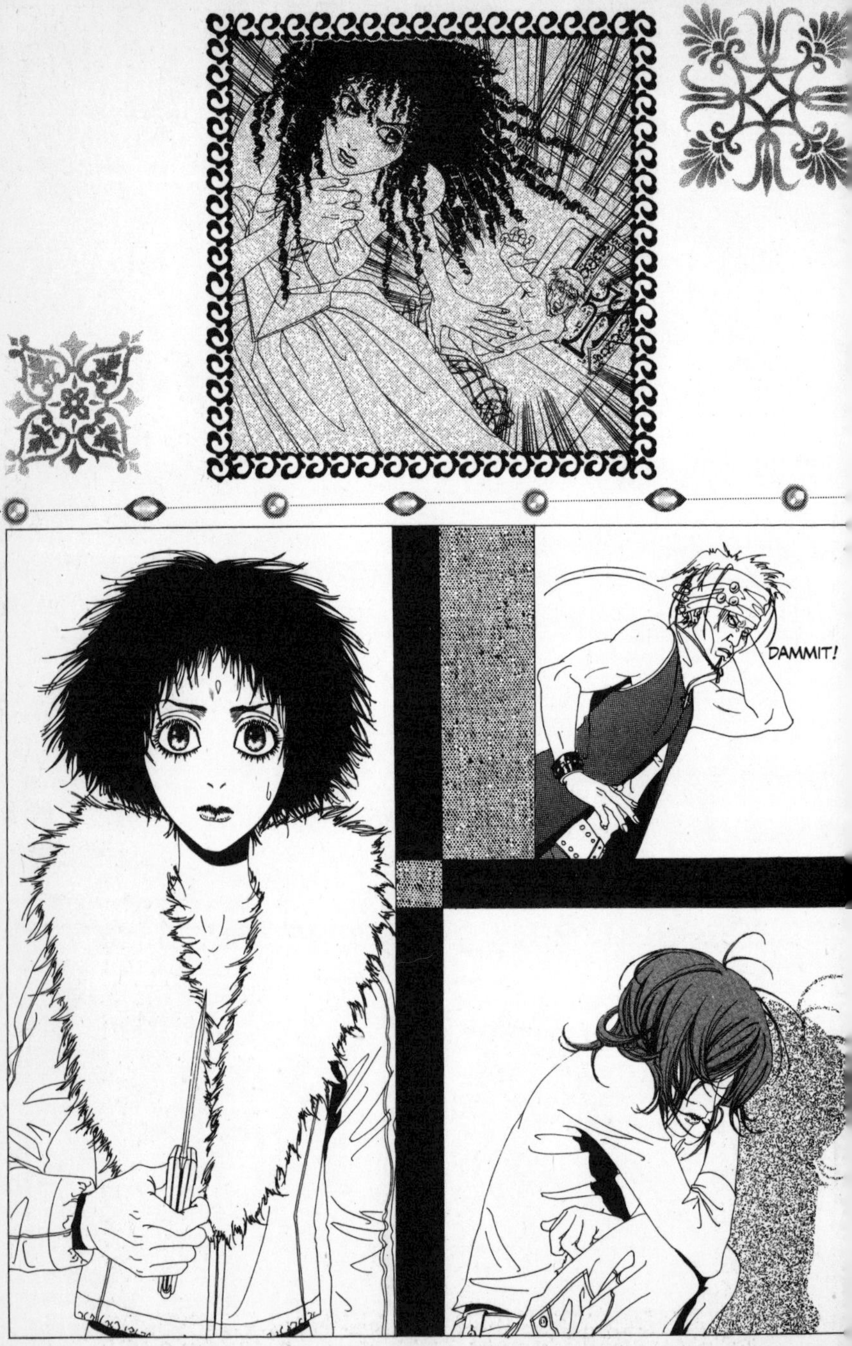
DAMMIT!

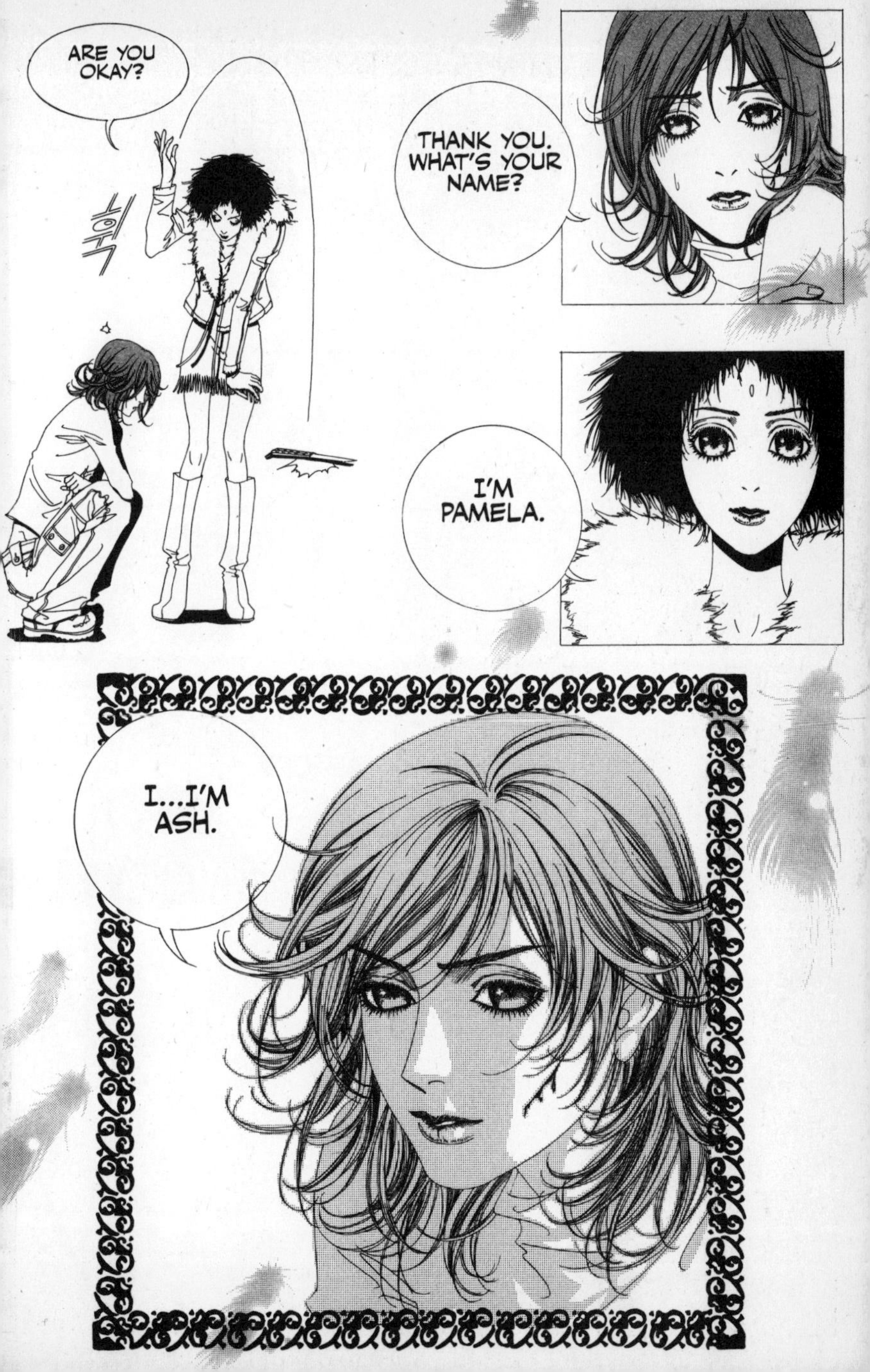
ARE YOU OKAY?
THANK YOU. WHAT'S YOUR NAME?
I'M PAMELA.
I...I'M ASH.

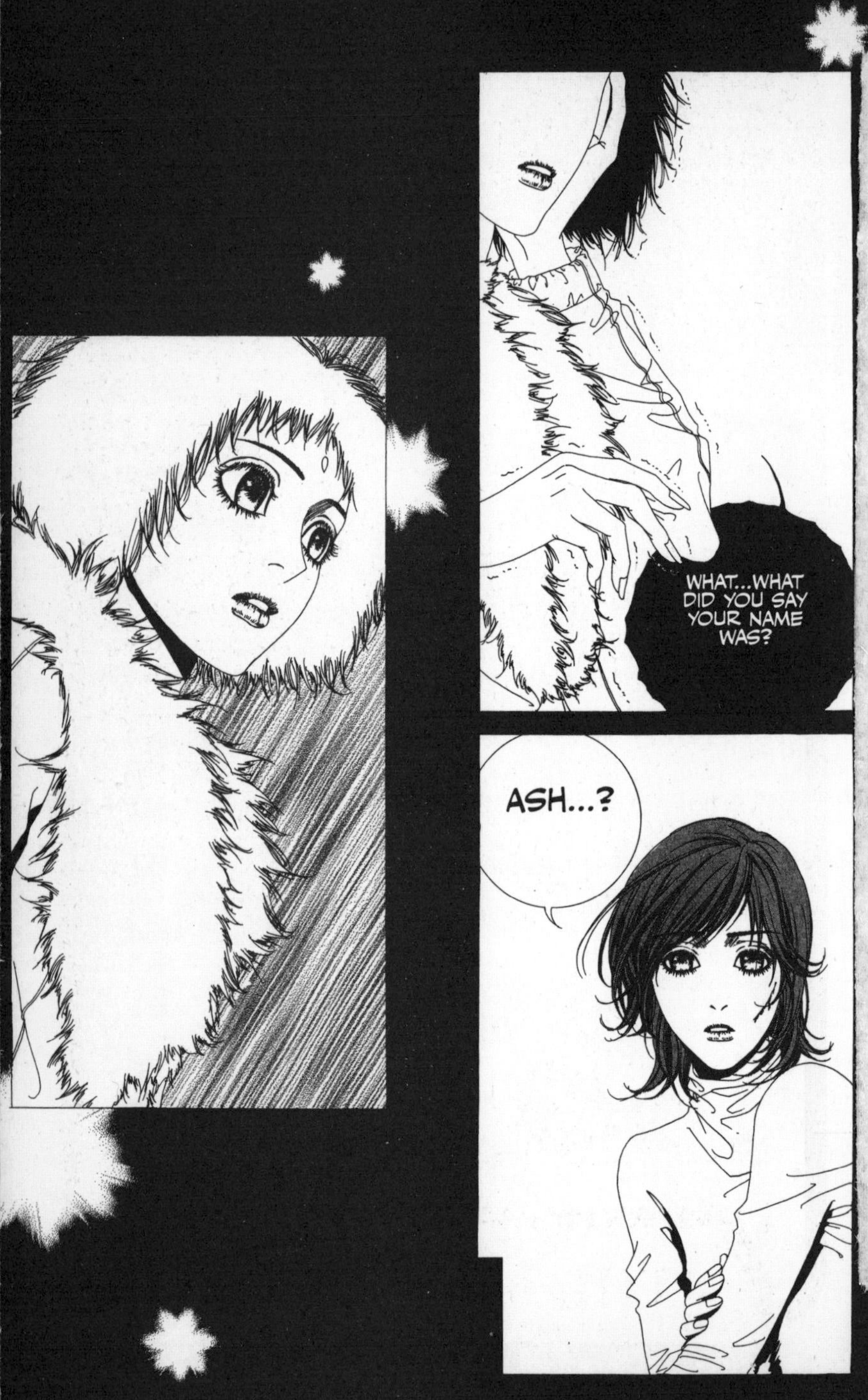
WHAT...WHAT DID YOU SAY YOUR NAME WAS?
ASH...?

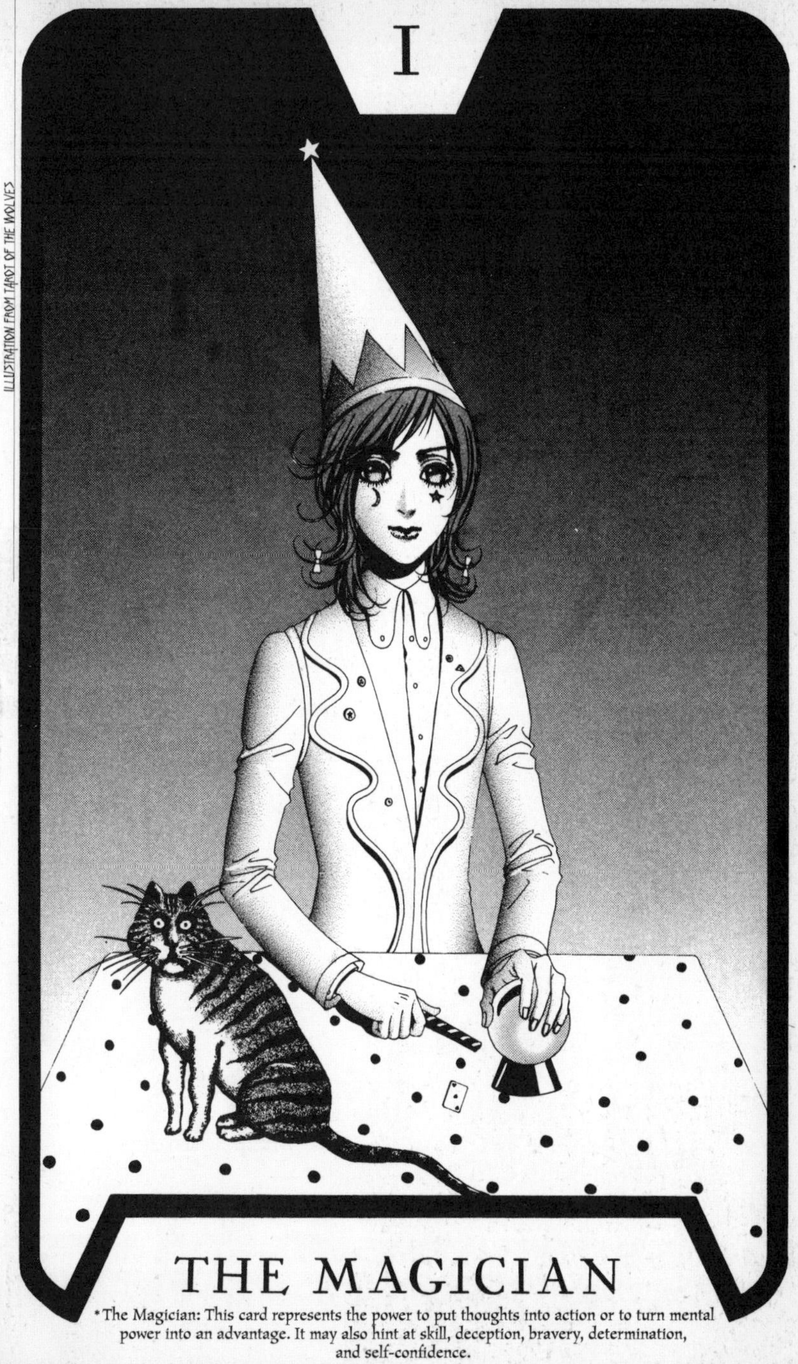
I
THE MAGICIAN

ILLUSTRATION FROM TAROT OF THE WOLVES

*The Magician: This card represents the power to put thoughts into action or to turn mental power into an advantage. It may also hint at skill, deception, bravery, determination, and self-confidence.

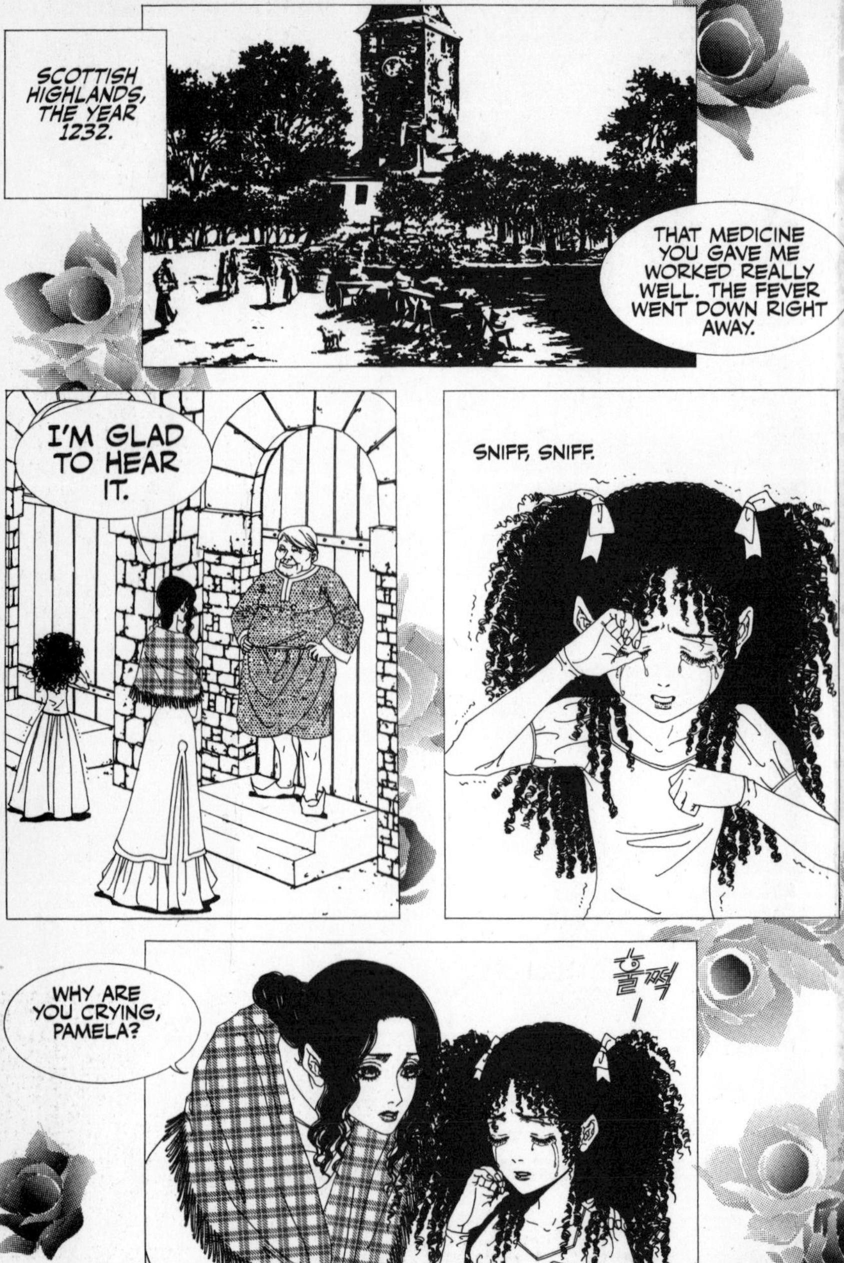
SCOTTISH HIGHLANDS, THE YEAR 1232.
THAT MEDICINE YOU GAVE ME WORKED REALLY WELL. THE FEVER WENT DOWN RIGHT AWAY.
I'M GLAD TO HEAR IT.
SNIFF, SNIFF.
훌쩍
WHY ARE YOU CRYING, PAMELA?

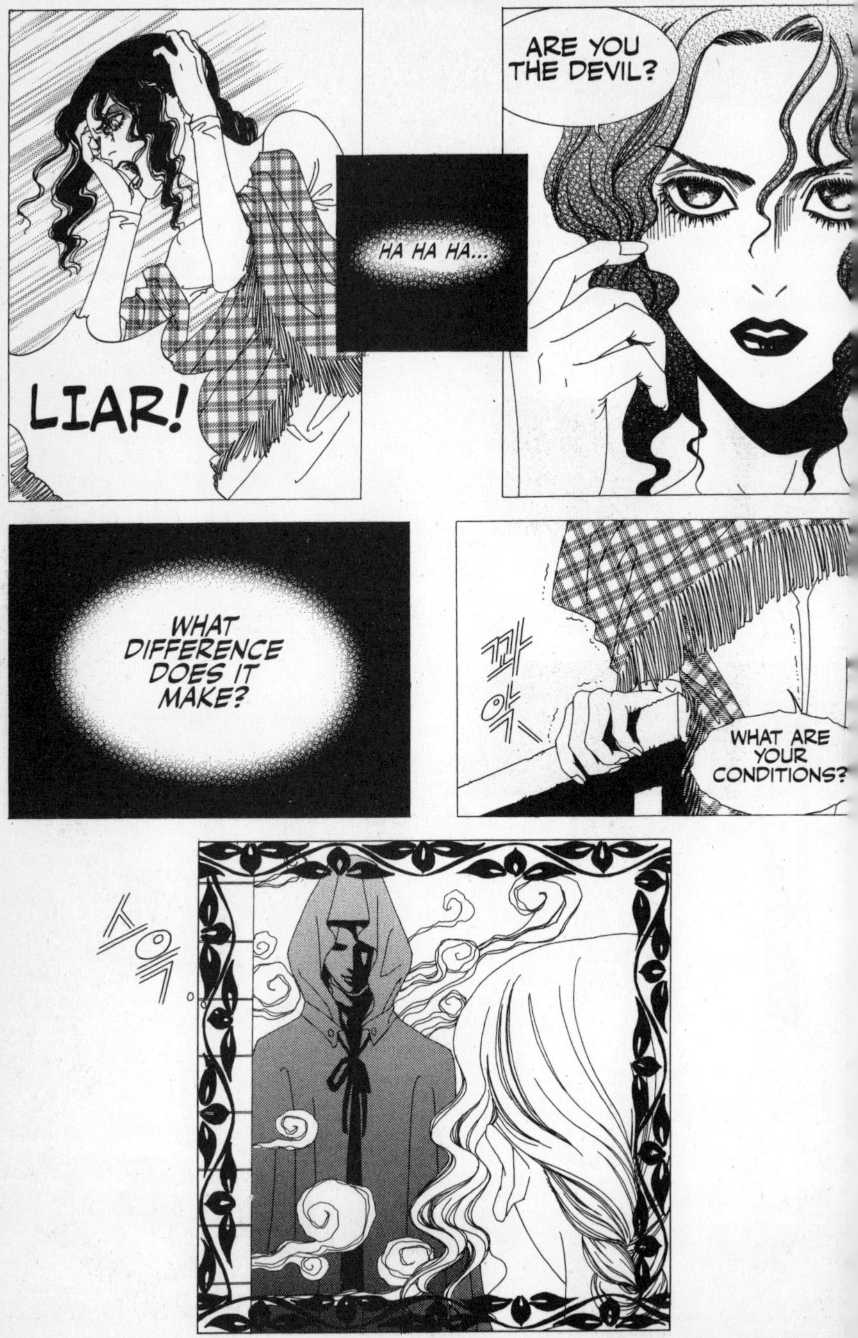
LIAR!
HA HA HA...
ARE YOU THE DEVIL?
WHAT DIFFERENCE DOES IT MAKE?
꽈악
WHAT ARE YOUR CONDITIONS?
스으윽

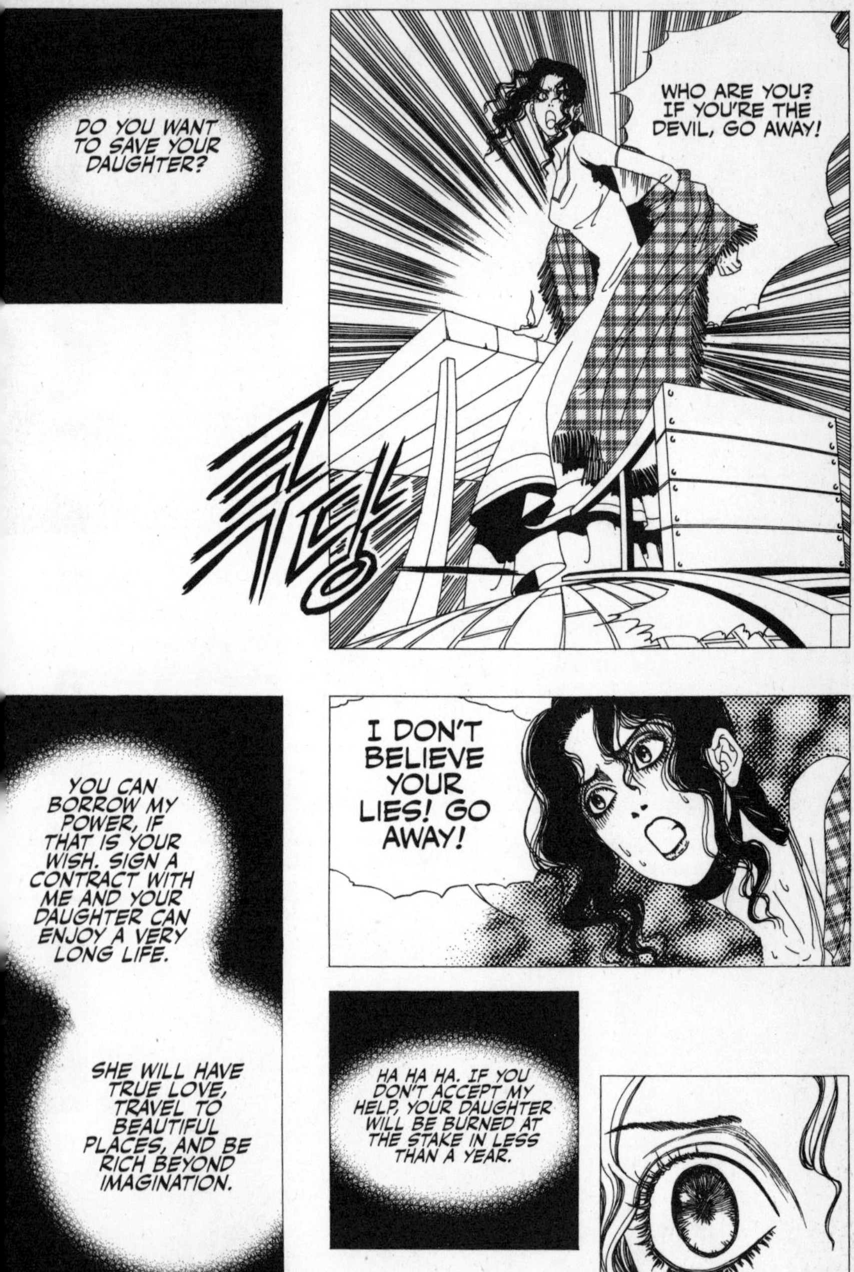
DO YOU WANT TO SAVE YOUR DAUGHTER?
WHO ARE YOU? IF YOU'RE THE DEVIL, GO AWAY!
YOU CAN BORROW MY POWER, IF THAT IS YOUR WISH. SIGN A CONTRACT WITH ME AND YOUR DAUGHTER CAN ENJOY A VERY LONG LIFE.
SHE WILL HAVE TRUE LOVE, TRAVEL TO BEAUTIFUL PLACES, AND BE RICH BEYOND IMAGINATION.
I DON'T BELIEVE YOUR LIES! GO AWAY!
HA HA HA. IF YOU DON'T ACCEPT MY HELP, YOUR DAUGHTER WILL BE BURNED AT THE STAKE IN LESS THAN A YEAR.

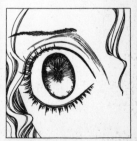

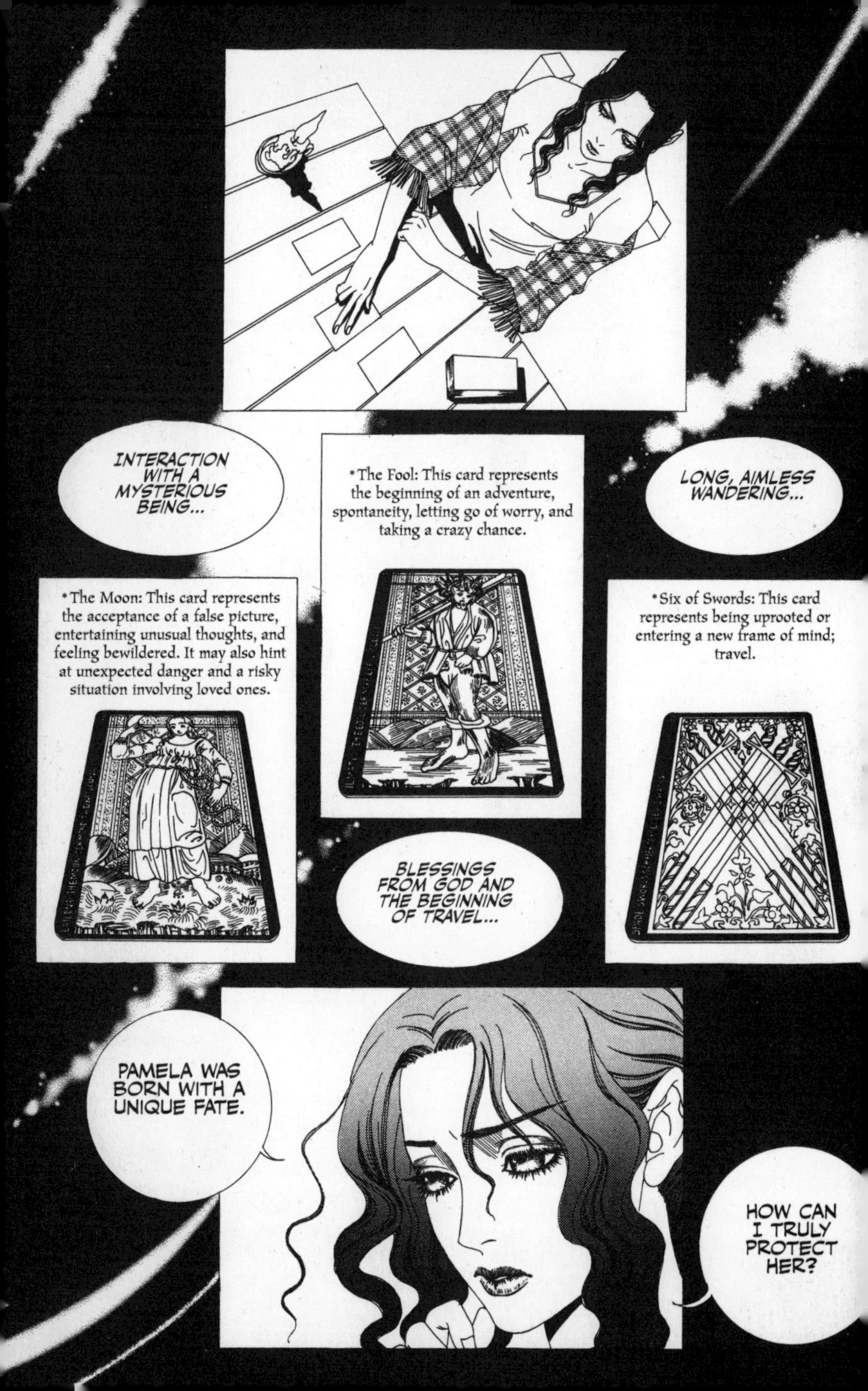
INTERACTION WITH A MYSTERIOUS BEING...
*The Fool: This card represents the beginning of an adventure, spontaneity, letting go of worry, and taking a crazy chance.
LONG, AIMLESS WANDERING...
*The Moon: This card represents the acceptance of a false picture, entertaining unusual thoughts, and feeling bewildered. It may also hint at unexpected danger and a risky situation involving loved ones.
*Six of Swords: This card represents being uprooted or entering a new frame of mind; travel.
BLESSINGS FROM GOD AND THE BEGINNING OF TRAVEL...
PAMELA WAS BORN WITH A UNIQUE FATE.
HOW CAN I TRULY PROTECT HER?

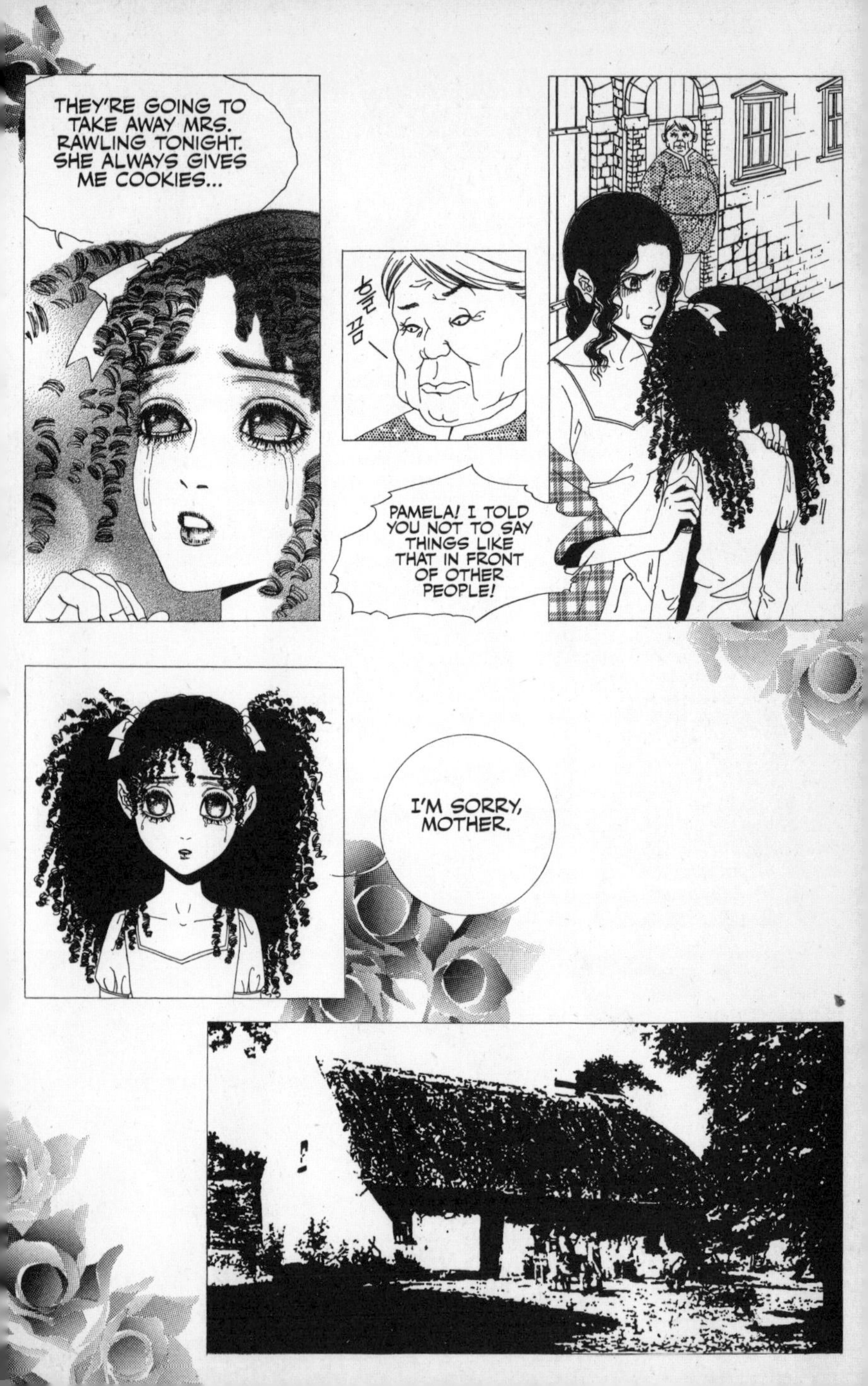
THEY'RE GOING TO TAKE AWAY MRS. RAWLING TONIGHT. SHE ALWAYS GIVES ME COOKIES...
흘끔
PAMELA! I TOLD YOU NOT TO SAY THINGS LIKE THAT IN FRONT OF OTHER PEOPLE!
I'M SORRY, MOTHER.

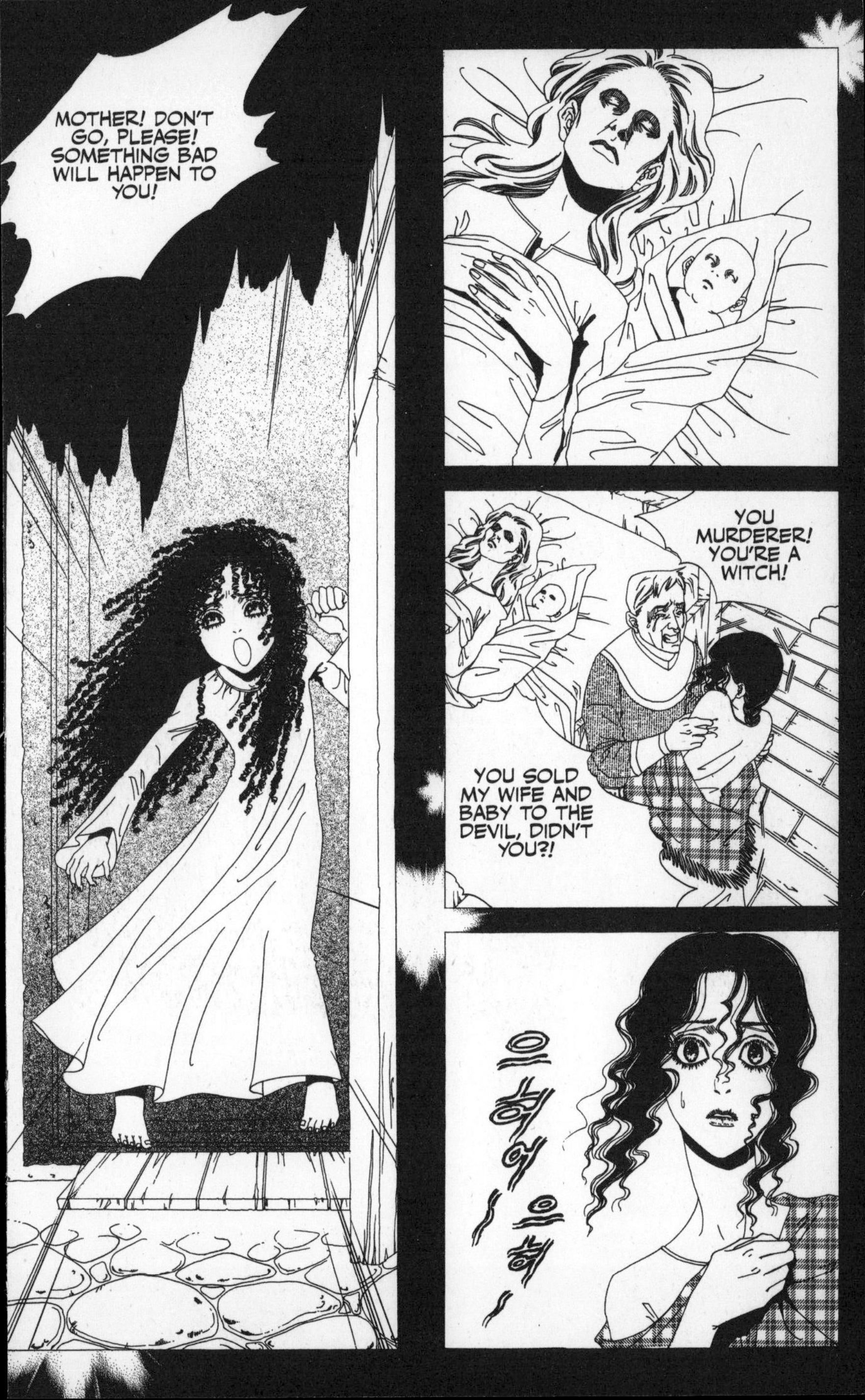
MOTHER! DON'T GO, PLEASE! SOMETHING BAD WILL HAPPEN TO YOU!
YOU MURDERER! YOU'RE A WITCH!
YOU SOLD MY WIFE AND BABY TO THE DEVIL, DIDN'T YOU?!

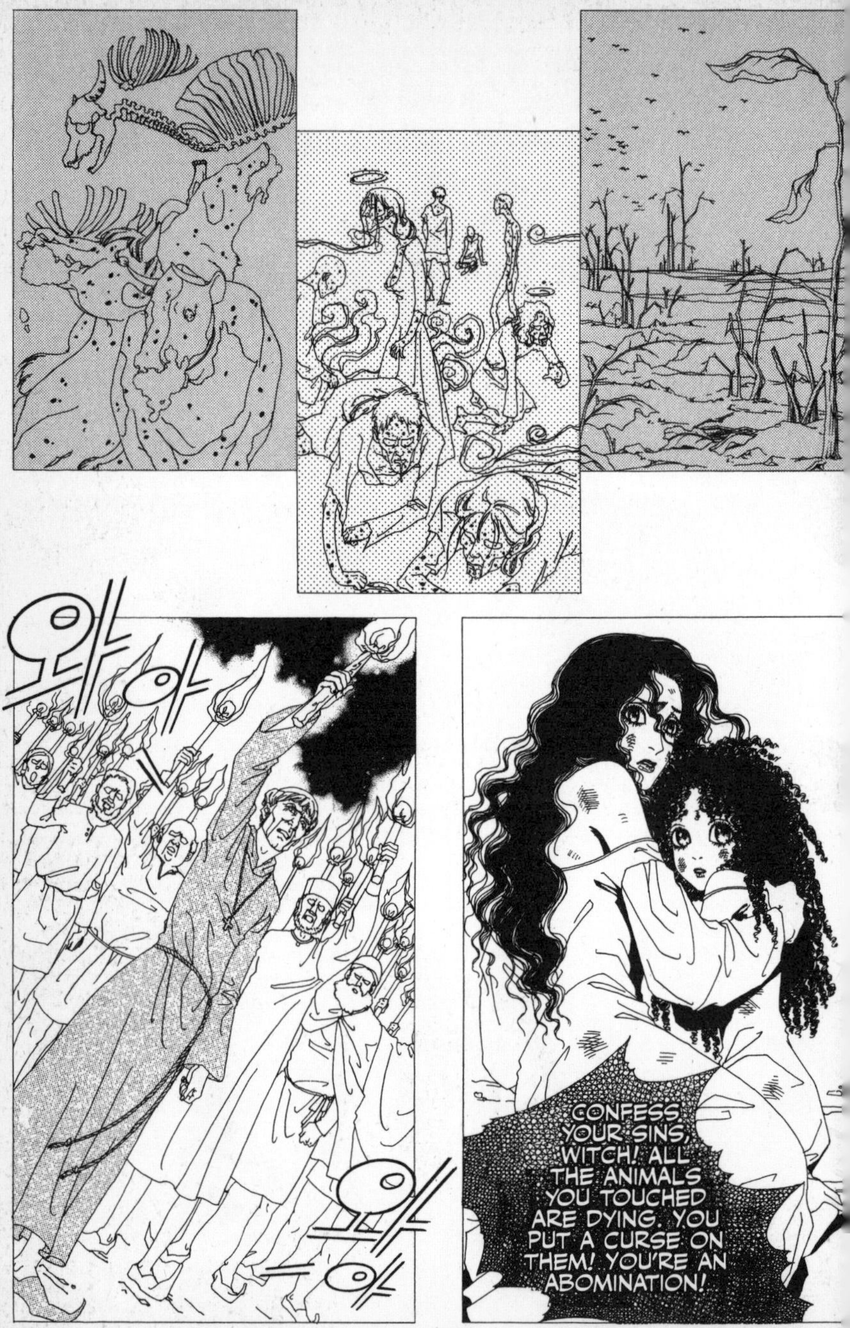
와아
와아
CONFESS YOUR SINS, WITCH! ALL THE ANIMALS YOU TOUCHED ARE DYING. YOU PUT A CURSE ON THEM! YOU'RE AN ABOMINATION!

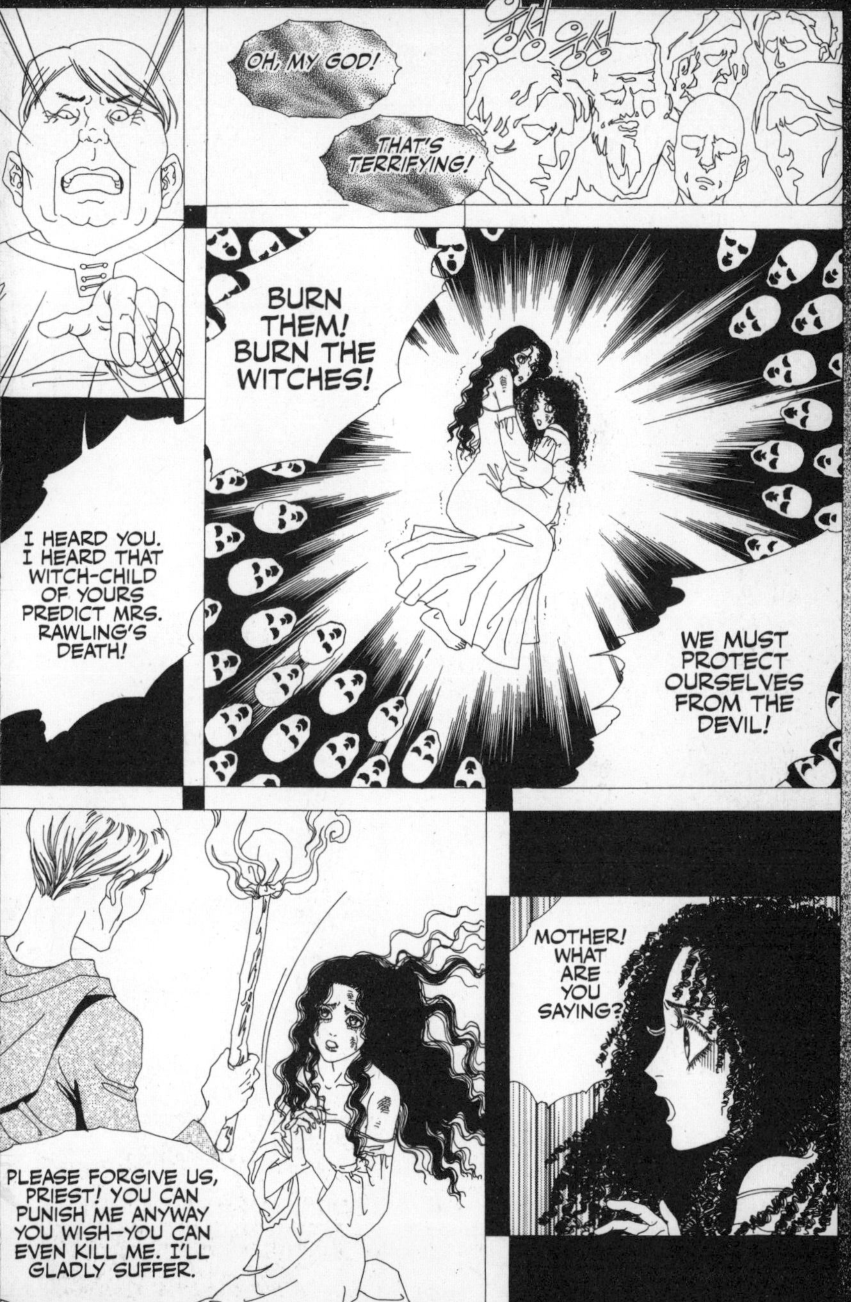
OH, MY GOD!
THAT'S TERRIFYING!
웅성 웅성
BURN THEM! BURN THE WITCHES!
I HEARD YOU. I HEARD THAT WITCH-CHILD OF YOURS PREDICT MRS. RAWLING'S DEATH!
WE MUST PROTECT OURSELVES FROM THE DEVIL!
PLEASE FORGIVE US, PRIEST! YOU CAN PUNISH ME ANYWAY YOU WISH–YOU CAN EVEN KILL ME. I'LL GLADLY SUFFER.
MOTHER! WHAT ARE YOU SAYING?

BUT MY DAUGHTER IS FREE OF SIN. SHE'S ONLY ELEVEN YEARS OLD.

PLEASE SPARE HER. I ALONE AM RESPONSIBLE FOR ALL THE DISASTERS.

MOTHER, WHAT ARE YOU SAYING? YOU DIDN'T DO ANYTHING WRONG!

A CHILD OF A WITCH IS ALSO A WITCH!

THE CHILD IS THE DEVIL'S SPAWN!

NO, NO! PRIEST, SAVE HER! I BEG OF YOU!

SINCE SHE HAS CONFESSED HER CRIME, THIS WOMAN SHALL BE PUT TO DEATH.

BUT THE CHILD STILL HAS A CHANCE FOR REDEMPTION. I'LL TAKE HER TO THE MONASTERY TO SEE WHAT HAPPENS.

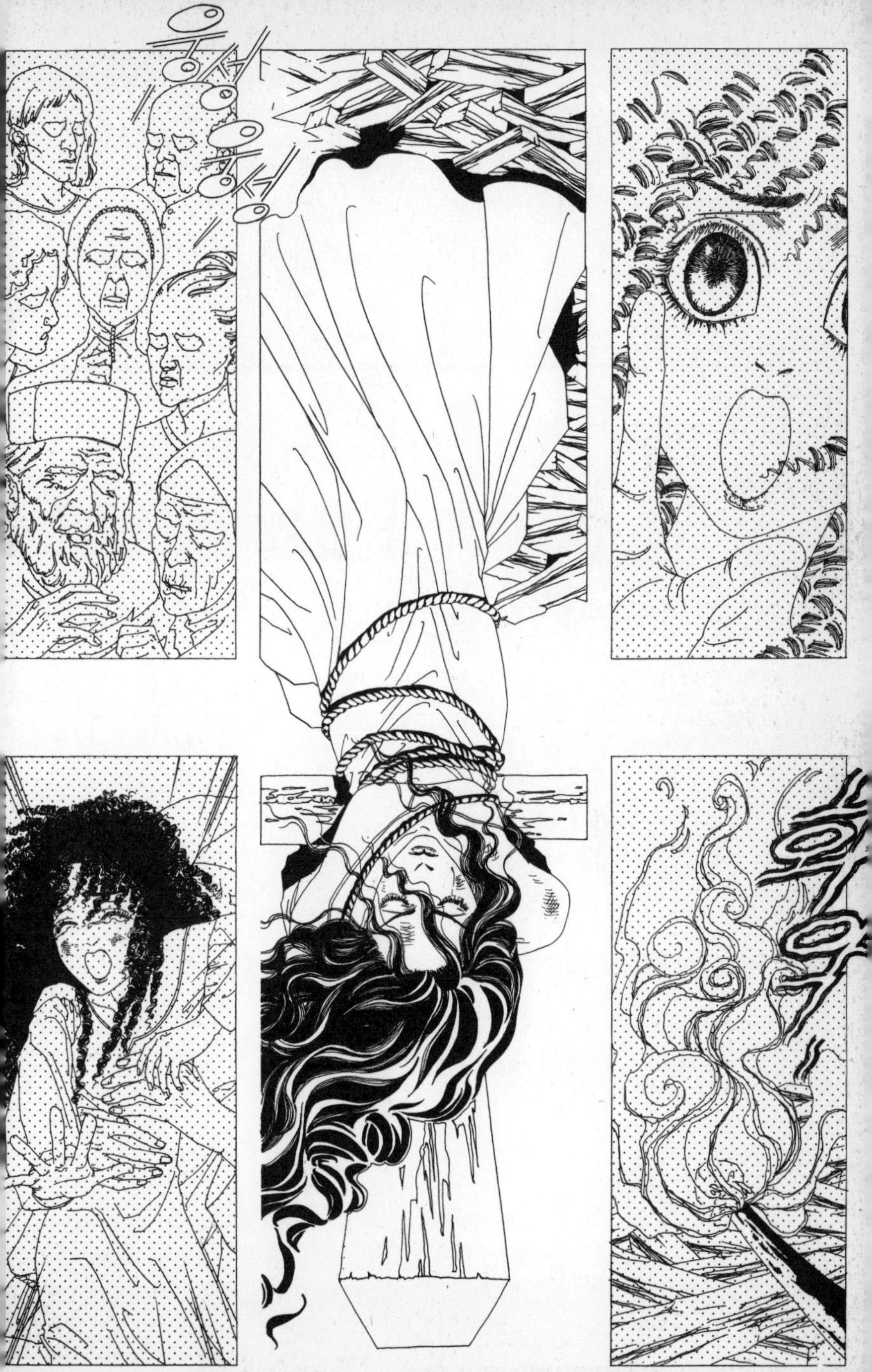
웅성웅성

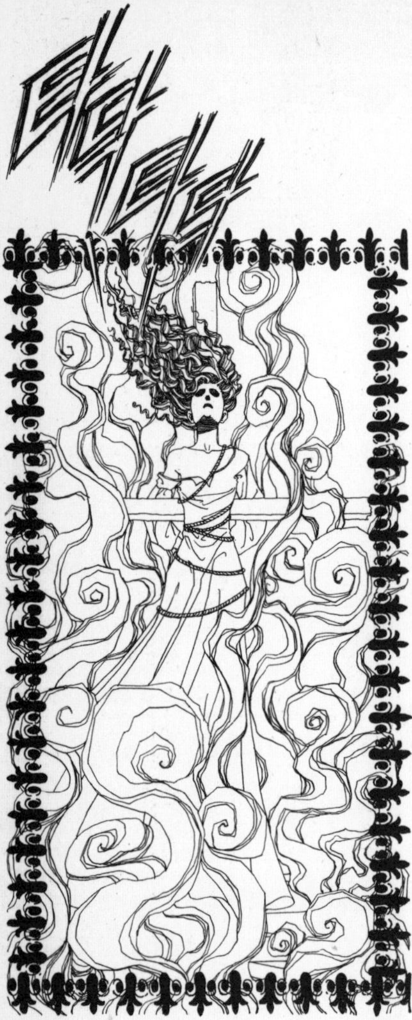
타닥 타닥
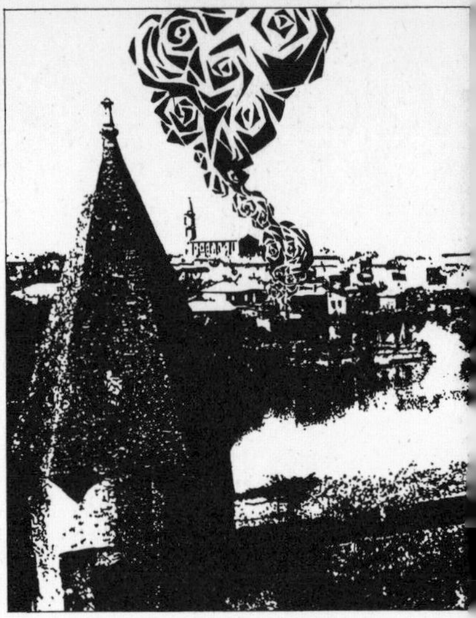
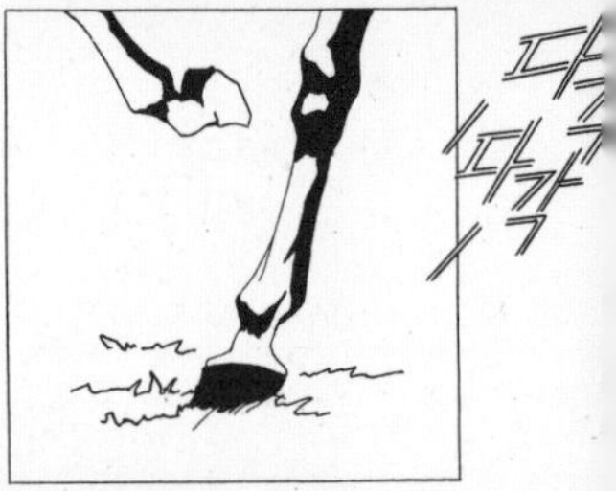
다각 다각
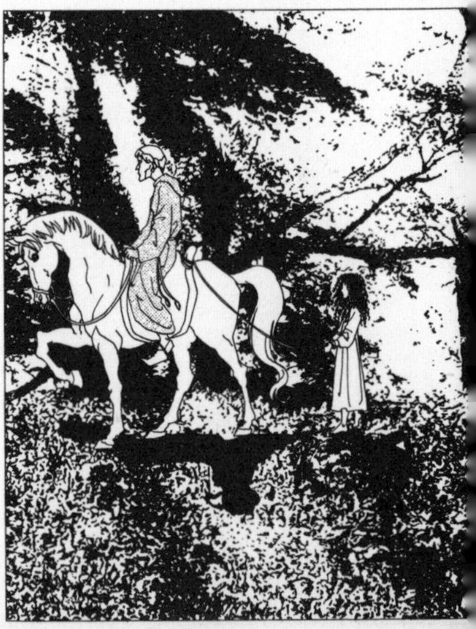

I'VE SEEN YOU BEFORE. YOU'RE NO PRIEST.

......

WHOA...

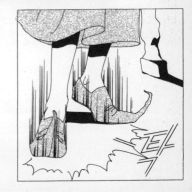

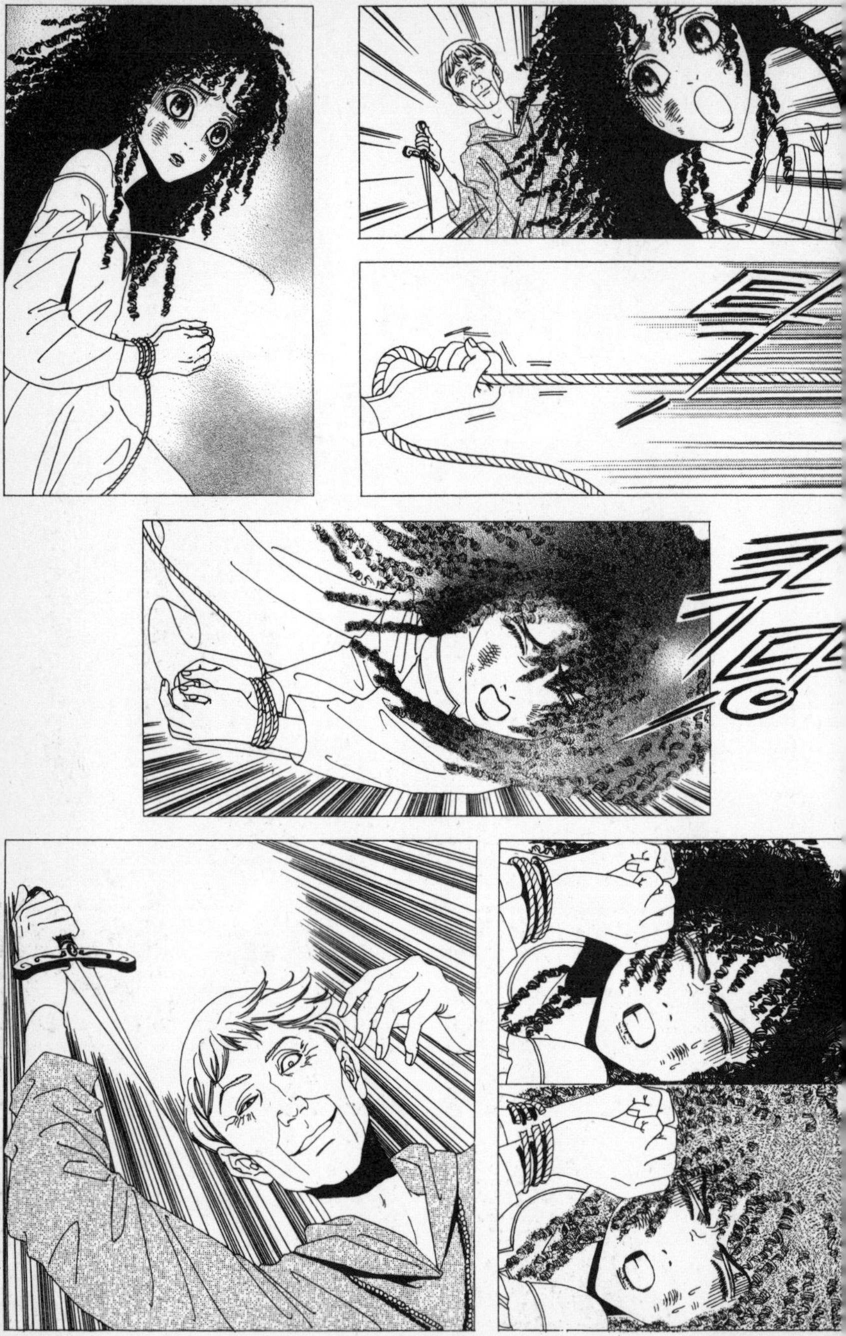
투
쿠당

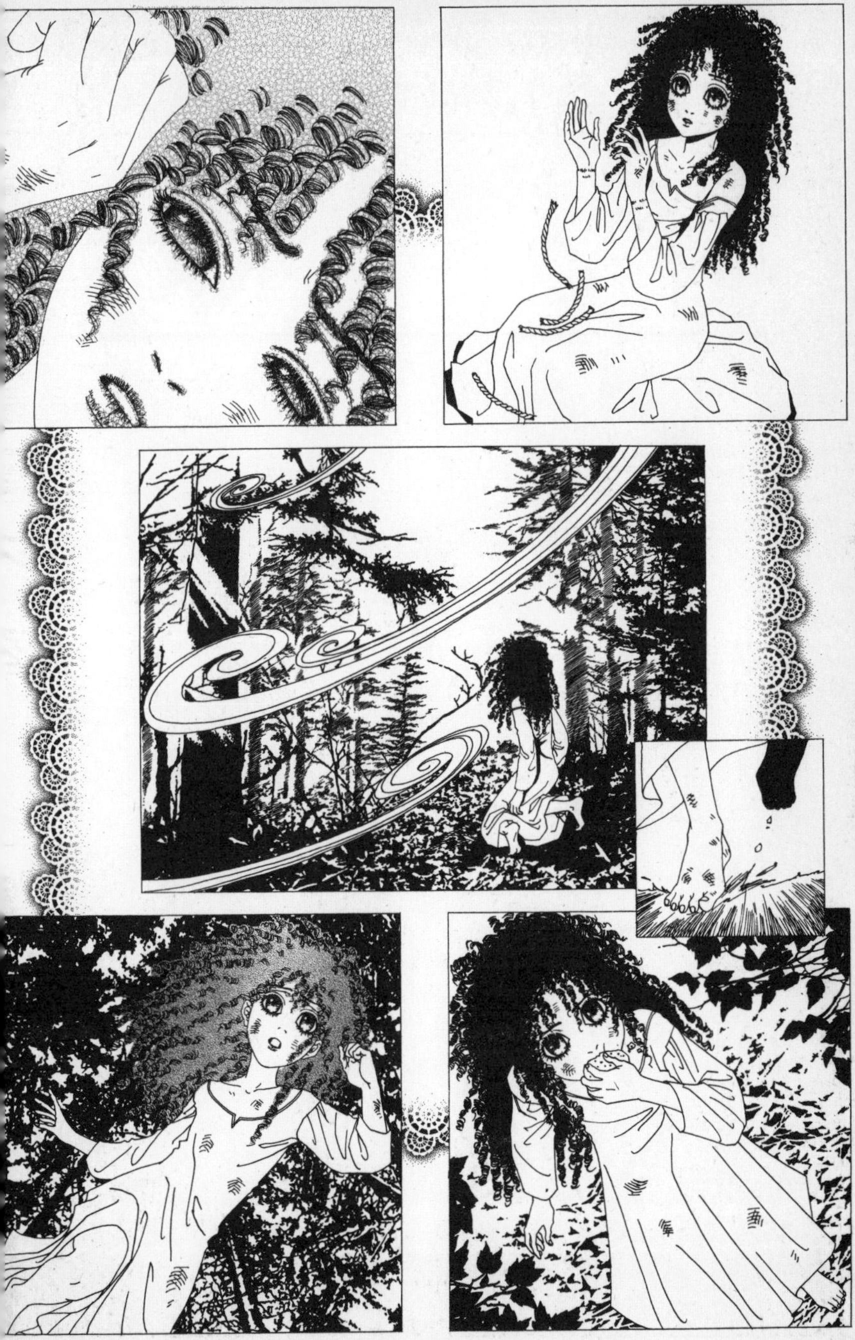

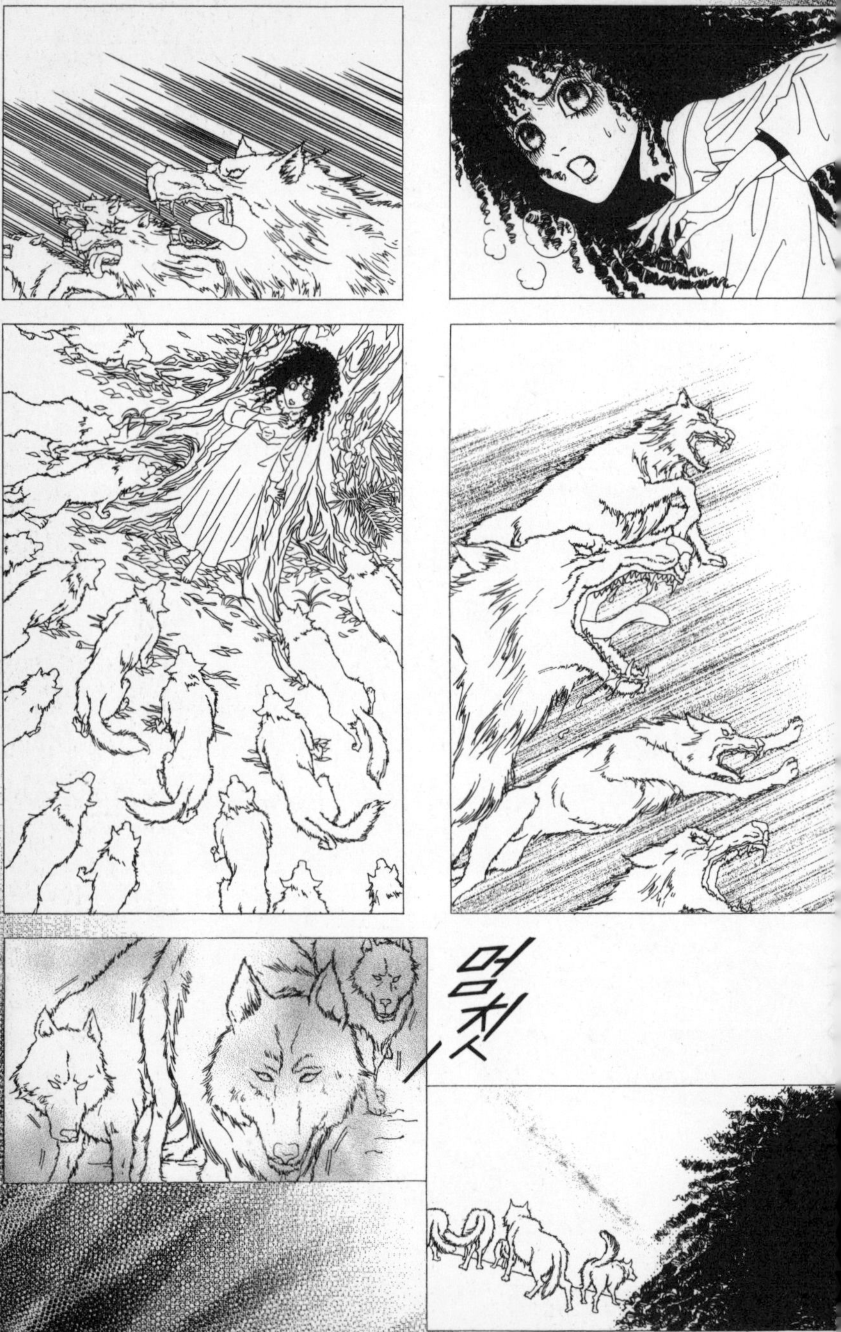
멈칫!

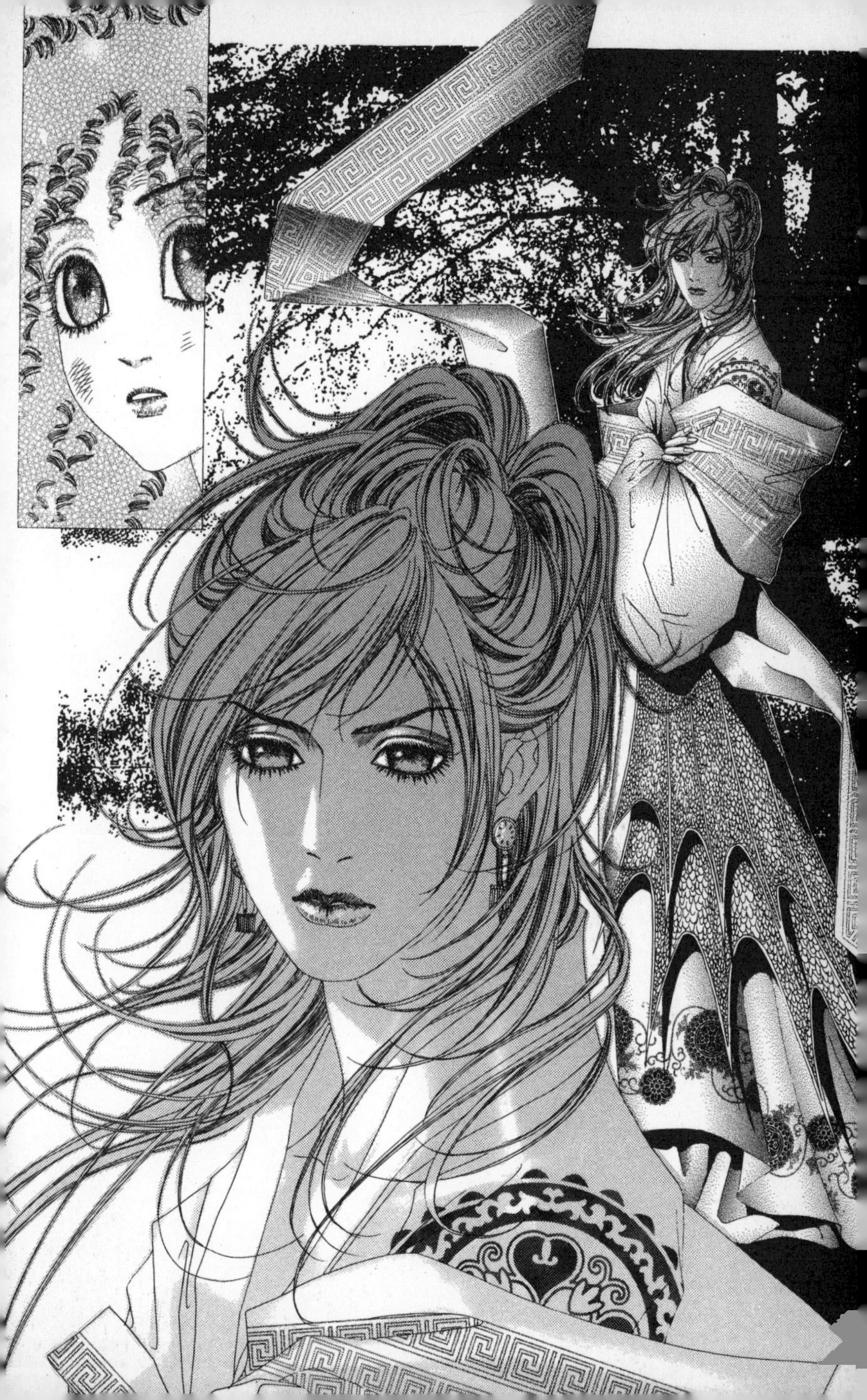

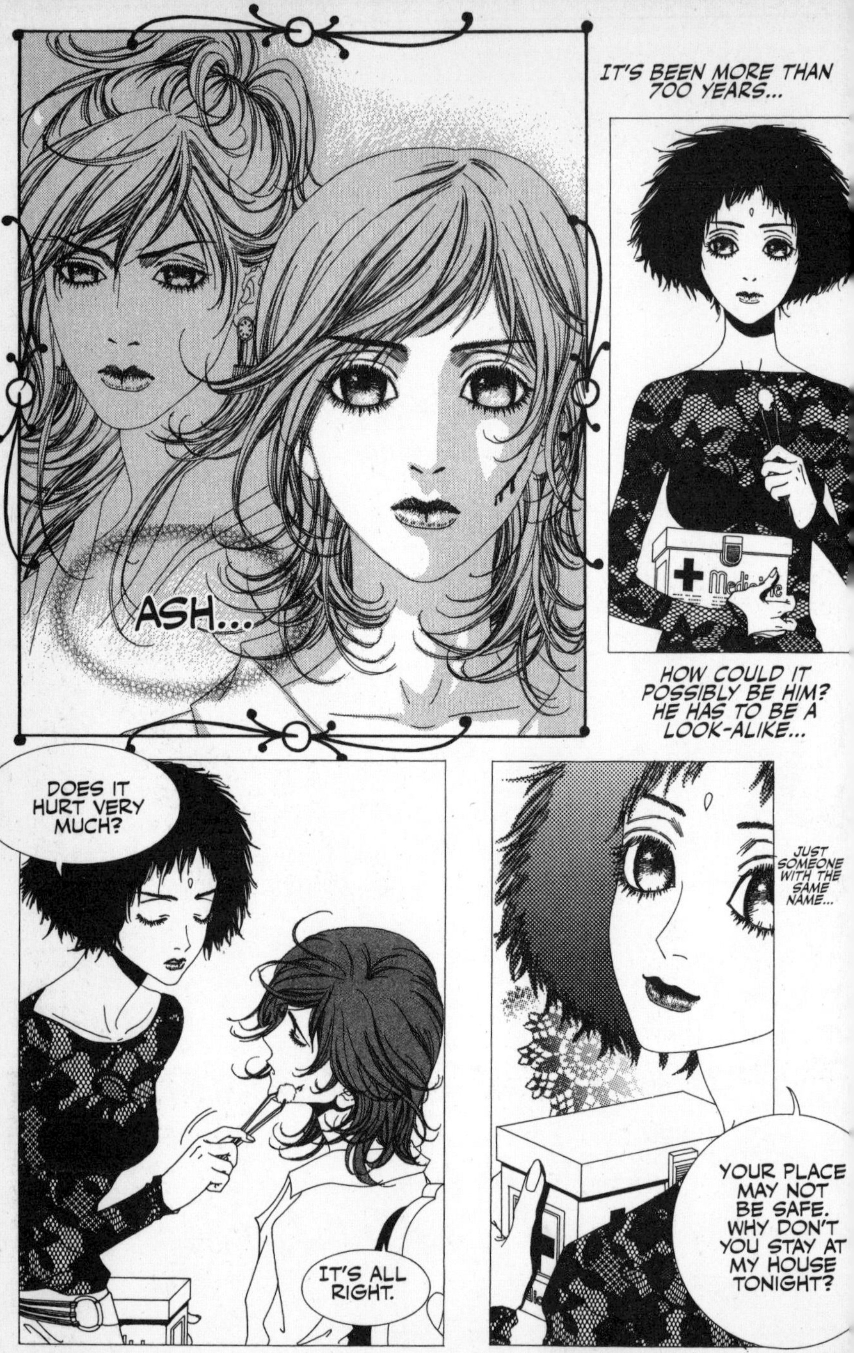
ASH...
IT'S BEEN MORE THAN 700 YEARS...
HOW COULD IT POSSIBLY BE HIM? HE HAS TO BE A LOOK-ALIKE...
DOES IT HURT VERY MUCH?
IT'S ALL RIGHT.
JUST SOMEONE WITH THE SAME NAME...
YOUR PLACE MAY NOT BE SAFE. WHY DON'T YOU STAY AT MY HOUSE TONIGHT?

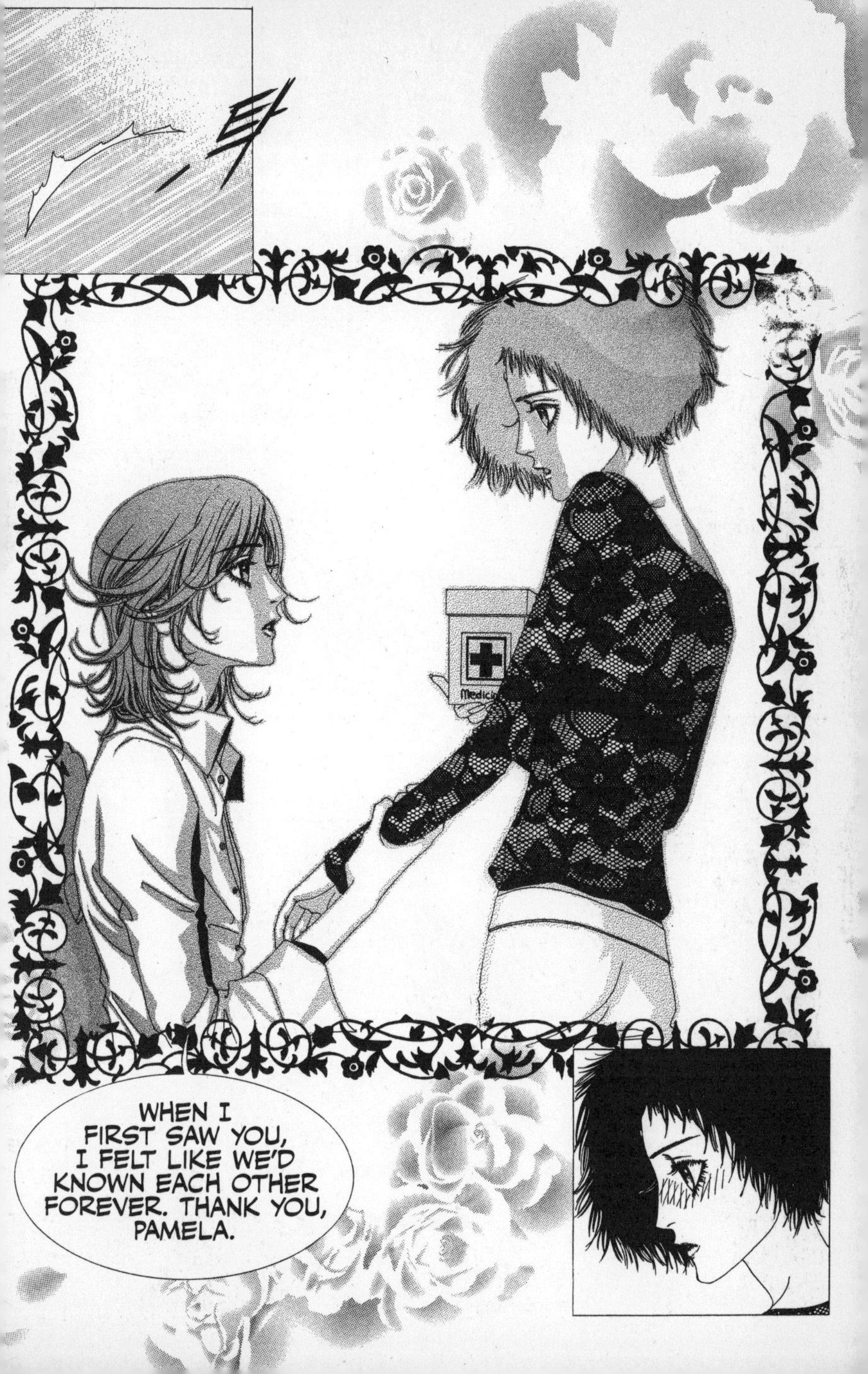
WHEN I FIRST SAW YOU, I FELT LIKE WE'D KNOWN EACH OTHER FOREVER. THANK YOU, PAMELA.

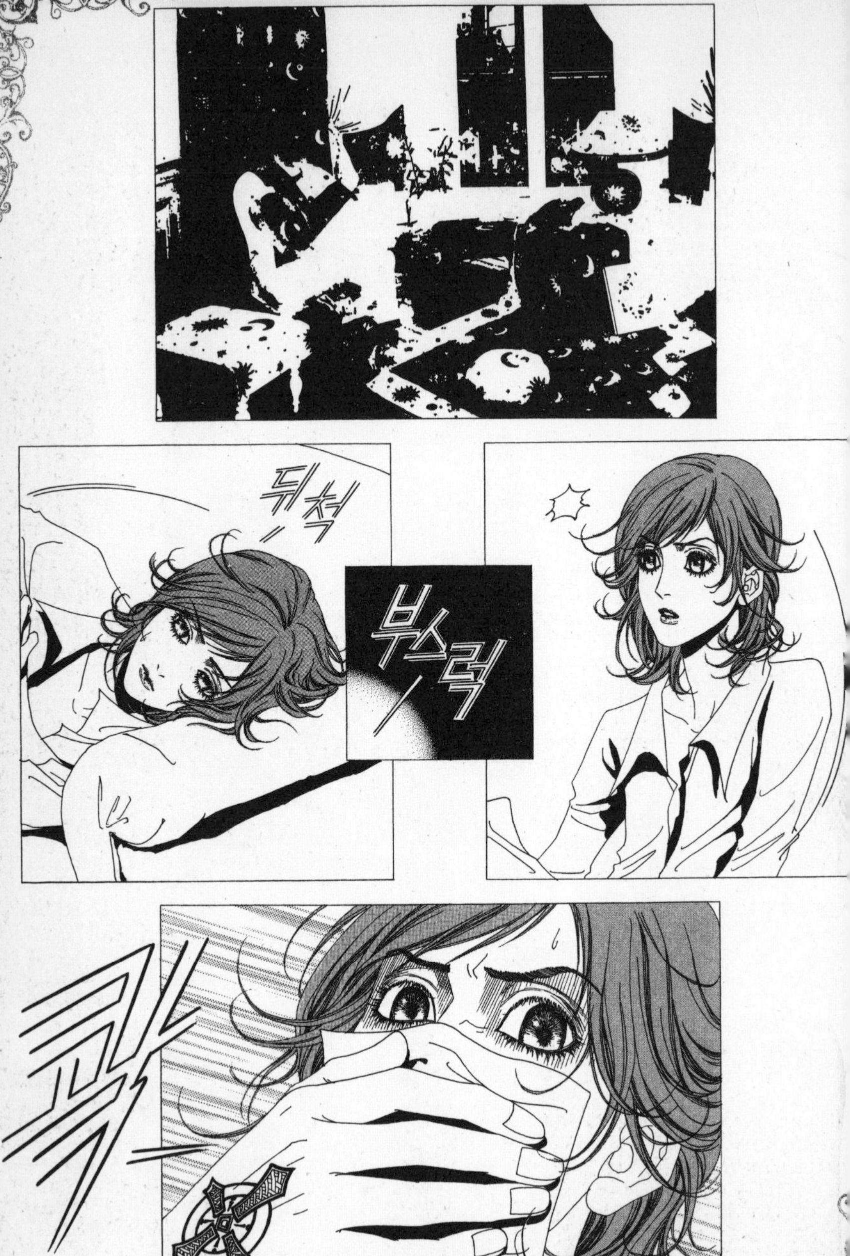
뒤척
부스럭
콱

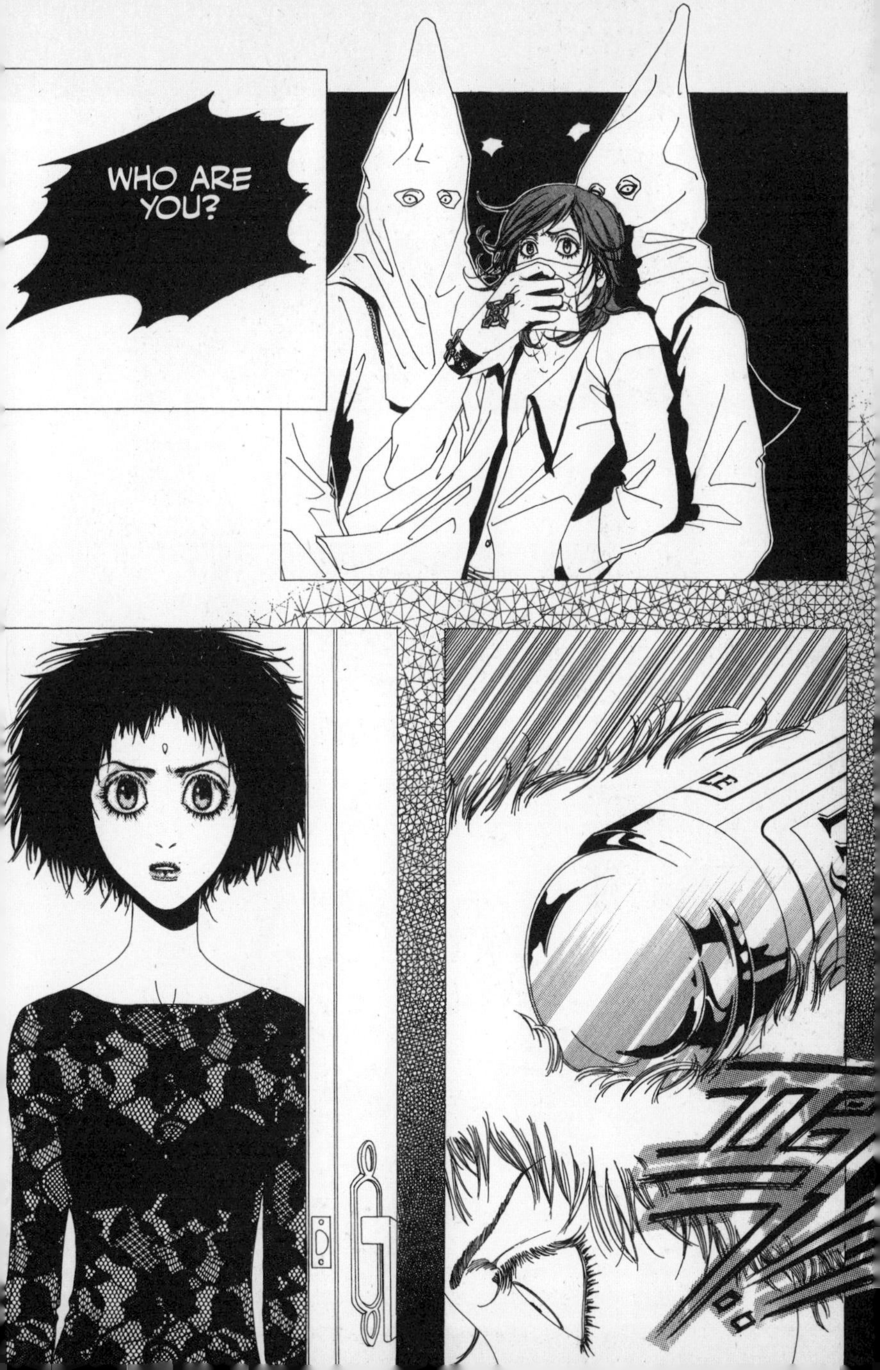
WHO ARE YOU?

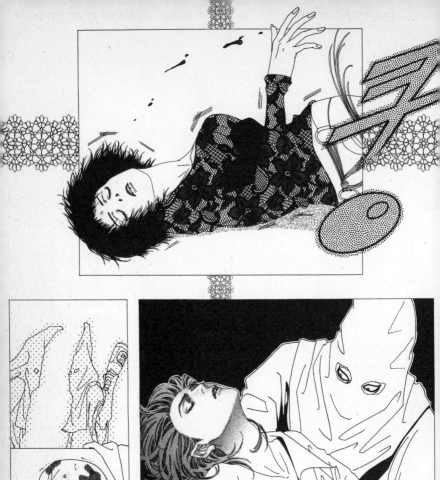

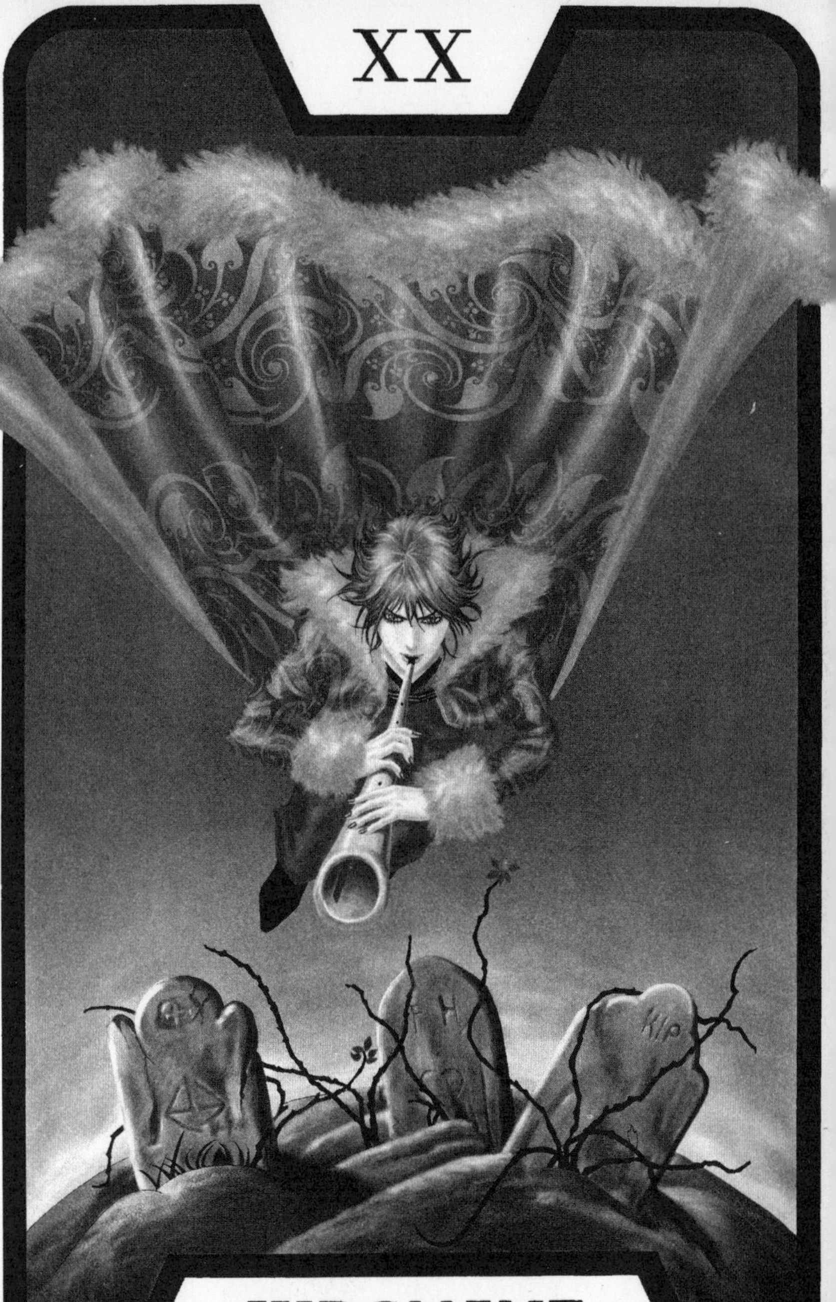
XX
JUDGMENT

ILLUSTRATION FROM TAROT OF THE WITCHES

*Judgment: This card signifies making hard choices, feeling reborn, knowing what you must do, and atonement for past mistakes; forgiveness.

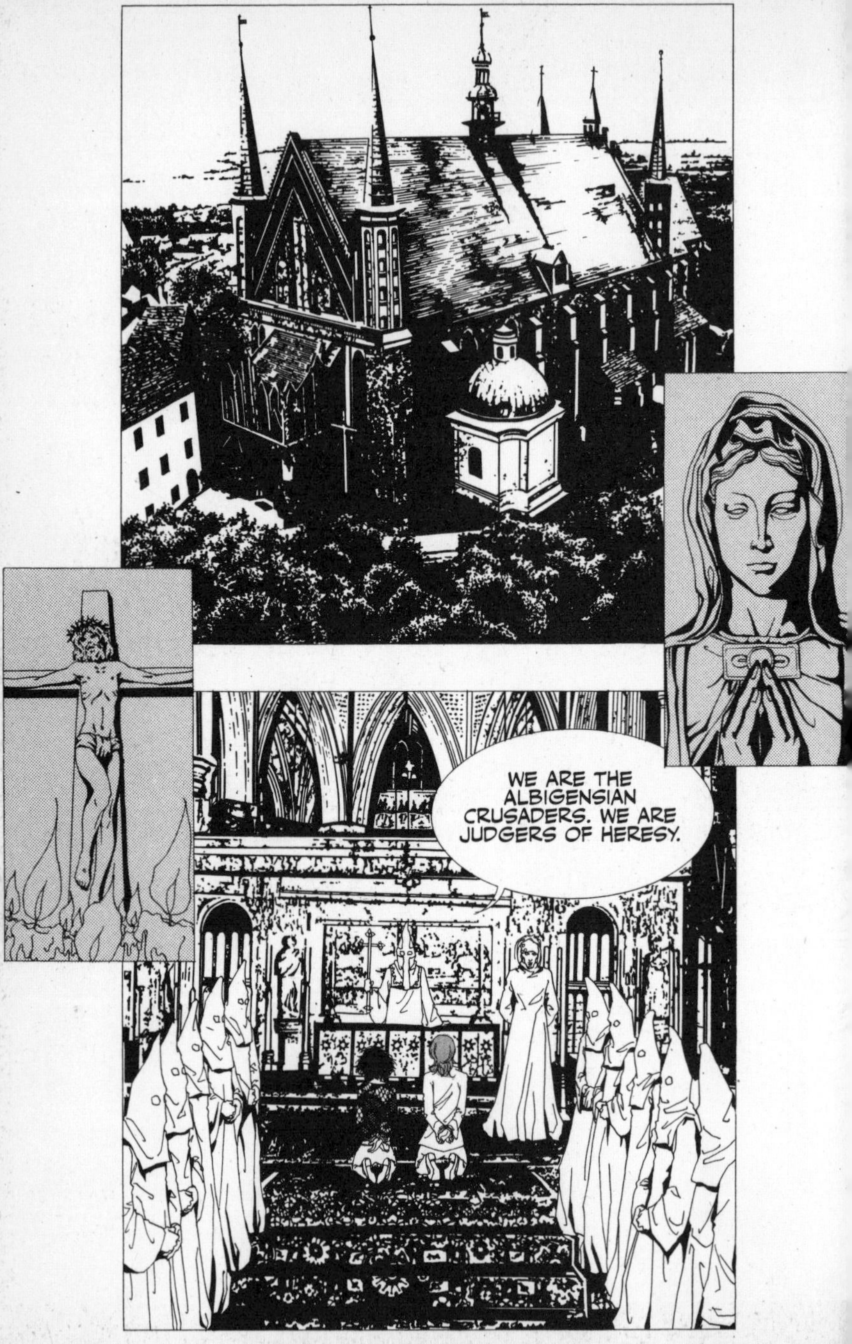
WE ARE THE ALBIGENSIAN CRUSADERS. WE ARE JUDGERS OF HERESY.

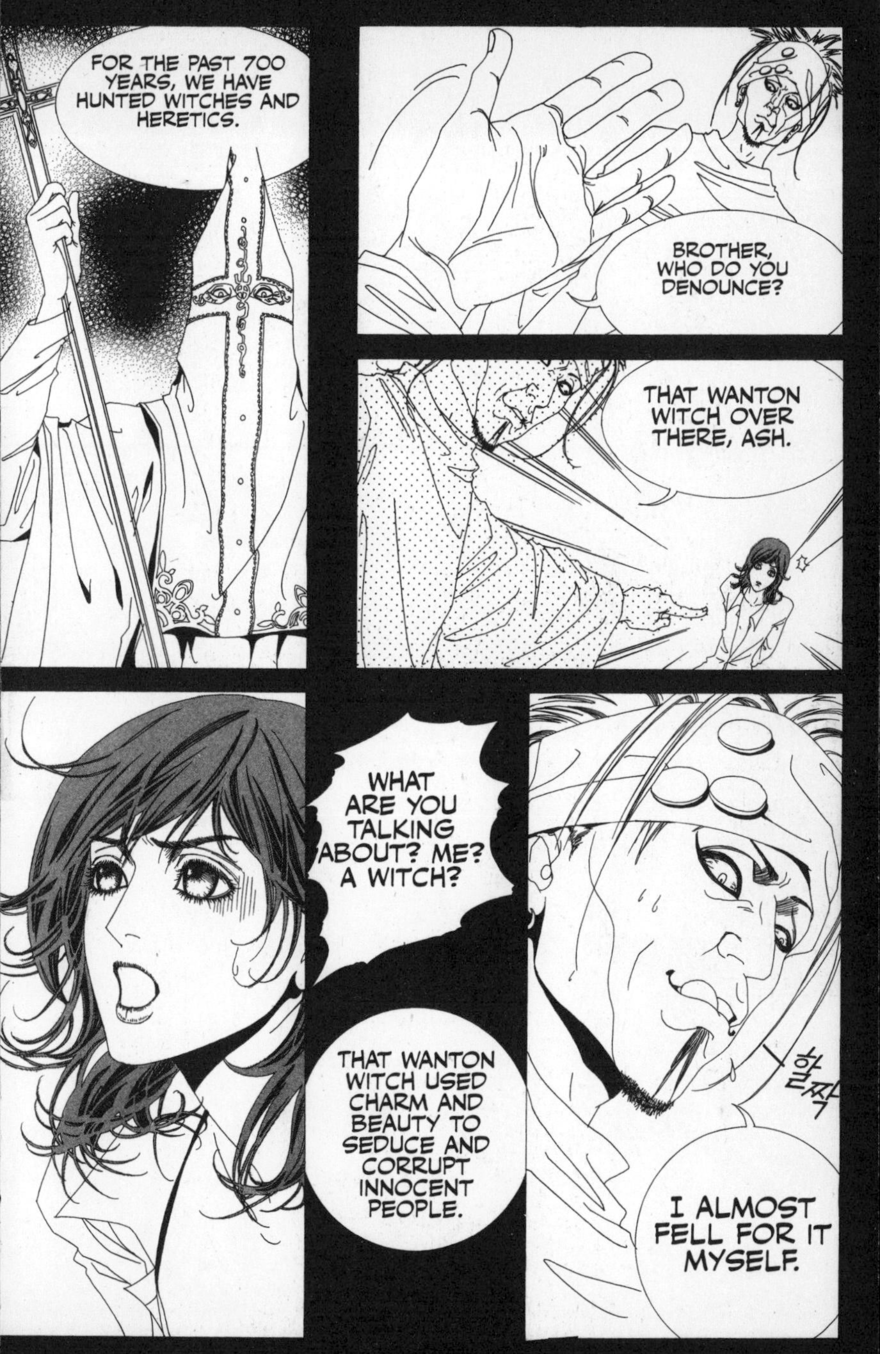

FOR THE PAST 700 YEARS, WE HAVE HUNTED WITCHES AND HERETICS.
BROTHER, WHO DO YOU DENOUNCE?
THAT WANTON WITCH OVER THERE, ASH.
WHAT ARE YOU TALKING ABOUT? ME? A WITCH?
THAT WANTON WITCH USED CHARM AND BEAUTY TO SEDUCE AND CORRUPT INNOCENT PEOPLE.
할짝
I ALMOST FELL FOR IT MYSELF.

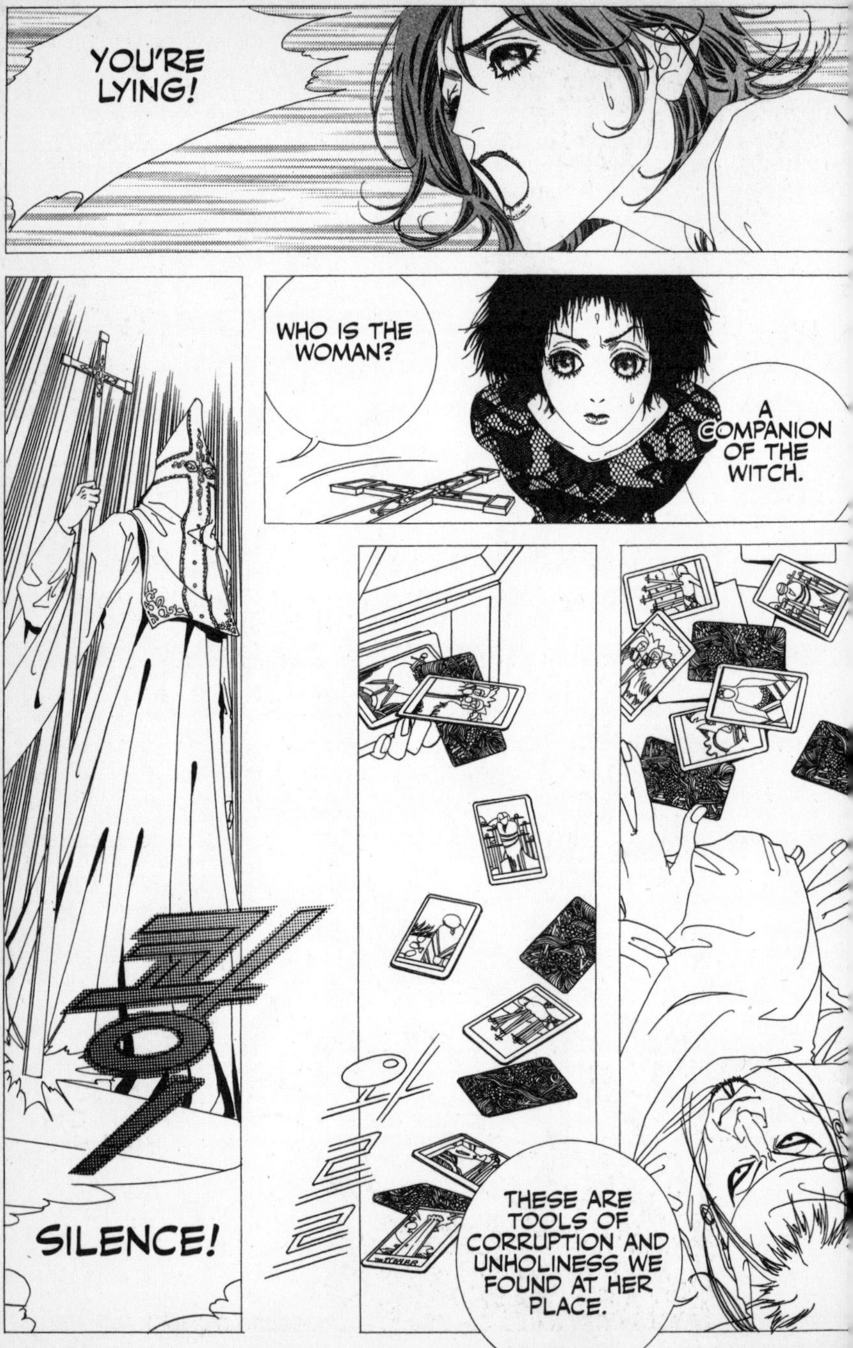
YOU'RE LYING!
SILENCE!
WHO IS THE WOMAN?
A COMPANION OF THE WITCH.
THESE ARE TOOLS OF CORRUPTION AND UNHOLINESS WE FOUND AT HER PLACE.

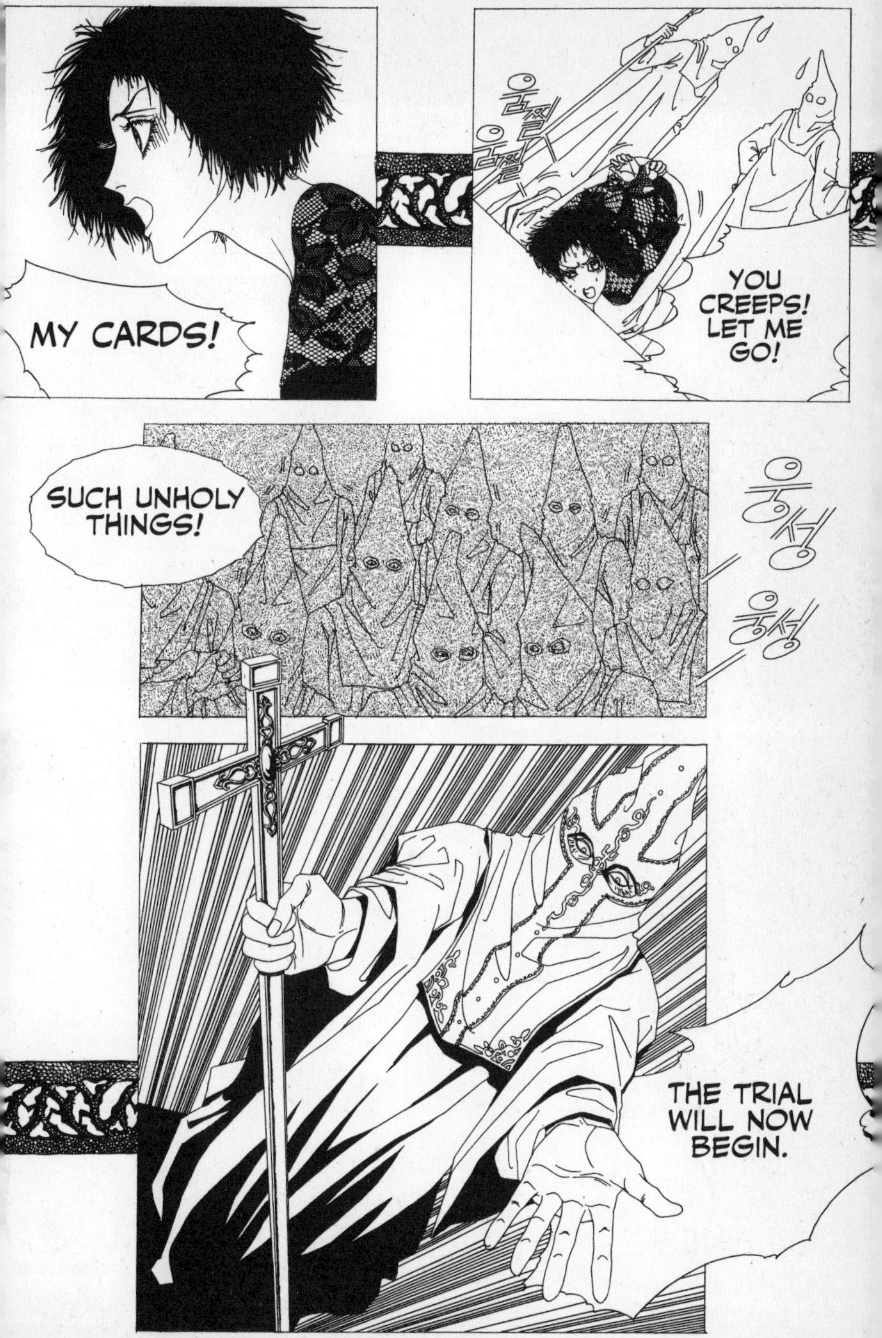
MY CARDS!
움찔 움찔
YOU CREEPS! LET ME GO!
SUCH UNHOLY THINGS!
웅성 웅성
THE TRIAL WILL NOW BEGIN.

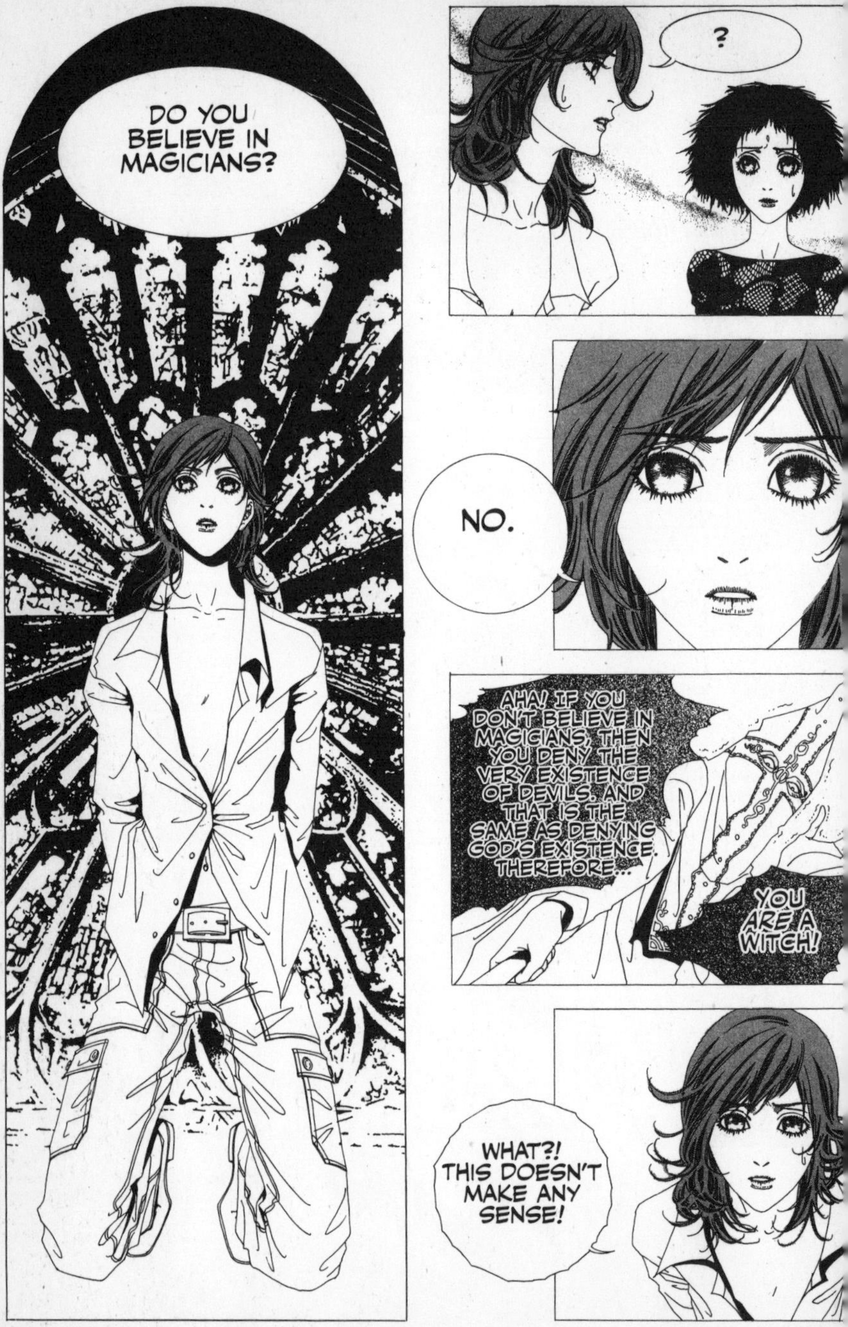
DO YOU BELIEVE IN MAGICIANS?
?
NO.
AHA! IF YOU DON'T BELIEVE IN MAGICIANS, THEN YOU DENY THE VERY EXISTENCE OF DEVILS. AND THAT IS THE SAME AS DENYING GOD'S EXISTENCE. THEREFORE...
YOU ARE A WITCH!
WHAT?! THIS DOESN'T MAKE ANY SENSE!

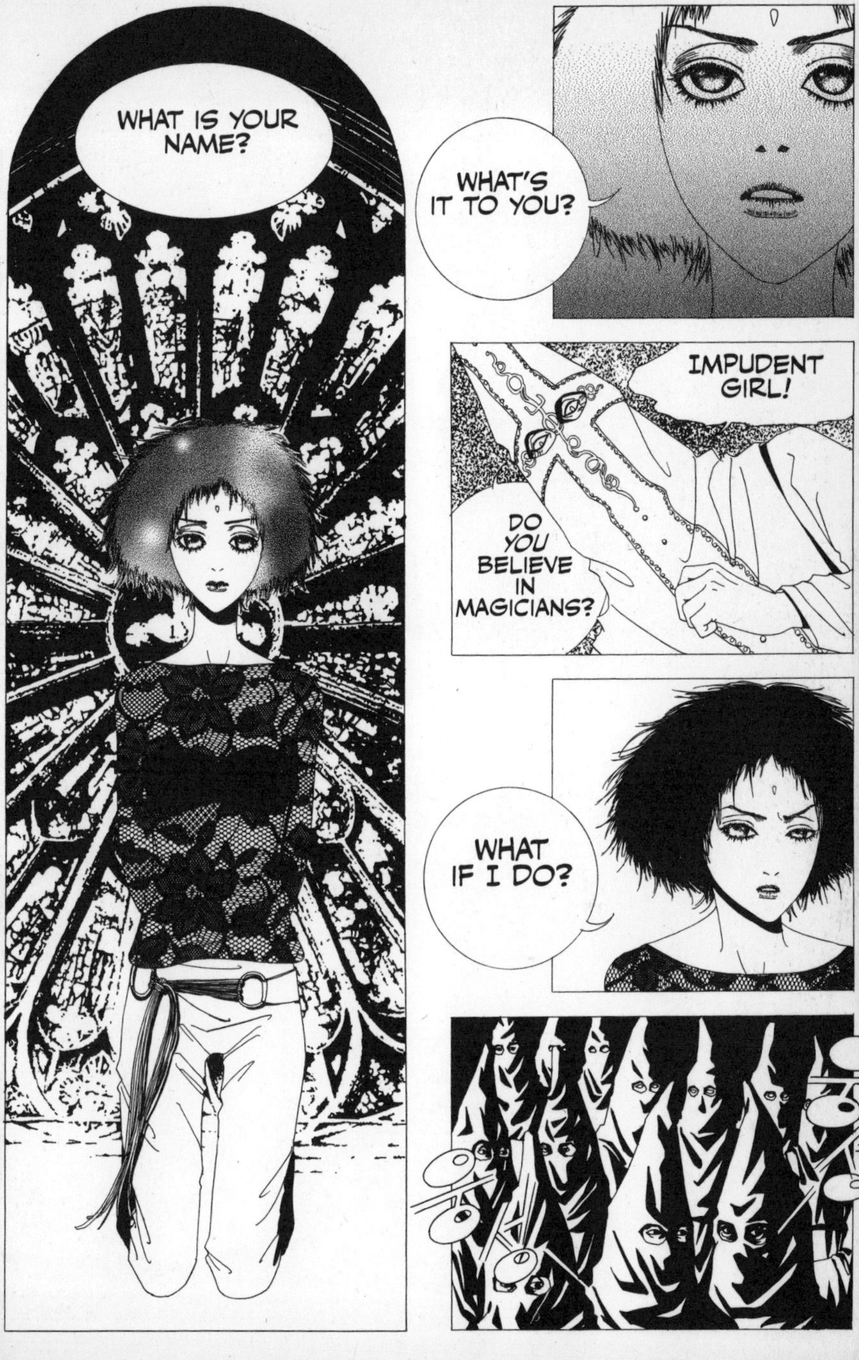
WHAT IS YOUR NAME?
WHAT'S IT TO YOU?
IMPUDENT GIRL!
DO YOU BELIEVE IN MAGICIANS?
WHAT IF I DO?

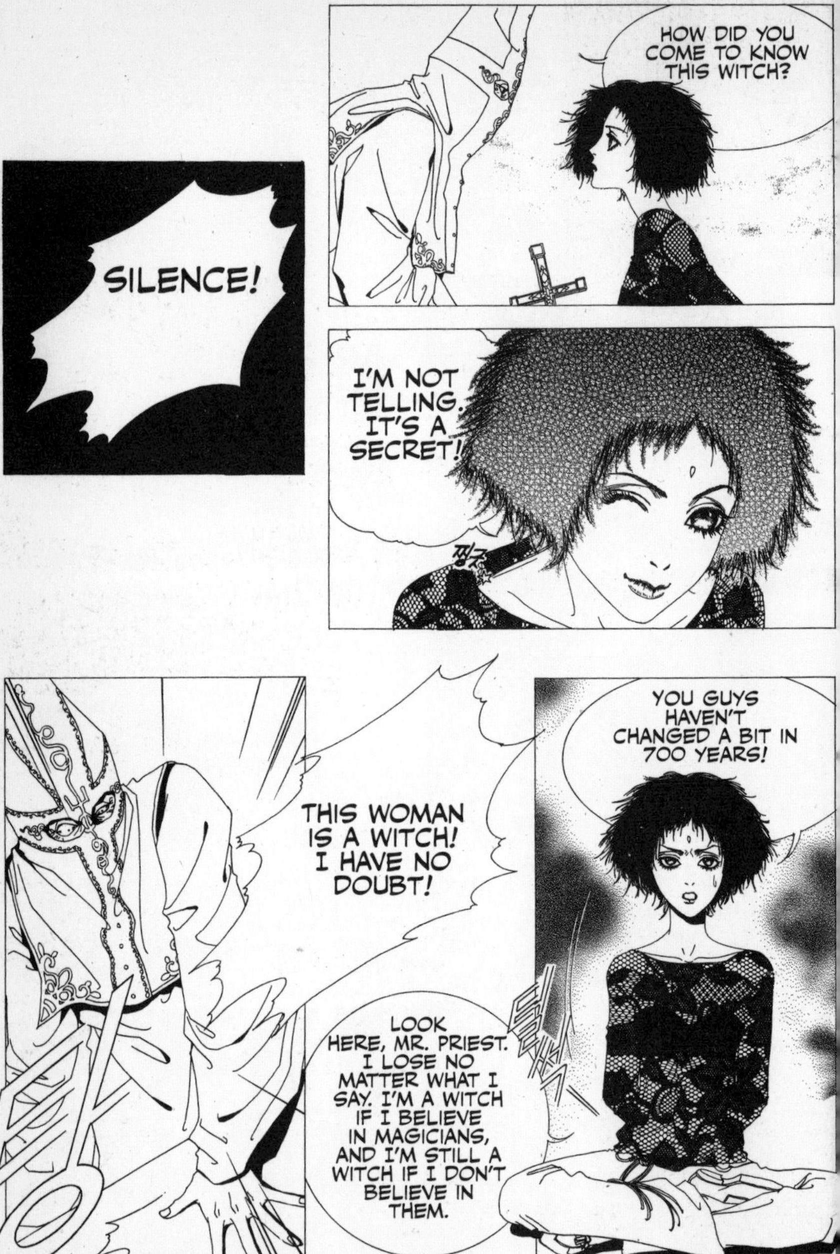
SILENCE!
HOW DID YOU COME TO KNOW THIS WITCH?
I'M NOT TELLING. IT'S A SECRET!
THIS WOMAN IS A WITCH! I HAVE NO DOUBT!
YOU GUYS HAVEN'T CHANGED A BIT IN 700 YEARS!
LOOK HERE, MR. PRIEST. I LOSE NO MATTER WHAT I SAY. I'M A WITCH IF I BELIEVE IN MAGICIANS, AND I'M STILL A WITCH IF I DON'T BELIEVE IN THEM.

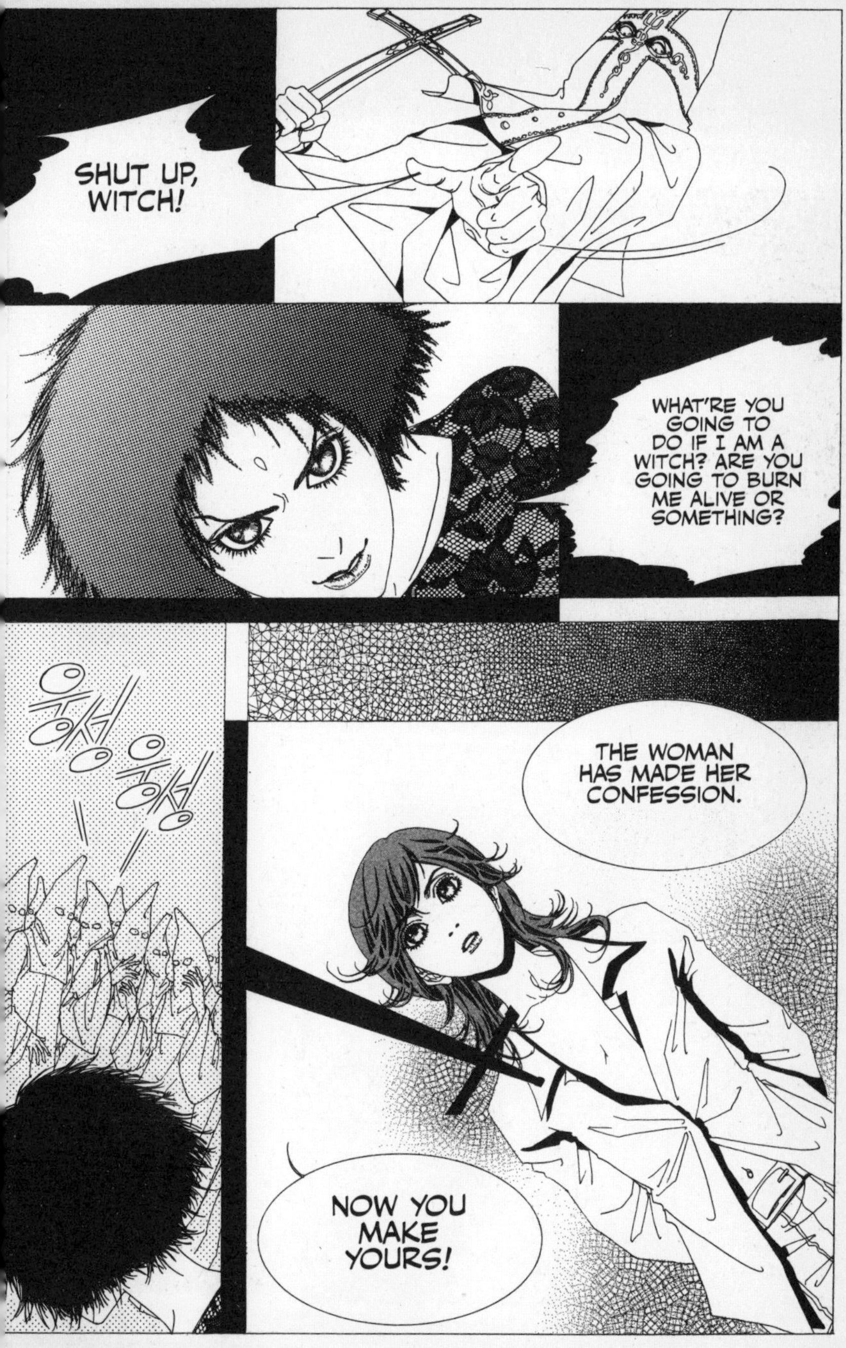
SHUT UP, WITCH!
WHAT'RE YOU GOING TO DO IF I AM A WITCH? ARE YOU GOING TO BURN ME ALIVE OR SOMETHING?
웅성 웅성
THE WOMAN HAS MADE HER CONFESSION.
NOW YOU MAKE YOURS!

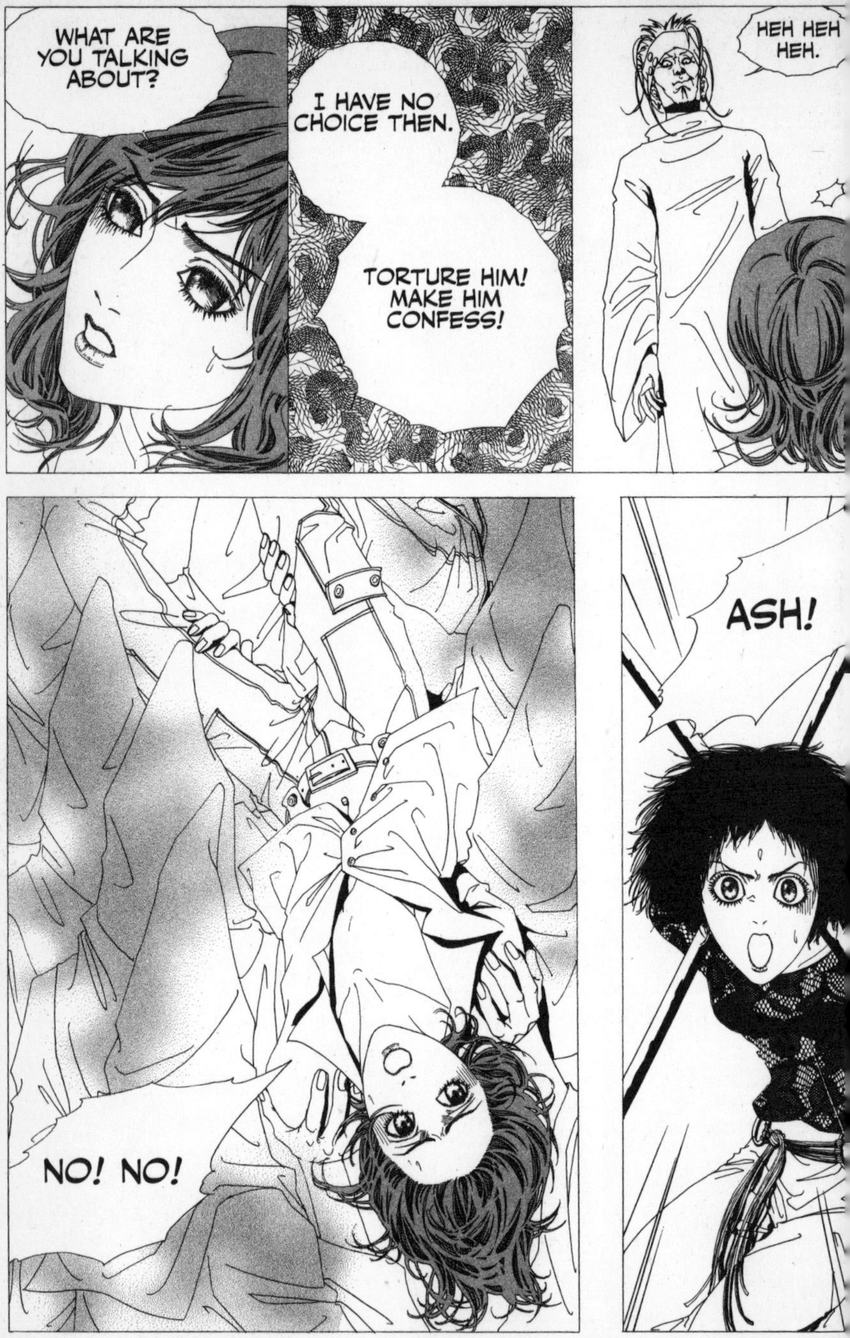
WHAT ARE YOU TALKING ABOUT?
I HAVE NO CHOICE THEN.
TORTURE HIM! MAKE HIM CONFESS!
HEH HEH HEH.
NO! NO!
ASH!

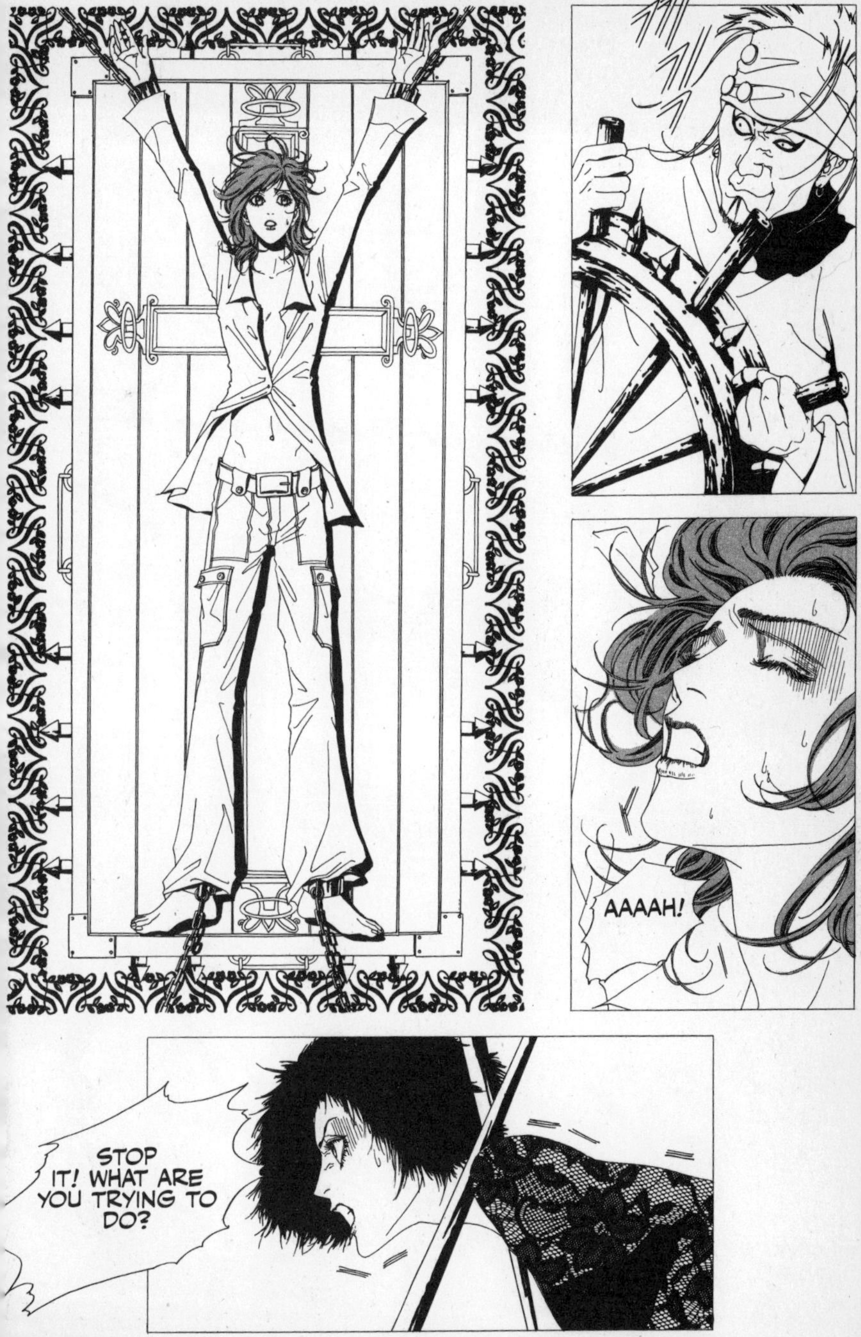
AAAAH!
STOP IT! WHAT ARE YOU TRYING TO DO?

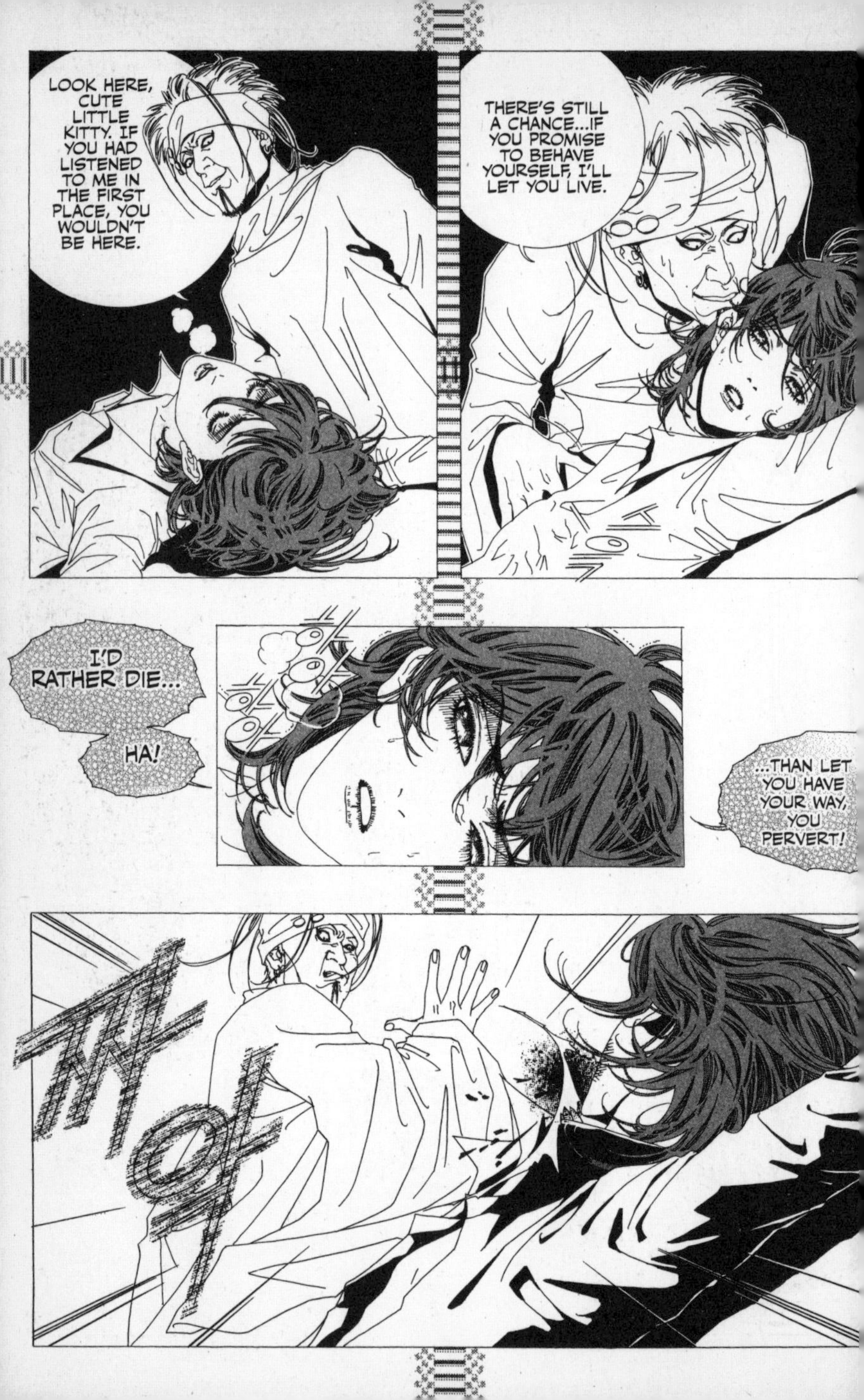
LOOK HERE, CUTE LITTLE KITTY. IF YOU HAD LISTENED TO ME IN THE FIRST PLACE, YOU WOULDN'T BE HERE.
THERE'S STILL A CHANCE...IF YOU PROMISE TO BEHAVE YOURSELF, I'LL LET YOU LIVE.
I'D RATHER DIE...
HA!
...THAN LET YOU HAVE YOUR WAY, YOU PERVERT!

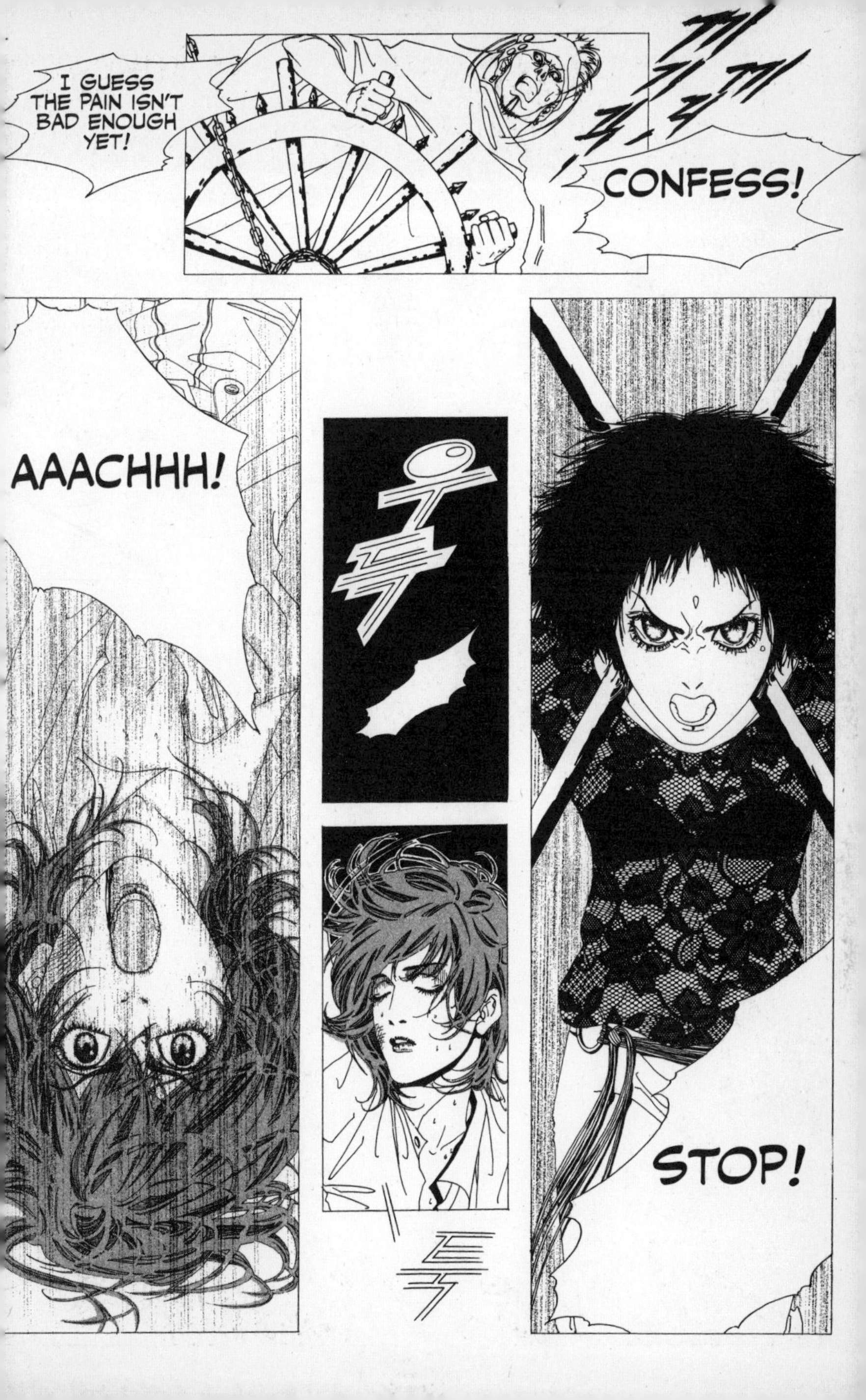
I GUESS THE PAIN ISN'T BAD ENOUGH YET!
CONFESS!
AAACHHH!
STOP!

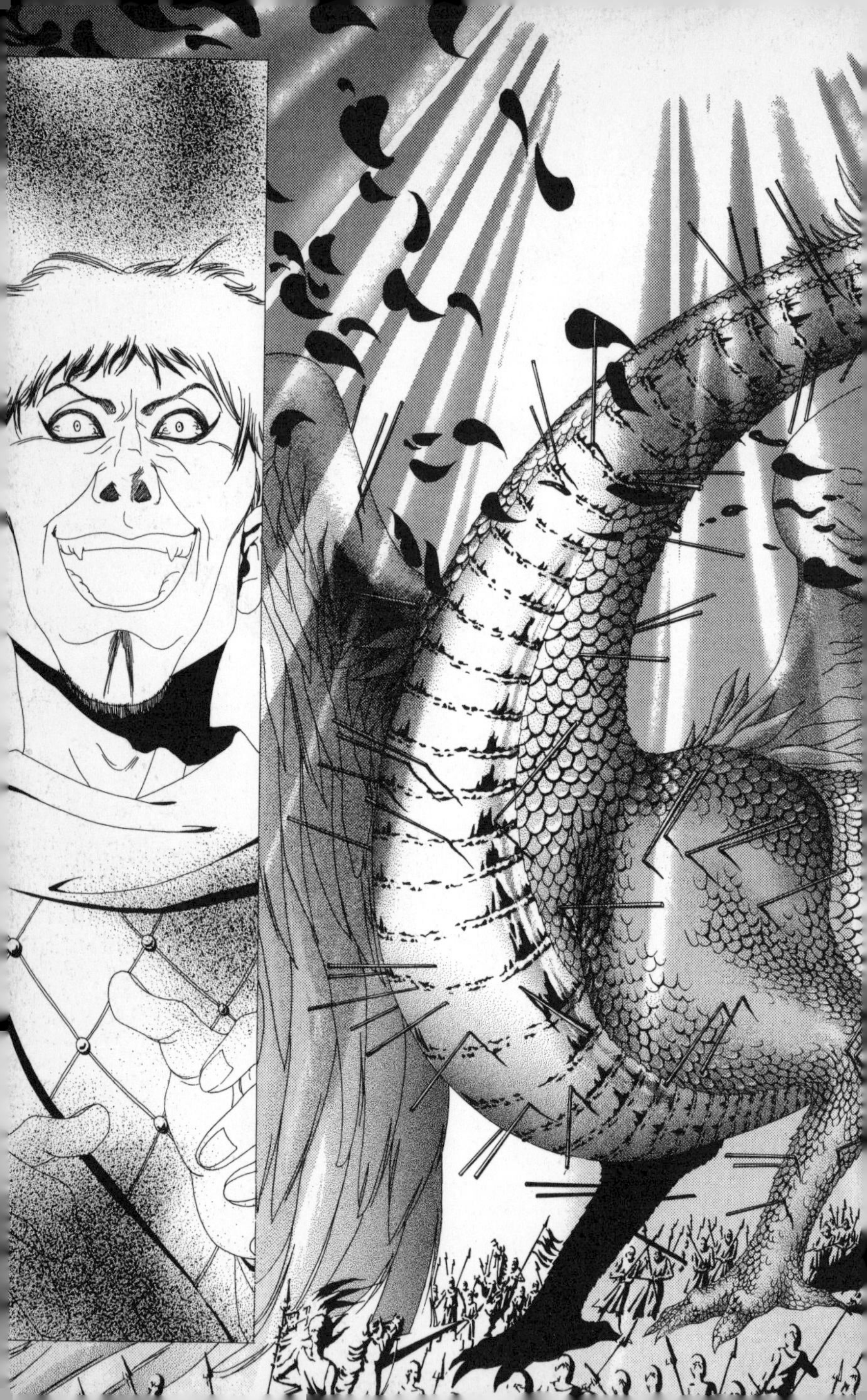

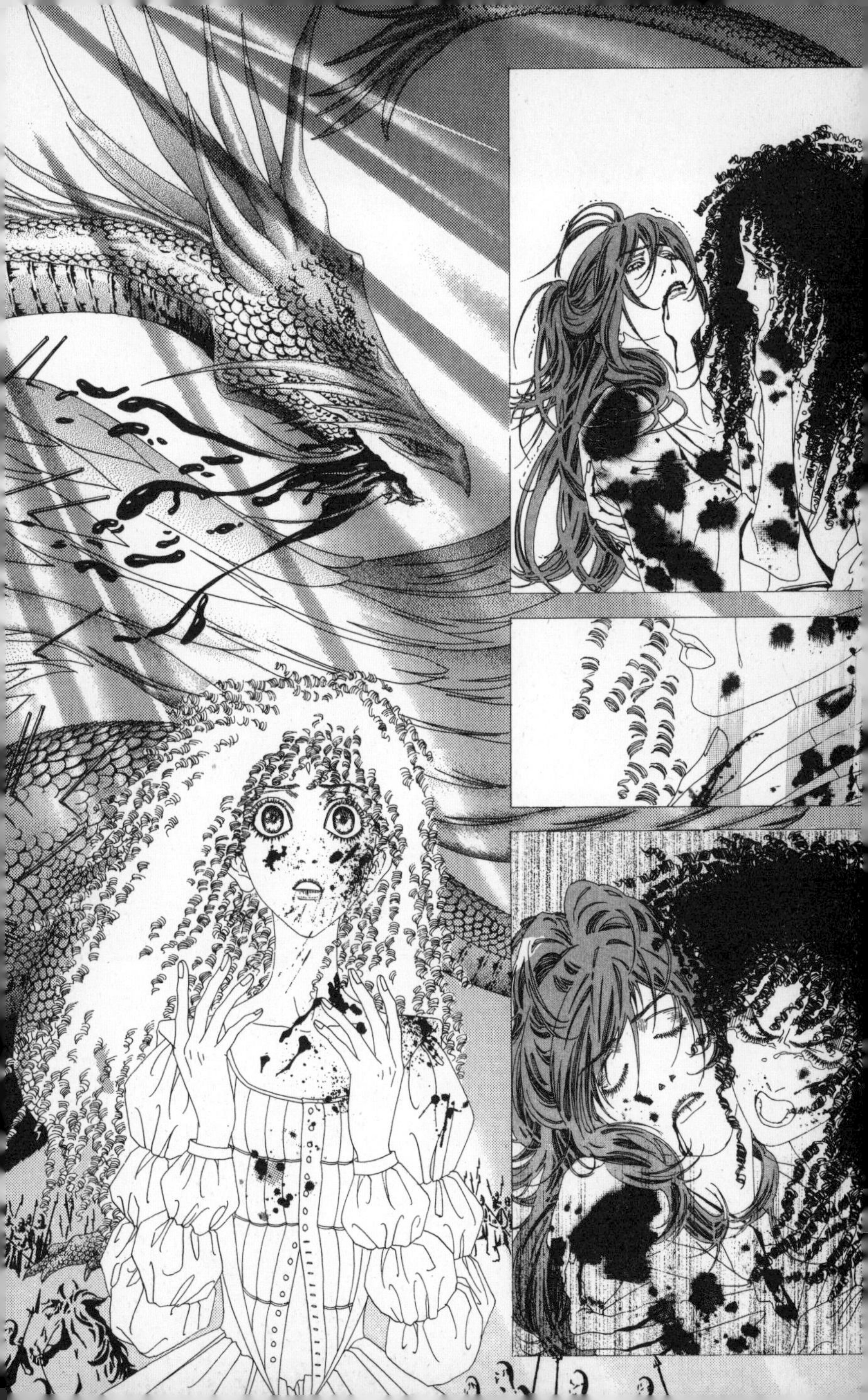

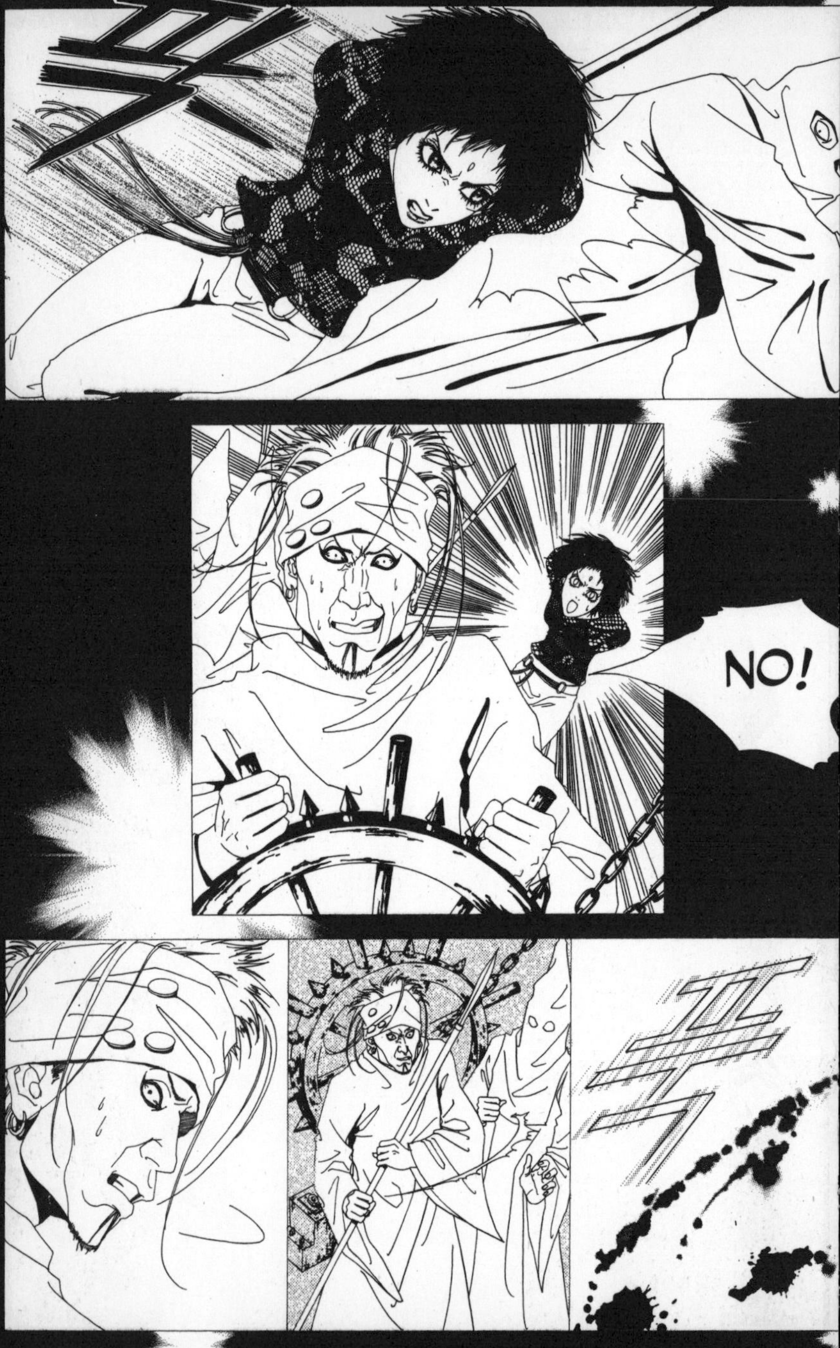
NO!

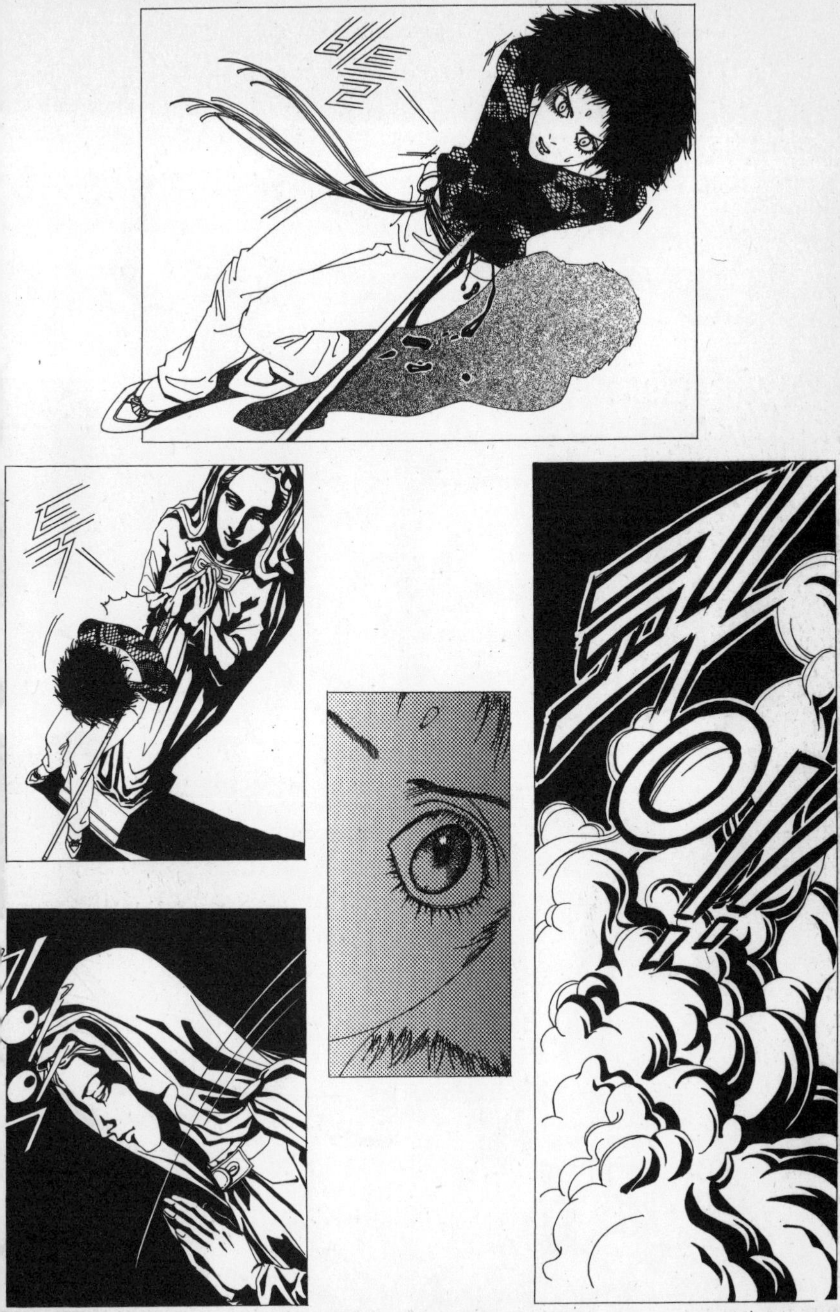
비틀
툭

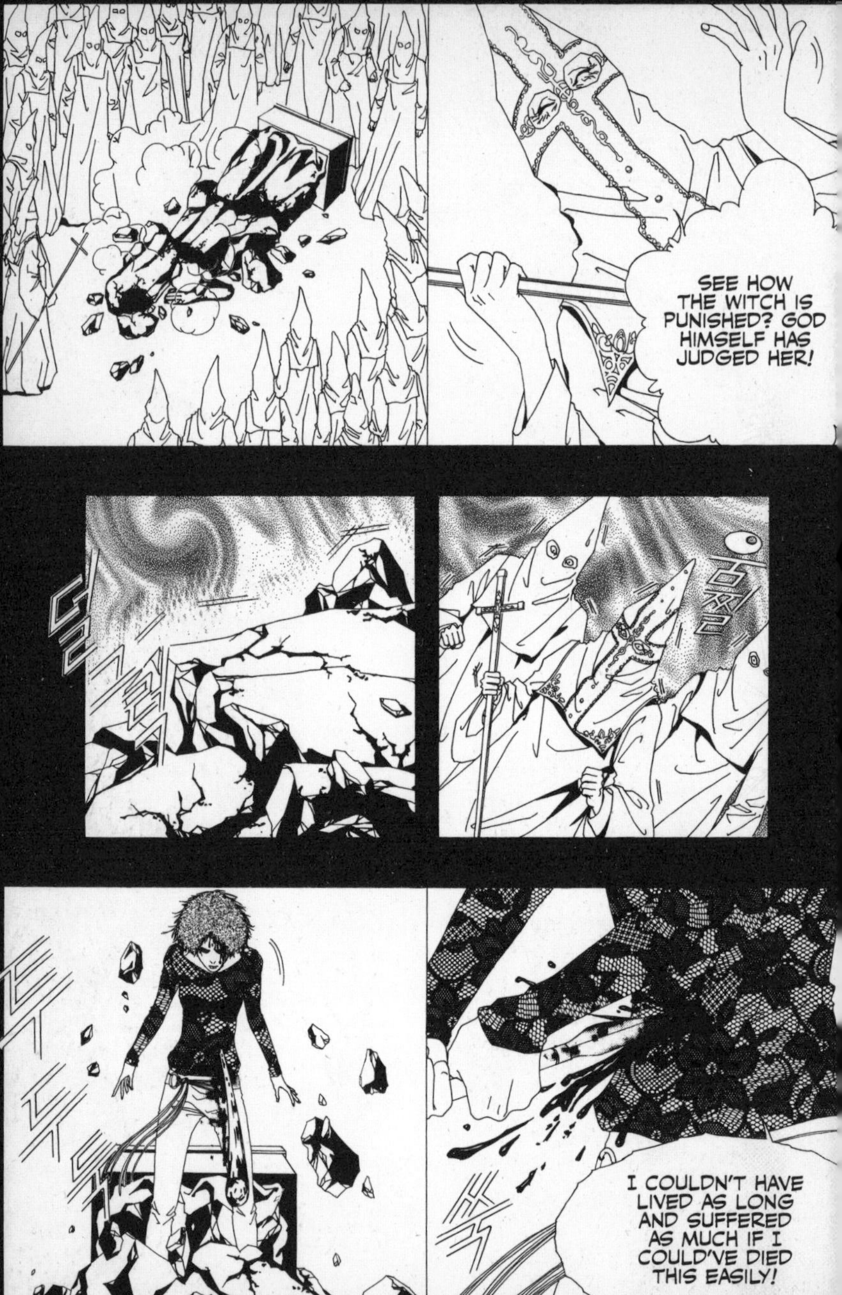
SEE HOW THE WITCH IS PUNISHED? GOD HIMSELF HAS JUDGED HER!
I COULDN'T HAVE LIVED AS LONG AND SUFFERED AS MUCH IF I COULD'VE DIED THIS EASILY!

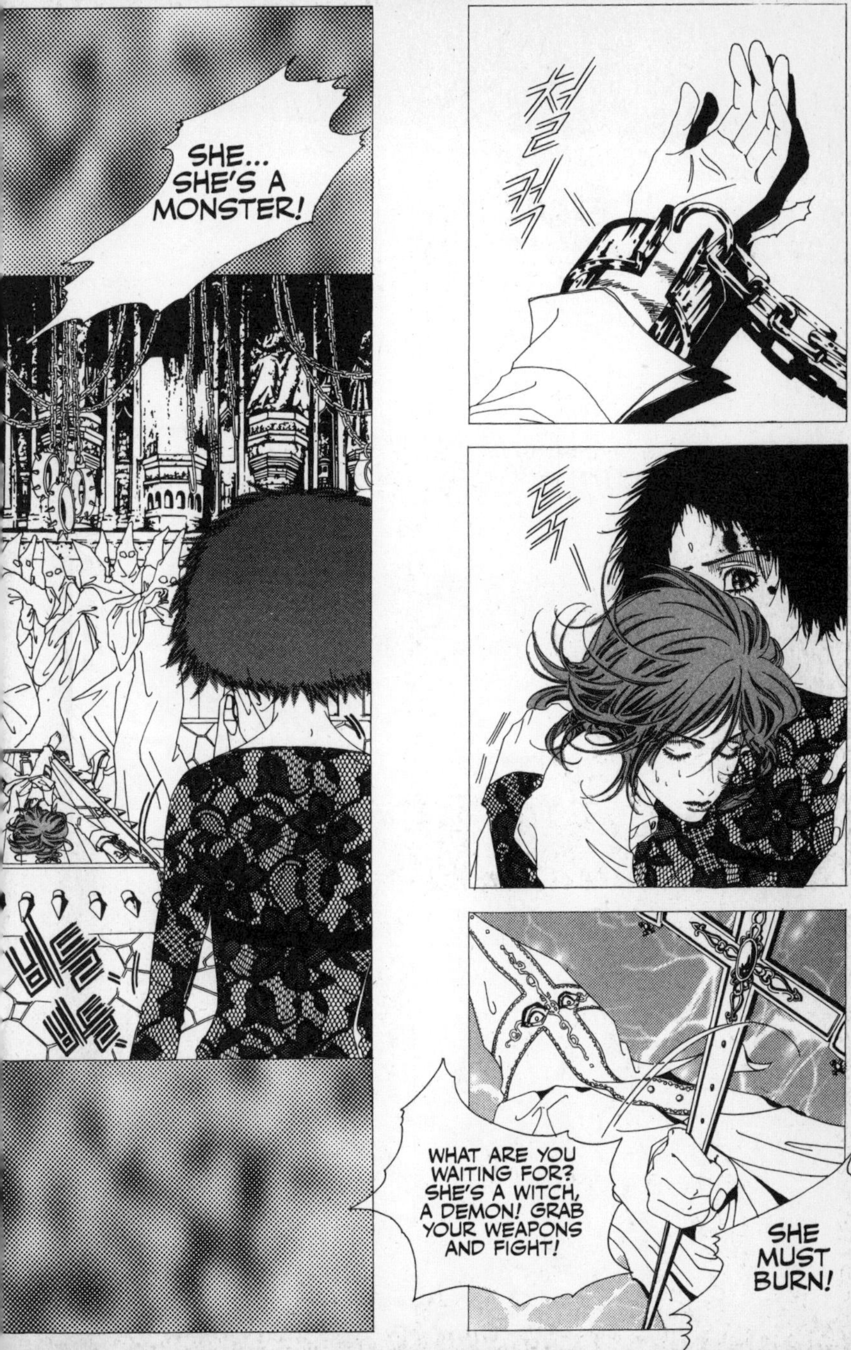
SHE... SHE'S A MONSTER!
WHAT ARE YOU WAITING FOR? SHE'S A WITCH, A DEMON! GRAB YOUR WEAPONS AND FIGHT!
SHE MUST BURN!

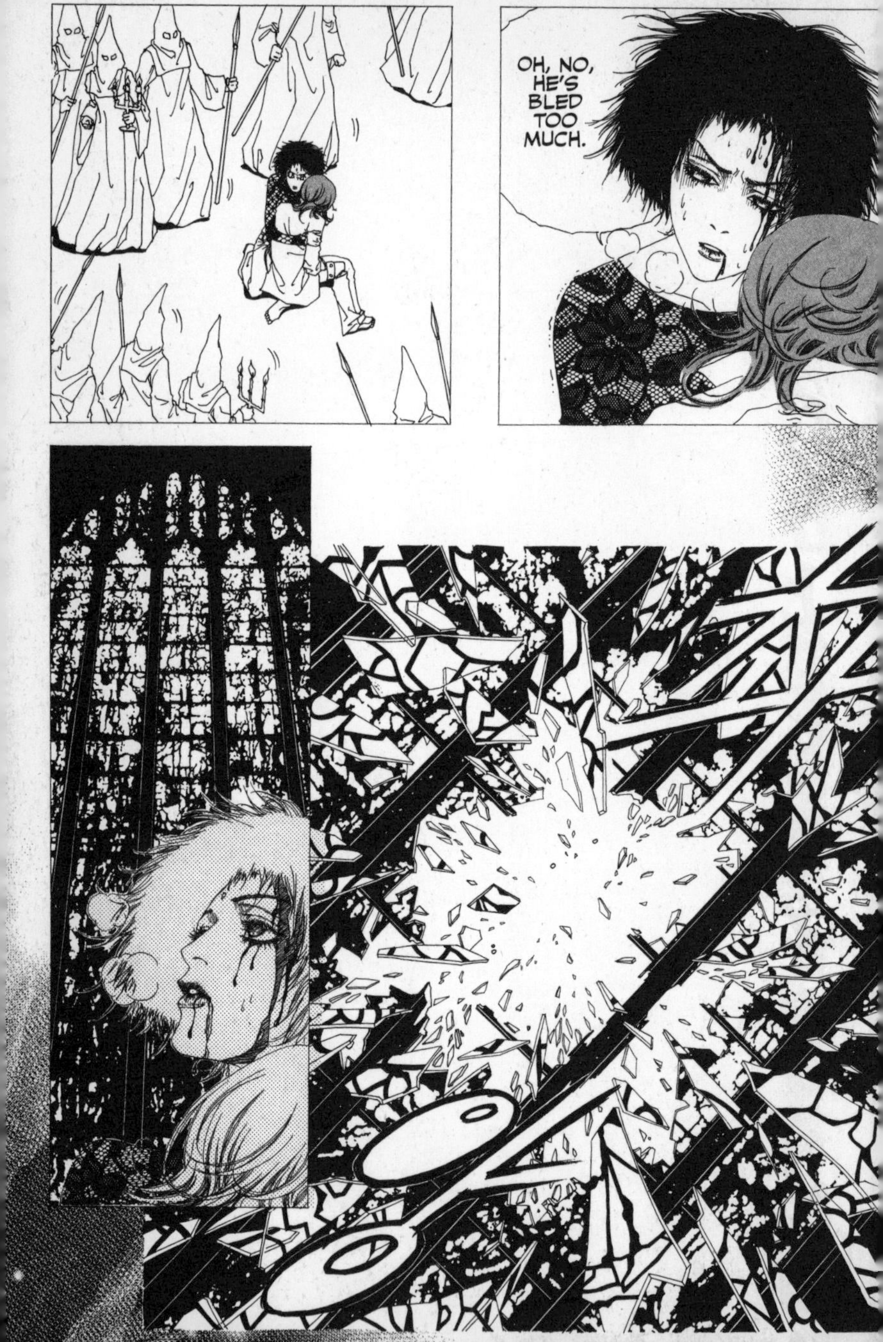
OH, NO, HE'S BLED TOO MUCH.

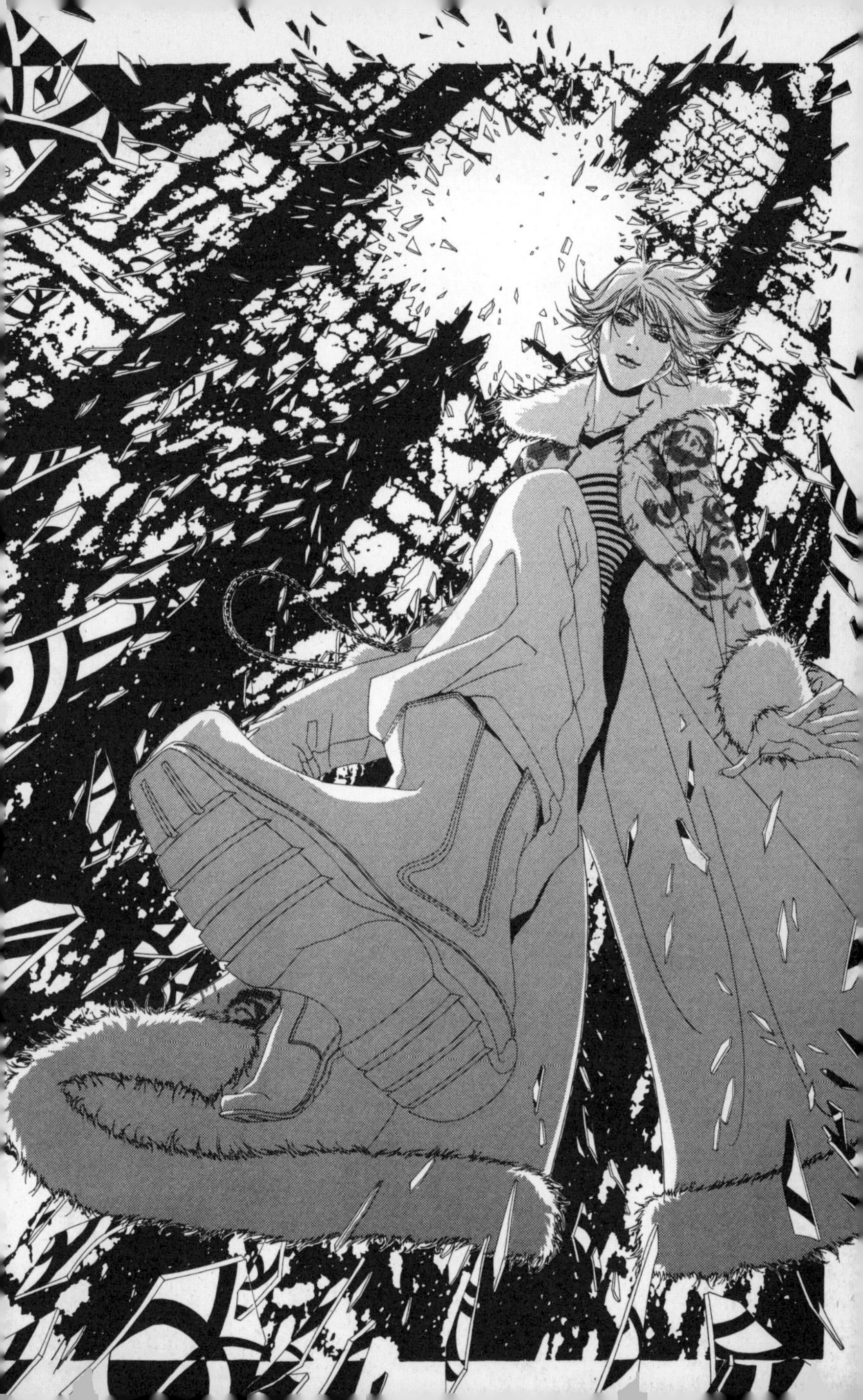

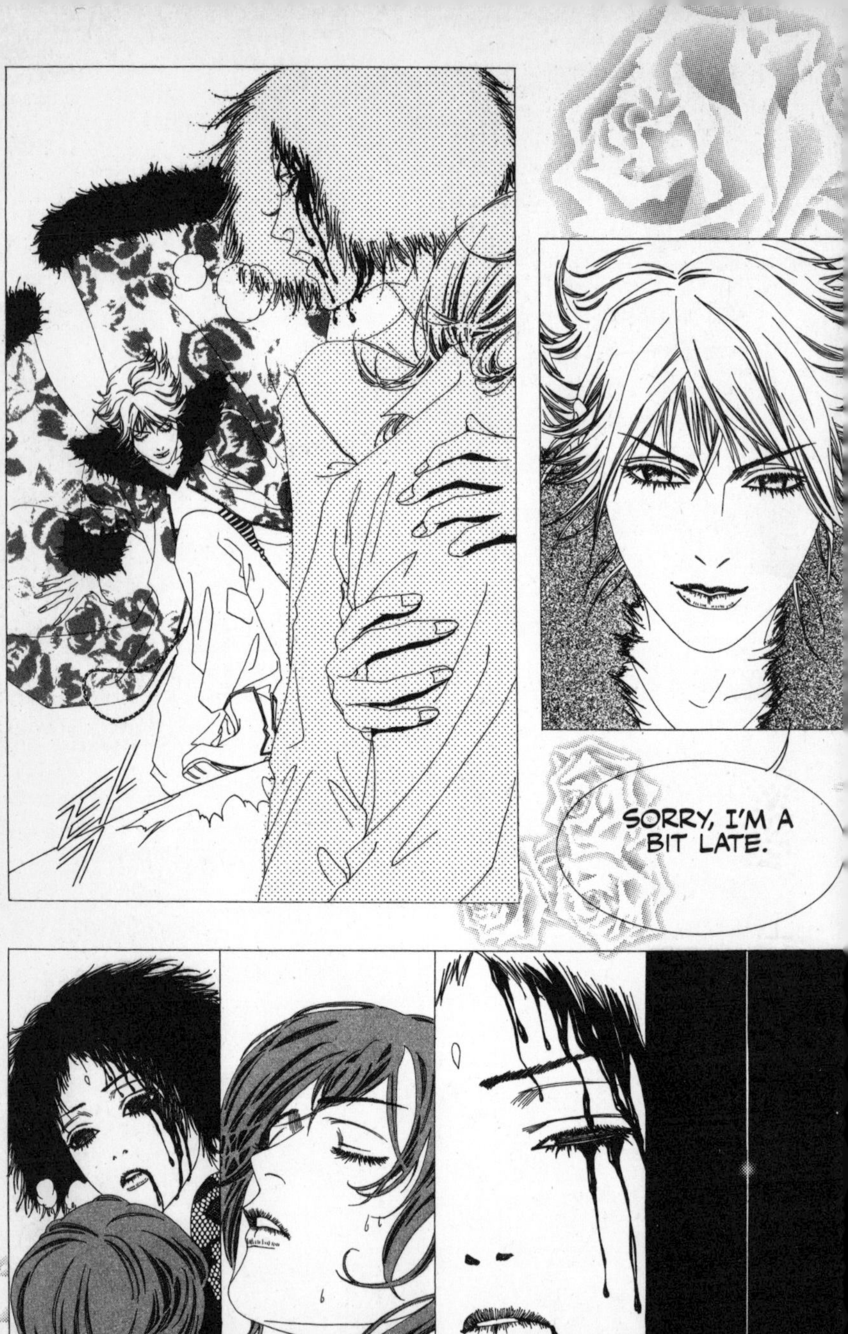
SORRY, I'M A BIT LATE.

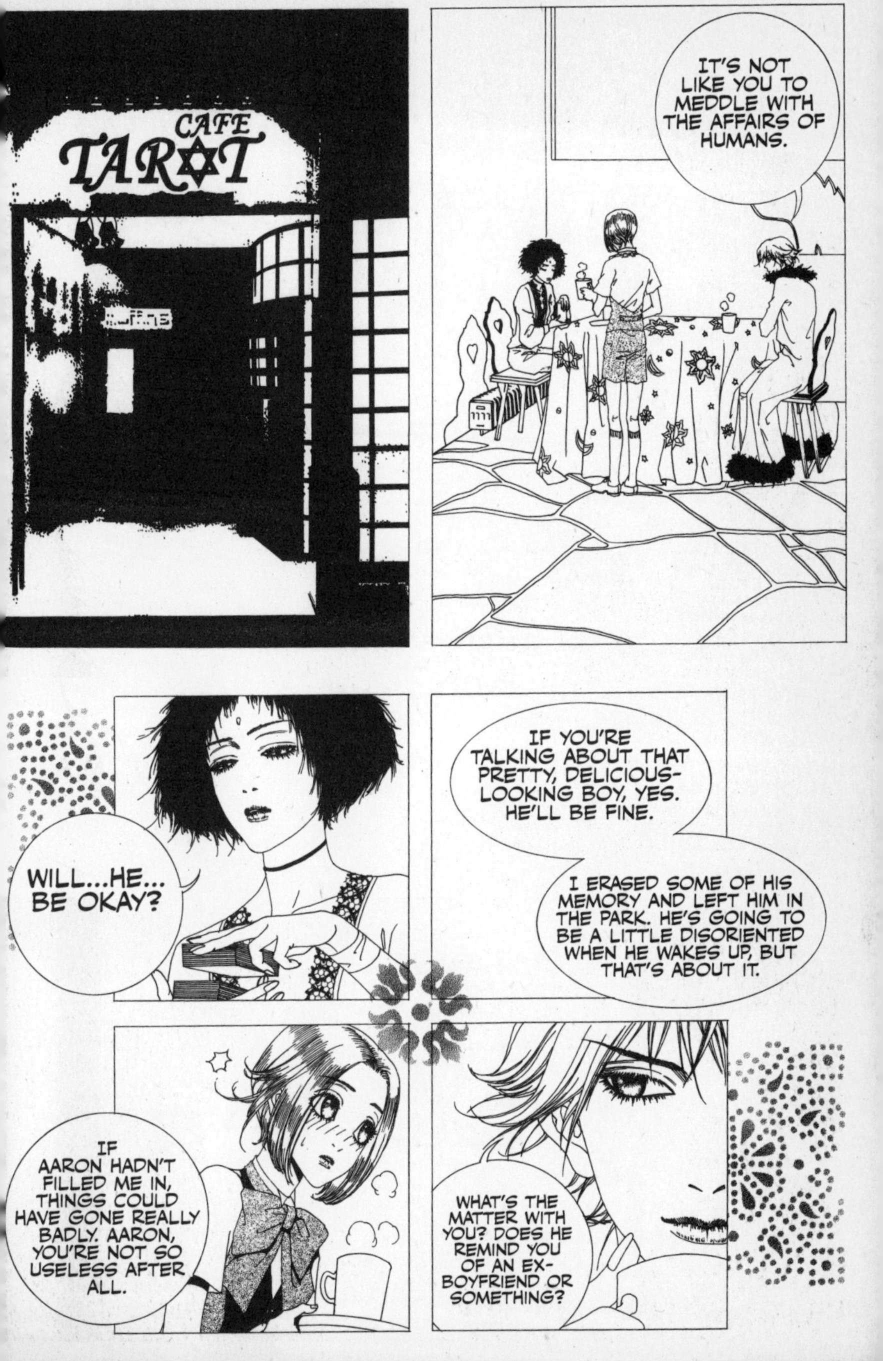
CAFE TAROT
IT'S NOT LIKE YOU TO MEDDLE WITH THE AFFAIRS OF HUMANS.
WILL...HE... BE OKAY?
IF YOU'RE TALKING ABOUT THAT PRETTY, DELICIOUS-LOOKING BOY, YES. HE'LL BE FINE.
I ERASED SOME OF HIS MEMORY AND LEFT HIM IN THE PARK. HE'S GOING TO BE A LITTLE DISORIENTED WHEN HE WAKES UP, BUT THAT'S ABOUT IT.
IF AARON HADN'T FILLED ME IN, THINGS COULD HAVE GONE REALLY BADLY. AARON, YOU'RE NOT SO USELESS AFTER ALL.
WHAT'S THE MATTER WITH YOU? DOES HE REMIND YOU OF AN EX-BOYFRIEND OR SOMETHING?

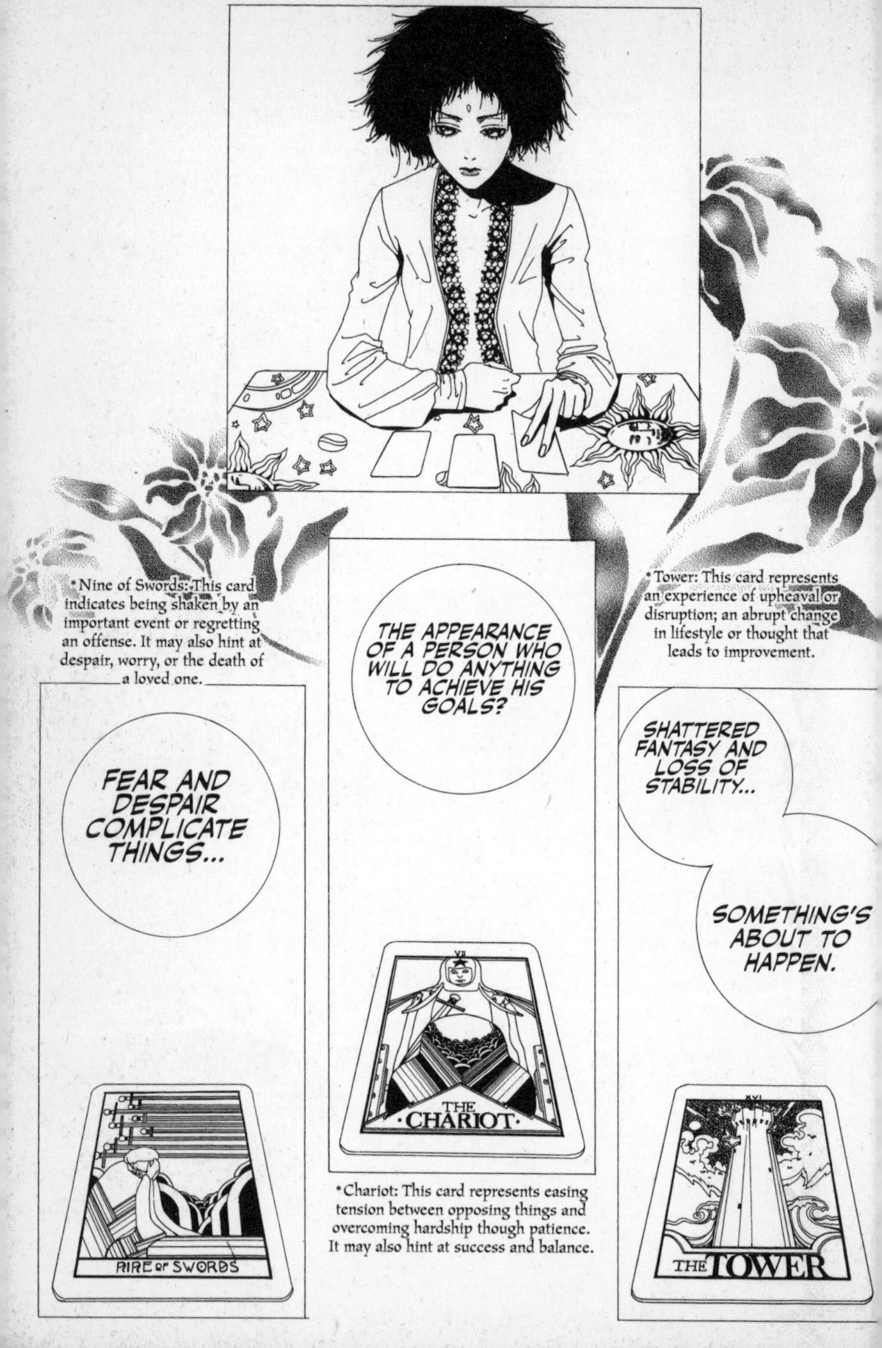
*Nine of Swords: This card indicates being shaken by an important event or regretting an offense. It may also hint at despair, worry, or the death of a loved one.
FEAR AND DESPAIR COMPLICATE THINGS...
NINE OF SWORDS
THE APPEARANCE OF A PERSON WHO WILL DO ANYTHING TO ACHIEVE HIS GOALS?
VII
THE CHARIOT
*Chariot: This card represents easing tension between opposing things and overcoming hardship though patience. It may also hint at success and balance.
*Tower: This card represents an experience of upheaval or disruption; an abrupt change in lifestyle or thought that leads to improvement.
SHATTERED FANTASY AND LOSS OF STABILITY...
SOMETHING'S ABOUT TO HAPPEN.
XVI
THE TOWER

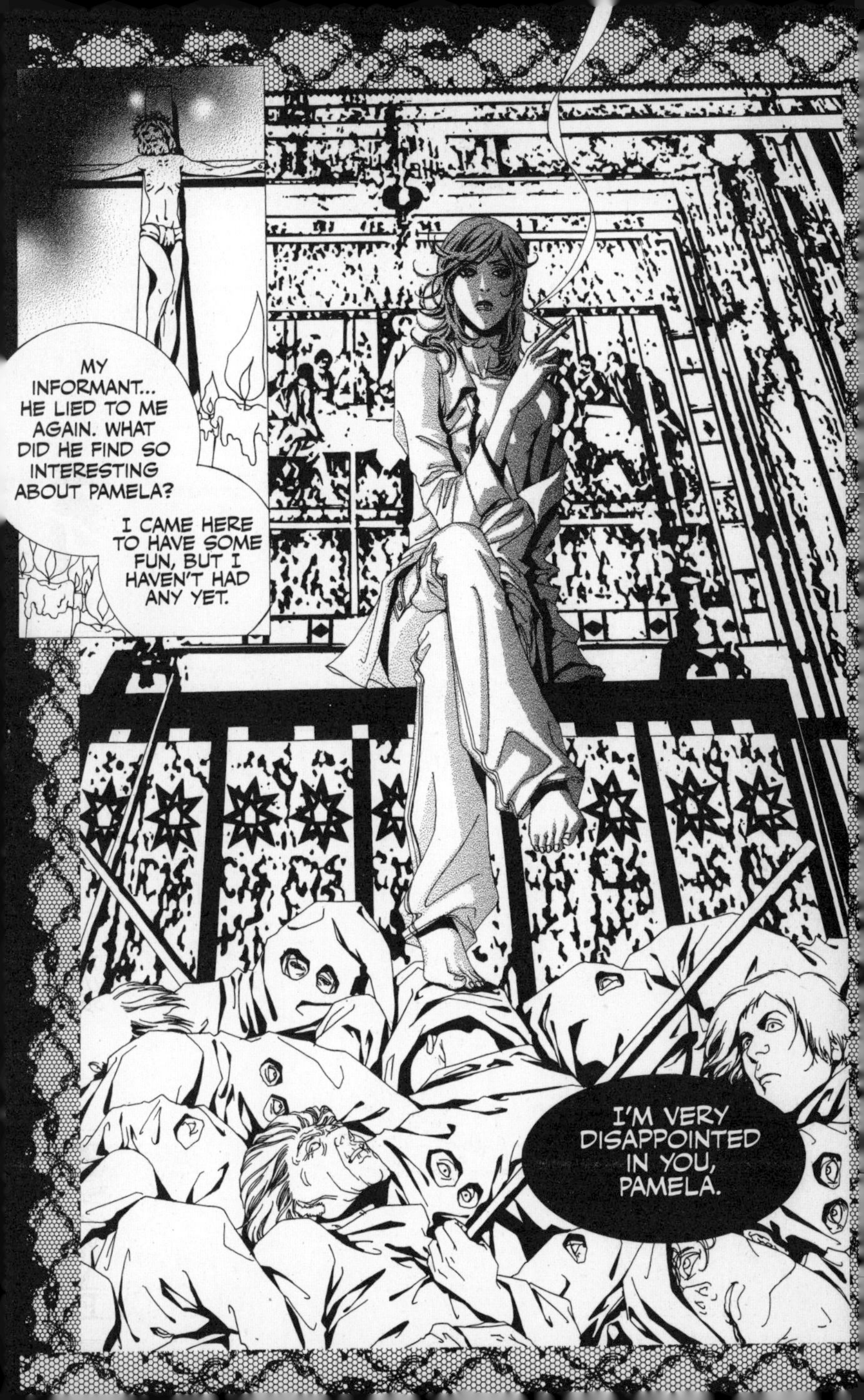
MY INFORMANT... HE LIED TO ME AGAIN. WHAT DID HE FIND SO INTERESTING ABOUT PAMELA?
I CAME HERE TO HAVE SOME FUN, BUT I HAVEN'T HAD ANY YET.
I'M VERY DISAPPOINTED IN YOU, PAMELA.

IN THE NEXT VOLUME OF

The Tarot Café

THE TAROT CAFÉ TELLS THE
PARANORMAL TALE OF PAMELA, A
TAROT CARD READER WHO IS FATED
TO HELP SUPERNATURAL BEINGS
LIVING IN THE HUMAN WORLD. A
SULTAN WHO WISHES FOR NOTHING
MORE THAN TO LEARN WHAT HAS
BECOME OF HIS FIRST LOVE ... AN
IMPOVERISHED STUDENT FALLS IN
LOVE WITH A LAKE FAIRY ... TWO 700-
YEAR-OLD DRAGONS ATTEMPT TO
REKINDLE AN ANCIENT FRIENDSHIP ...
MORE PARANORMAL TALES
FROM THE TAROT CAFÉ.

TOKYOPOP SHOP

PRINCESS AI

A Diva Torn from Chaos
A Savior Doomed to Love

Volume 2
Lumination

Ai continues to search for her place in our world on the streets of Tokyo. Using her talent to support herself, Ai signs a contract with a top record label and begins her rise to stardom. But fame is unpredictable—as her talent blooms, all eyes are on Ai. When scandal surfaces, will she burn out in the spotlight of celebrity?

Preview the manga at:
www.TOKYOPOP.com/princessai

TEEN
AGE 13+

© & TM TOKYOPOP Inc. and Kitty Radio, Inc.

SPOTLIGHT TOKYOPOP MANGA SUPPLEMENT

BECK: MONGOLIAN CHOP SQUAD

OT
OLDER TEEN
AGE 16+

ROCK IN MANGA!

BECK
MONGOLIAN CHOP SQUAD™
TOKYOPOP
Harold Sakuishi
1

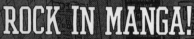

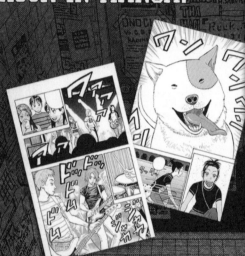

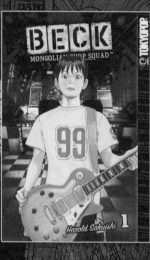

Yukio Tanaka is one boring guy with no hobbies, a weak taste in music and only a small vestige of a personality. But his life is forever changed when he meets Ryusuke Minami, an unpredictable rocker with a cool dog named Beck. Recently returned to Japan from America, Ryusuke inspires Yukio to get into music, and the two begin a journey through the world of rock 'n' roll dreams! With cameos of music's greatest stars—from John Lennon to David Bowie—and homages to supergroups such as Led Zeppelin and Nirvana, anyone who's anyone can make an appearance in *Beck*...even Beck himself! With action, music and gobs of comedy, *Beck* puts the rock in manga!

HAROLD SAKUISHI'S HIGHLY ADDICTIVE MANGA SERIES THAT SPAWNED A HIT ANIME HAS FINALLY REACHED THE STATES!

FOR MORE INFORMATION VISIT: WWW.TOKYOPOP.COM

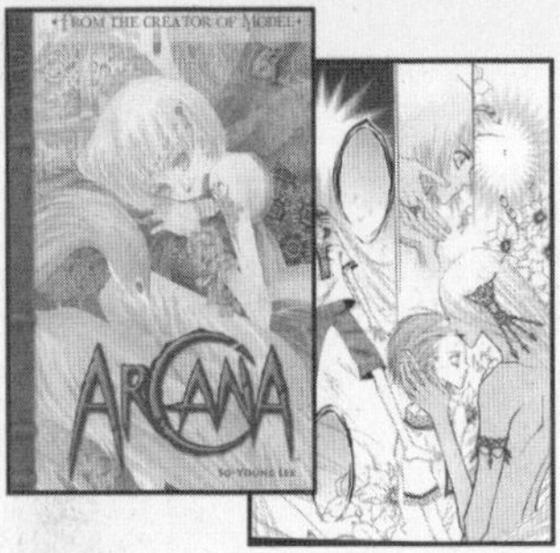
FROM THE CREATOR OF MODEL
ARCANA
SO-YOUNG LEE

ARCANA

BY SO-YOUNG LEE

Inez is a young orphan girl with the ability to communicate with living creatures of all kinds. She is the chosen one, and a great destiny awaits her! Inez must bring back the guardian dragon to protect her country's fragile peace from the onslaught of a destructive demon race.

From the creator of TOKYOPOP's *Model* comes an epic fantasy quest filled with wizards, dragons, deception and adventure beyond your wildest imagination.

T TEEN AGE 13+

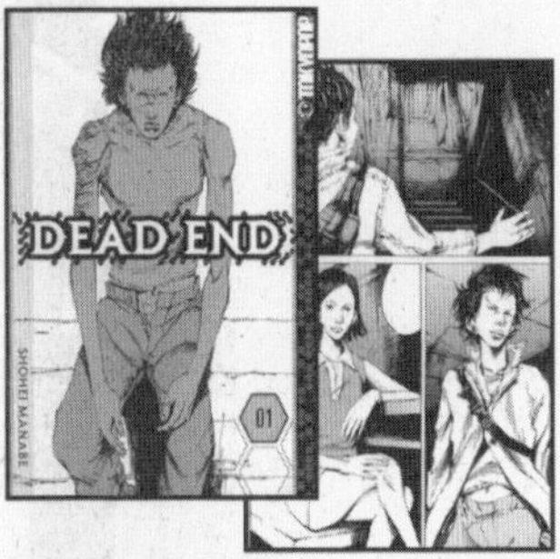
DEAD END
SHOHEI MANABE
01

DEAD END

BY SHOHEI MANABE

When Shirou's memory is suddenly erased and his friends are brutally murdered, he is forced to piece together clues to solve a shocking and spectacular puzzle. As we follow Shirou's journey, paranoia assumes an air of calm rationality and the line between tormenter and prey is often blurred.

OT OLDER TEEN AGE 16+

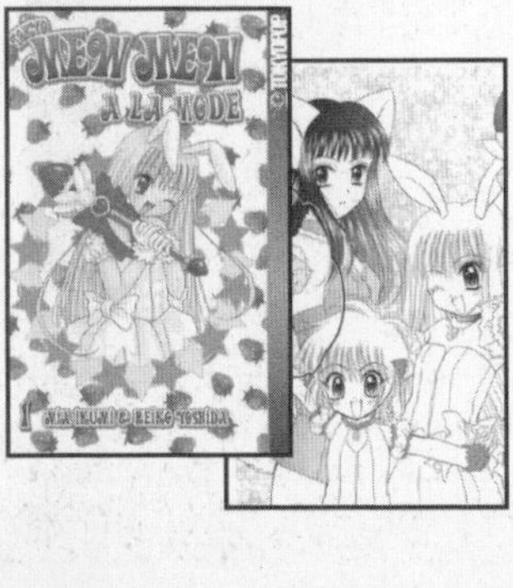
MEW MEW
A LA MODE

TOKYO MEW MEW A LA MODE

BY MIA IKUMI AND REIKO TOSHIDA

The cats are back, and a new Mew emerges—the first Mew Mew with *two* sets of animal genes. Half cat, half rabbit, Berry joins the Mew Mew team just in time: a new gang is about to appear, and its leader loves wild game like rabbit—well done and served for dinner!

The highly anticipated sequel to *Tokyo Mew Mew* (*Mew Mew Power* as seen on TV)!

Y YOUTH AGE 10+